Broken

GENDER AND JUSTICE

Edited by Claire M. Renzetti

This University of California Press series explores how the experiences of offending, victimization, and justice are profoundly influenced by the intersections of gender with other markers of social location. Cross-cultural and comparative, series volumes publish the best new scholarship that seeks to challenge assumptions, highlight inequalities, and transform practice and policy.

# Broken

*Women's Stories of Intimate and*
*Institutional Harm and Repair*

## Lisa Young Larance

UNIVERSITY OF CALIFORNIA PRESS

University of California Press
Oakland, California

© 2024 by Lisa Young Larance

Library of Congress Cataloging-in-Publication Data

Names: Young Larance, Lisa, author.
Title: Broken : women's stories of intimate and
    institutional harm and repair / Lisa Young Larance.
Other titles: Gender and justice (University of California
    Press) ; 12.
Description: Oakland, California : University of
    California Press, [2024] | Series: Gender and justice ;
    12 | Includes bibliographical references and index.
Identifiers: LCCN 2023052483 (print) | LCCN 2023052484
    (ebook) | ISBN 9780520392328 (cloth) | ISBN
    9780520392335 (paperback) | ISBN 9780520392342
    (ebook)
Subjects: lcsh: Intimate partner violence—United States. |
    Women—Violence against—United States. | Abused
    women—Rehabilitation—United States. | Abused
    women—United States—Psychology. | Feminists—
    United States.
Classification: LCC HV6626.2 .Y676 2024  (print) | LCC
    HV6626.2  (ebook) | DDC 362.82/920973—dc23/
    eng/20240214
LC record available at https://lccn.loc.gov/2023052483
LC ebook record available at https://lccn.loc
    .gov/2023052484

33   32   31   30   29   28   27   26   25   24
10   9   8   7   6   5   4   3   2   1

*To the women who have courageously told their stories,*
*all who still have stories to tell,*
*and those who never got the chance.*

. . .

*In memory of my phenomenal mother,*
*Floy Ella Muender Young*
*1935–2023*

If you are broken inside, for whatever reason why you're broken, it's going to come out in all of those relationships, especially your closest intimate relationships. So if you are someone who is broken, I think it pays to know that you are broken before you really land in these situations; because a broken person who ends up with an abusive person? . . . That's just a life of turmoil and then you're creating more work because you're still going to have to heal.

—Sage

# Contents

# Illustrations

# Acknowledgments

I owe my deepest gratitude to the women who participated in this project. With limited time and energy you made space to tell me your stories, believing I would write them in ways that would help others. May you recognize your contributions and continue to heal and move forward.

My appreciation for the support I received to write *Broken* spans decades. My undergraduate years at Smith College changed the trajectory of my life. Thank you, Susan Van Dyne. At Smith, I gained a keen awareness of how we all suffer when the stories of those marginalized by sexism, racism, classism, homophobia, and transphobia go untold. Debra Carney, thank you for the care you took tooling 18-year-old me with the necessary skills to begin writing those stories.

Thank you to those who supported my pursuit of an MSW at Washington University's Brown School. The degree made it possible for me to be invited into hundreds of lives. Karen Cochran Kelly, thank you for our friendship and your writing support. Michelle Shoresman, the Fulbright provided a gateway for me to learn from rural Bangladeshi women, my first teachers in the field. Thank you.

I was fortunate to begin my direct-practice work on behalf of systems-involved women among pioneering feminist practitioners and researchers who continue to work tirelessly for change. Thank you all for our conversations and collective work. Conversations with movement leaders who have passed away informed my early practice and theoretical frameworks in ways that only these leaders could—Andrea Bible, Anne Marshall, Sister Mary Nerney, and Ellen Pence, thank you.

My thanks to my many colleagues and friends for our conversations and collaborations over decades. My gratitude to those who have also offered feedback on earlier versions of this work: Susan Miller, Shamita Das Dasgupta, Jane Shivas, Allison Hoffman-Ruzicka, Lisa MacGray, Maryann Lane Porter, Melissa Scaia, Lotus Seeley, Quetita Cavero, Aubrey Sitler, Bryan Victor, Christine Watson, Anne Blumenthal, and Morgan Simpson.

The University of Michigan joint doctoral program in social work and sociology was an outstanding place to explore practice-based ideas while absorbing theoretical concepts as well as research knowledge and skills. Workshop and writing group conversations and graduate student instructor positions provided me a glimpse of a hoped-for future. Elizabeth Armstrong and Rich Tolman, you were exceptional advisors. Thank you, Erika Childs, for your care with the women's words.

Thanks to my dissertation committee for feedback on the dissertation that evolved into *Broken*. Cochairs Elizabeth Armstrong and Rich Tolman, and members Alexandra Murphy, Karen Staller, and Paige Sweet, your guidance and scholarship are evident throughout my work.

To my kindred spirits in advocacy organizations, on police forces, in the judiciary, in probation offices, with child protection caseloads, and in antiviolence intervention spaces—who are, wish to, or must remain unnamed—thank you for all you do to make a difference in the lives of systems-involved women, their families, and their communities. And thank you for our conversations and your reviews of this work as it evolved.

My gratitude to Bryn Mawr College's provost, Tim Harte, and the Graduate School of Social Work and Social Research's (GSSWSR) dean, Janet Shapiro, for your institutional support. Dean Shapiro and GSS-WSR faculty and staff, it is a privilege to be part of our dynamic social justice focused practitioner-scholar community.

My thanks to Claire Renzetti and Maura Roessner for believing in this project, Sam Warren, for your editorial assistance, the anonymous reviewers, editor Beth Sherouse, production editor Stephanie Summerhays, Gabriel Bartlett for your exceptional copyediting, and Emily LeGrand for your detailed indexing.

It is my extraordinarily good fortune to be Floy and Earl Young's daughter. You both shaped my life in such beautiful ways. Leslie Young, somehow the stars aligned to make us sisters and beloved friends. My dear Buckland cousins, who are more like siblings, I love you. Richard, thank you for asking me to dance. We've never stopped. You, Colvin, Hayden, and Ruel are my rays of sunshine.

. . .

As I was putting the finishing touches on *Broken,* my phenomenal mother, Floy Ella Muender Young, passed away. I am devastated. I will forever miss your physical presence in my life, momma. May your spirit shine through me, my children, and this work.

# Introduction

"It was the only time I stood up for myself. . . . I asked him to *please* leave me alone," Essence tearfully explained.[1] But Essence's former partner refused to give her space. Instead, he grabbed her by the throat and slammed her slim body into the wall. All the while, he kept

> his hands on my throat. He just kind of swung me down [the wall] into the bathroom floor and he was choking me. He had my arms pinned. At the same time he's doing this, he's yelling, "Stop, Essence! Stop! You're out of control! Stop! What are you doing? You're going to hurt yourself!" . . .
>
> The only thing I could do was cough, so to my kids [who were downstairs] it [sounded] like I'm out of control; he's trying to save me, when actually, he was choking[2] me to the point where I was going to lose consciousness. So, when I started coughing, I think he realized this is getting serious; I need to let her go. He got up. I grabbed my phone. [I] called the police.

When the police officer entered the house to question Essence, it was clear that the officer had already spoken to her former partner. Essence explained the officer "knew my history that I'd been molested. He knew that I suffer from depression from time to time, and he knew that I had panic attacks." She shared her story with me while we sat side by side on her sofa. With folded arms and tears in her eyes, Essence expressed shock that the officer asked very little about what happened before or during the incident or even if she was hurt. Instead, Essence explained, "It was just the whole mental illness thing!" She knew her former partner leveraged her race, childhood sexual assault history, and mental health diagnosis against her by talking to the officer first and portraying Essence as a "crazy" Black woman.[3] And because he had a scratch on his chest, a self-defensive abrasion resulting from Essence's struggle to free herself when he swung her down the wall by her throat, *she* was arrested. From Essence's perspective, his ability to use her "broken past" against her and gaslight her in the presence of her children and police officers made her feel "so broken." Moreover, Essence being identified by the criminal legal system (CLS)[4] as an offender meant that the harm of him strangling her, including possible brain injury, went unaddressed.

Several factors led to Essence's domestic violence conviction: her community's compliance with a mandatory arrest regime; the police officer's approach to questioning; her former partner withholding information about his actions during the incident; and her public defender encouraging her to accept a no-contest plea. As an offender, Essence was under a probation officer's surveillance for two years, and was court ordered to attend fee-for-service antiviolence intervention (AVI) over 30 consecutive weeks. And the court, probation, and intervention costs? Those were hers to pay. Because her children were home during the incident, child protective services (CPS) became involved, exposing Essence to the coercive power of a CPS caseworker "who never got [her] side of the story at all." Essence was wrongfully arrested for defending herself and was at risk of losing custody of her children.

. . .

"You guys got to stop this!" warned the security guard patrolling the community space. Valerie yelled back, "You don't understand! Leave me alone! You don't know what he's put me through! I don't care what you say or do or anything!" Again, the security guard warned, "Well, if you keep it up, I have to call the police!" Valerie shouted back, "Go ahead and call the police!" When the police officers arrived, they found Valerie, in her words, "punching [her partner] in the face repeatedly." She was arrested, jailed, and convicted of domestic violence.

Valerie and her boyfriend had been together for years. Housing was always uncertain. They lived on the street, in shelters, and between low-budget motel rooms. As we talked, Valerie's hair was tucked behind her ears, the fluorescent Motel 6 light highlighting the freckles on her nose. We sat on the edge of the squeaky motel room bed while she detailed the times he had beaten her. At one point, he strangled Valerie and punched her in the face so severely that she was hospitalized. But he still would not stop. "They kicked him out . . . because he was still putting his hands on me in the hospital," Valerie explained. Advocates offered Valerie refuge at the local domestic violence shelter, "but [she] didn't wind up going." He threatened that if he could not find her, he would kill her mother and grandmother. When released from the hospital, Valerie hoped things would be different. She and her boyfriend continued to cycle through motel rooms at night and public spaces during the day. Then one day Valerie saw him out in town with "*that* woman"—the one he had denied having a sexual relationship with, the one whose children Valerie had babysat and "done everything for," hoping her instincts were wrong. Seeing them together, Valerie knew he had lied. Valerie "chased him down" in a community space and assaulted him. The betrayal was too much.

With determination in her voice and on her face, she insisted, "I let it happen . . . [it] is my fault!" Her matter-of-fact tone made it clear that she was responding to his infidelity, physical beatings, threats, and gaslighting. Valerie then described herself as "just a very rebellious kid" who "never wanted to listen to the rules, was always fighting, always getting kicked out of group homes." In this context, by physically responding to her partner's abuse, she was also lashing out against a long sequence of past harms endured in foster homes and as a teenage rape survivor. Her arrest and conviction made sense. She smiled and proclaimed that she was "*beautifully* broken"—*because* of all she had overcome.

Whereas Essence was wrongfully arrested, Valerie assaulted her boyfriend in front of the responding police officers. Now systems-identified as an "offender," Valerie, like Essence, was under a probation officer's surveillance for two years, and was court ordered to attend fee-for-service AVI over 30 consecutive weeks. Just as with Essence, the court, probation, and court-ordered AVI fees were hers to pay. Owing to her boyfriend's previous violence against her, CPS caseworkers removed Valerie's children. She described herself as "homeless" and reliant on public transportation. How would she comply with the court orders? How would she work toward reunification with her children? And where would she live should she get her children back? Did Valerie's identities as a young white woman with a history of domestic and sexual violence survivorship matter?

. . .

The US legal response to domestic violence is meant to keep victims safe and hold offenders accountable. For Essence and Valerie, however, the response seemed to achieve the opposite. *Broken* takes an in-depth look at the collateral damage of this legal process for women with histories of domestic and sexual violence survivorship who used nonfatal self-defensive actions when responding to imminent harm. *Broken* also illuminates less-considered experiences of women, like Valerie, arrested for using nonfatal non-self-defensive force, who became systems-identified offenders and also had histories of enduring intimate harm. By bringing attention to the stories of legal systems-involved women in the community who have had AVI contact owing to their (alleged) use of force, *Broken* offers an examination of cumulative community-based carceral responses—probation, CPS, and AVI—which are typically excluded from analysis and conversations about "mass incarceration."[5]

*Broken* details the first-person accounts of 33 women who participated in AVI by criminal or family court mandate, or voluntarily.[6] Although many AVIs have a supportive component, they are fee-for-service surveilled spaces where most of the participants are women convicted of domestic violence and complying with court orders to avoid jail. Rather than describing themselves as "victims" or "offenders," however, these women described themselves as being, or feeling, "broken," indicating both the harms they endured and those they caused. Informed by my years of fieldwork focused on learning from systems-involved women and two decades as an AVI practitioner, *Broken* challenges the victim-offender binary—that is, how the legal system, CPS, and AVIs categorize people as either victims or offenders and intervene accordingly. I argue that this binary inflicts further harm in the lives of women, like those in this book, who have survived domestic and sexual violence and are wrongfully arrested, as well as those who are legal systems-involved for using nonfatal, non-self-defensive force. These women's (alleged) use of force obscures their relationship histories, and often results in wrongful or disproportionate systems responses, effectively weaponizing their survivorship. In this process, the women in *Broken* were criminal or family court ordered or both to complete and pay for AVI and a range of obligations in the community before they could be released from state surveillance and, in some cases, have their children returned to their care. What practitioners and researchers largely fail to consider is the exacting physical, emotional, and financial toll this process has on the well-being of low-income women with diverse identities.

While bringing attention to how the victim-offender binary affected these women by exacerbating their self-described "breakage"—psychological, physical, and social experiences of harm before and during carceral systems contact—*Broken* also highlights their personal agency in healing from and repairing this breakage. This work centers systems-involved women's voices, integrating feminist sociological and social work frameworks. This view challenges current carceral approaches, urging responses beyond the binary that attend to the complexity of the human experience. To situate the victim-offender binary's evolution, I provide an overview of early US battered women's movement messaging and alliance with law enforcement as well as how that alliance ushered in CPS involvement. I then explain why I use the term *domestic violence*, and what I mean by it. I continue by explaining who I am, as well as the context within which I learned from these women, which provides the necessary foundation for how this project evolved and how I developed the theoretically informed concept of "breakage," derived from the women's words. This introductory chapter ends with my explanation of breakage, detailed examples from the women's lives, and an overview of the chapters that follow.

## THE VICTIM-OFFENDER BINARY'S EVOLUTION: US MOVEMENT MESSAGING AND ALLIANCES

The US-based battered women's movement grew out of grassroots social justice efforts, including Rosa Parks's 1940s work with the National Association for the Advancement of Colored People focused on ending white men's rape of Black women (McGuire, 2010), and the early 1970s middle-class white feminist antirape movement (Schechter, 1982). The battered women's movement recognized men's sexual and physical violence against women as a tool of social control. Co-occurring identities, such as race, class, and sexuality, however, largely went unaddressed, despite women of color, lesbians, transgender, and low-income people's engagement in the work (Goodmark, 2013; McGuire, 2010; Richie et al., 2021; Schechter, 1982). The battered women's movement was pivotal in not only saving women's lives, but in reframing domestic violence from a private family issue into a significant social problem—an historical turning point.[7] The movement involved a range of efforts, including public messaging that domestic violence "can happen to anyone" (Richie, 2000). This messaging shaped ideas about who domestic violence victims are and what their common experiences might entail. This approach was meant to strategically encourage movement cohesion, bring attention to the dire circumstances that many women faced, and promote accountability for those who had harmed their partners (Schechter, 1982; Sokoloff and Dupont,

2005). The strategy evolved alongside some movement leaders' efforts to forge formal alliances with law enforcement. Women of color and their allies warned against these efforts, however, owing to the troubled history between law enforcement and marginalized communities (Kim, 2013; Miller, 1989; Richie, 2012).

According to sociologist Beth Richie (2000, p. 1134), messaging that violence against women "can happen to anyone" misinforms ideas around who *real* domestic violence victims are—namely, cisgender, able-bodied, heterosexual, middle-class, white women who, because of those identities, can easily seek and receive supportive intervention. This perception not only overlooks race, class, disability, sexuality, and gender identity; it leaves those marginalized by a range of intersecting oppressions at an increased risk of being misunderstood by legal and child protection systems. Social work professor Valli Kalei Kanuha (1996) explains that "everywoman" messaging diminishes the diversity of marginalized women's lives as well as analysis regarding the prevalence and impact of domestic violence. Because of the everywoman perception, any way that a woman can be perceived as responsible for the violence against her, particularly if she used violence herself, complicates her struggle to secure formal support.

Without context, the everywoman perception dangerously diverts attention away from a social justice-informed analysis (see Richie, 2012). It also perpetuates the idea of a "paradigmatic victim" (Goodmark, 2012), a "good girl" (McCorkel, 2013), a "good survivor" (Sweet, 2021), or what RyAnn and other women I interviewed for this project call a "*Lifetime* victim." As RyAnn explains, "All the women who are depicted [on *Lifetime* television] as domestic violence survivors or . . . victims are . . . passive women that are being beat, that cannot fight back, living in like terror and fear, and have no autonomy at all. They're just a victim."

This early messaging codified the real victim stereotype—a chaste, nondisabled, cisgender, heterosexual, middle-class, drug-free white woman who never used violence, is soft spoken and easy to work with. Thus, hegemonic white femininity has become the yardstick against which all other women are judged (Collins, 2004; Hamilton et al., 2019). While this messaging benefits those who align with the stereotype, it causes further harm to women who do not. As Richie (1996) points out, "The choices are harder and the consequences are more serious for women with low incomes, women of color, lesbians, women who become pregnant at a young age and others whose decisions, circumstances, and status violate the dominant culture's expectations or offend hegemonic images of 'womanhood'" (p. 2). By definition, women who have caused harm in their relationships cannot be "real victims." Instead, they are women who, as RyAnn put it, "talk back . . . get a little unruly" and make their "presence known".

Movement messaging in the mid-1970s and early 1980s worked in tandem with activists' efforts to forge formal alliances with law enforcement. The hope was that men who perpetrated harm against their intimate female partners would finally be held legally accountable.[8] This desire for accountability was situated in the frustration that arrest policies for domestic violence cases rarely existed in the early 1970s.[9] Because men's violence against women was considered a private matter, responding officers treated it as such. Therefore, less formal parameters dictated police decisions about whether or not to arrest. For example, some police officers responding to "a domestic" in the 1970s relied on an informal "stitch rule," arresting violent husbands only if they had injured their wives severely enough to require an anticipated number of surgical sutures (Eisenberg and Micklow, 1977; Pleck, 2004). Laws in some jurisdictions did not allow responding officers to arrest a person for a misdemeanor not committed in their presence (Goodmark, 2012). Police officer reluctance or inability to arrest arose because of the combination of limited laws guiding arrest procedures and police training manuals that encouraged crisis intervention and separation, such as asking one partner to walk around the block and cool down before returning home (International Association of Chiefs of Police, 1967).

Pursuing safety for women physically harmed by their partners, many battered women's movement activists argued that police should make arrests whenever there was probable cause. Their arguments were motivated by the belief that criminalizing violence against women would result in those actions finally being treated like any other crime, with the goal of shifting the onus for survivor safety from women who had been harmed to the community. Some lauded criminalizing violence against women as an achievement for the women's rights movement similar to reproductive or divorce legislation (Shepard and Pence, 1999); others, however, felt that this turn toward the carceral state was "a betrayal of the movement's emancipatory roots" (Kim, 2013, p. 1277).

Early outcomes of the Minneapolis Domestic Violence Experiment, which suggested that arrest was an effective deterrent to future violence, reinforced the belief that criminalizing men's violence against women was a promising intervention (Sherman and Berk, 1984). Researchers cautioned, however, that the experiment needed replicating before they could draw a definitive conclusion about a generalizable positive impact (Sherman et al., 1992). Nonetheless, jurisdictions across the United States largely adopted mandatory arrest laws and policies in the late 1980s through the 1990s.

In 1994, mandatory arrest laws and policies became an integral aspect of addressing domestic violence cases in the original version of the Violence Against Women Act (VAWA), which required states receiving grant funding to adopt these policies (Larance et al., 2019b). Although the 2000 version of the VAWA removed the requirement and allowed either mandatory (must arrest) or preferred (should arrest) arrest policies, many states had already implemented the former. With either of these mandates, according to criminologist Susan Miller (2005), "people in violent situations are dichotomized into 'victim' and 'perpetrator' categories, with the context of the situation left unexamined . . . [so that] a single act of a woman's violence eclipses her entire history of victimization" (pp. 9–10). Lost were the "in-betweens," which a contextual view could allow (Miller, 2018). Women of color, undocumented immigrants, and disabled, low-income, and LGBTQIA+ people became particularly at risk of wrongful arrest (Ballan and Frye, 2012; Kelley, 2017; Potter, 2008; Richie, 1996, 2012; Sokoloff and Dupont, 2005; Swan and Snow, 2003; West, 2009). Battered women's advocates[10]—many of them middle-class white women—celebrated these incident-based, violence-focused policies as a victory for abused women who had long suffered violence at the hands of the men with whom they partnered (Goodmark, 2012; Pleck, 2004; Shepard and Pence, 1999). Those who found mandatory arrest laws and policies desirable did so precisely because they removed police discretion in determining whether or not to arrest. The goal was to promote systems-identified victims' safety, while holding offenders accountable.

For Essence and Valerie, these policies were not as effective as the advocates had hoped they would be. Although arrest deterred repeated domestic violence offenses in some jurisdictions, it had no effect in others, and may have even increased domestic violence in some communities (Berk et al., 1992; Dunford et al., 1990; Garner et al., 1995; Pate and Hamilton, 1992). Mandatory arrests have also had unintended consequences for women, with their arrest rates rising (Dichter, 2013; Hirshel et al., 2007). Sociologist Alesha Durfee (2012) found that these increases occurred because of the policies, not an increase in women's violence, suggesting that the additional arrests were not justified. Also problematic was the rise in arrests of both people at the incident (Hirschel et al., 2007; Martin, 1997).

For some marginalized women, the combination of public messaging and law enforcement's alliance with early battered women's movement leaders became an "intersectional failure" (Crenshaw, 2016). Centering the perspectives and experiences of mainly middle-class white women brought unintended consequences for women who did not align with the real victim stereotype. It also reified the victim-offender binary that continues to dictate systems responses to violence-involved women (Larance et al., 2022).

In jurisdictions where police serve as mandatory reporters, they must notify the state's child welfare agency of any incident where children are present because of the possibility that the children may have been exposed to violence. Therefore, a police response to such situations typically ushers in a CPS investigation whereby a caseworker determines whether the children are at any risk of harm or not and whether or not to open a formal case. Detractors point out that CPS involvement promotes increased state surveillance of already marginalized families across coercive systems rather than resource-enhancing therapeutic interventions that support their right to self-determination, even after cases are closed (Fong, 2020; Roberts, 2014). Thus, the criminal, civil, and family legal systems reinforce one another through a combination of approaches to mandatory interventions in vulnerable families.

*Broken* is grounded in my appreciation for the US battered women's movement's history and victories. It simultaneously recognizes how the "carceral creep" (Kim, 2015) between law enforcement and feminist activists has led to activists' subordination and the rise of carceral power (Bernstein, 2010). For example, the emphasis on domestic violence protections and increased surveillance of families has disproportionately advantaged middle-class cisgender heterosexual white women and especially disadvantaged low-income women of color and others marginalized by ableism, racism, sexism, transphobia, and homophobia. Thus, the movement's turn toward what Miller (2005) calls a "conservative criminal control model" has meant that the larger movement goals—income equality, housing, and childcare—became ancillary to the movement's focus on relationship building across and within the carceral system.

With this recognition, *Broken* is also grounded in my commitment to intersectional feminist social work and sociology that underscore the critical importance of recognizing how interlocking, overlapping individual identities shape the way marginalized women experience systems of power (see Crenshaw, 1991).[11] The bodies people inhabit, whom they love, their access to money, and their extended social networks profoundly affect how the carceral system responds to their needs. From this perspective, *Broken* intentionally challenges the victim-offender binary by detailing diverse women's lived experiences navigating community-based criminal, legal, and child protection systems. This reliance on the binary has led to voluntary trauma-informed remedies at no cost for those who align with the real victim stereotype, with largely punitive court-ordered fee-for-service measures for systems-identified offenders. Lost in the process, as *Broken* will show, is a formal systems-wide acknowledgement that would make it possible to understand and effectively intervene in the lives of those who have both survived and caused harm.

## COURT-ORDERED ANTIVIOLENCE INTERVENTIONS

US-based battered women's movement messaging about domestic violence and legal alliances evolved into a coordinated community response protocol (Shepard and Pence, 1999). In practice, an aspect of this protocol in domestic assault cases involves encouraging the victim (typically a woman) to voluntarily seek confidential, trauma-informed counseling at a domestic violence agency.[12] The offender (typically a man) is court ordered to participate in a battering intervention program (BIP). BIPs are court ordered, probation-officer-monitored, fee-for-service groups specifically developed to address the gendered underpinnings of heterosexual men's violence, power, and control used against the women with whom they partner or partnered.

With a growing number of women facing arrest after mandatory arrest laws and policies were implemented in the 1990s, domestic violence shelter-based services became unavailable to them even though many had survived domestic and sexual violence. Activist Sue Osthoff (2002) remembers that shelters would not serve women with survivorship histories once they were "charged with crimes (especially if the alleged crime was an assault against a partner) because, they say, they cannot or will not work with 'perpetrators'" (p. 1527). Thus, owing to the victim-offender binary, convicted women are increasingly court ordered to BIPs. Many feminist practitioners and scholars actively resist this turn of events as they recognize that women's referrals to programs designed for men are ineffective and potentially revictimizing (Dasgupta, 2002; Larance and Miller, 2017; Larance et al., 2019b; Pence and Dasgupta, 2006). Gradually, practitioners established interventions tailored to the needs of women who had caused harm, and often had histories of surviving harm, in communities across the United States (Larance et al., 2019b). As *Broken* will show, however, these tailored interventions may inadvertently perpetuate the carceral system's monetary-based punishment culture (Harris, 2016), while replicating the intimate coercion the women survived.

## LANGUAGE

In *Broken*, I use the term *domestic violence* to broadly refer to the range of harm the women suffered or caused in their intimate relationships. I use *domestic violence*, because it is the language the women used when telling their stories, commonly referring to "getting a domestic," or "in a domestic violence relationship."[13] It is also the term the criminal and family court systems typically use. But there are important distinctions between my use of this term in *Broken* and that used in the legal system. When I use the term *domestic violence*, I recognize that coercive control, sexual violence, and gaslighting are core components of patriarchal power (DeKeseredy, 2021; Saunders et al., 2022). Gendered power defines the intimate harm many of these women endure over the course of their lives. When women in heterosexual relationships use force, they typically did so in an effort to stop their partner's abuse, absent the structural power to effectively coercively control them. In contrast, the legal system in the research community defines "domestic violence" from an incident-based, violence focused perspective.

*Coercive control* is the hallmark of the intimate harm caused by abusive men against women in heterosexual relationships. Sociologist and forensic social worker Evan Stark (2007) defines coercion as "the use of force or threats to compel or dispel a particular response" (p. 228) and control as "structural forms of deprivation, exploitation, and command that compel obedience indirectly" (p. 229). Stark (2007) argues that coercive control is a "pattern of intimidation, isolation, and control . . . unique to men's abuse of women," and asserts that it is fundamental to explaining "why women become entrapped in abusive relationships in ways that men do not" (p. 102). The control aspect may continue long after the violence—if there is violence at all—subsides, and may feel more salient to the abused person than any physical harm. Particular to coercive control is how an abusive partner strategically uses "privileged access" (Stark and Hester, 2019) to the partner's personal and relationship-specific details.[14]

Expanding a gendered understanding, sociologist Kristin Anderson (2009) applies a multi-level theory (Ridgeway and Correll, 2004) to demonstrate the gendering of coercive control through interconnected levels of individual gender identity, interactions between people, and social structures. There are identity-based complexities. For example, criminologist Hillary Potter (2008) brings attention to how Black women must contend with the "strong Black woman" stereotype that foregrounds relentless resilience and tenacity while overlooking their daily challenges and institutional racism—both of which may make the coercive control they suffer invisible to those outside the relationship.

Coercive control can also be a component of harm between women in same-sex or lesbian relationships (Stark and Hester, 2019).[15] Social scientist Janice Ristock (2002) cautions against applying a heteronormative framework to violence between women in intimate relationships, as the dynamics include "multiple, overlapping, and compounding factors" (p. 63) unique to those relationships. Given this spectrum of understanding, it is important to note that only one woman in this work described having the ability to effectively control her partner. Suzie (see chapter 3) describes her wife's continued discomfort with her mere presence long after Suzie physically harmed her. Suzie's use of coercive control is also contextualized within her childhood sexual abuse history and surviving her former husband's harm.

*Gaslighting* is an integral component of coercive control. It is a type of psychological abuse that makes victims seem or feel that they are "crazy," or that the reality of the situation has been "flipped." Sociologist Paige Sweet (2019) explains that gaslighting "is rooted in power-laden intimate relationships, creates a sense of surreality, and mobilizes gender-based stereotypes, intersecting inequalities and institutional vulnerabilities against victims" (p. 869).[16] Coercively controlling partners use gaslighting in a range of settings to capitalize on their victim's vulnerabilities. While gaslighting is not unique to heterosexual relationships, men are more likely to use it effectively against women, given the structural power differences between them. Sweet (2019) points out that gender inequality between men and women is a necessary condition for gaslighting to be effective, as "it deprives women of the social power that would allow them to define men's realities" (p. 854). Not only are men less likely to fear women; they are less likely to change their behavior in response to women's attempts to coerce them through gaslighting. Psychologists Suzanne Swan and David Snow (2003) found that although women assaulted their partners, the women were also injured, experienced mental health challenges owing to the abuse, and lacked the power to coercively control their male partners. Similarly, Ashley Rousson and I (2016) observed a clear distinction between women wanting power and having power in their heterosexual relationships. We describe this difference as women seeking autonomy, in contrast to coercively controlling men exercising their authority. As a practitioner, I found that women often minimized the harm they had endured, masking extensive survivorship histories. Furthermore, women disclosed to me during individual and group sessions that when they tried to coerce or threaten their male partners, their partners would laugh at them and typically escalate their violence or coercive control or both. In contrast, men in BIPs I cofacilitated detailed success in controlling their female partners with a phrase or glance that had meaning within their relationship's culture. Consistent with others' work (Renzetti, 1992; Ristock, 2002), women in same-sex relationships have also described to me how they effectively controlled their partners through threats of outing their partner's undisclosed sexual orientation to friends, family, or colleagues. Because coercively controlling partners tailor the coercion and control to the context of the relationship, their tactics often remain invisible to those outside the relationship, making women seem or feel crazy while the abusive partner becomes further empowered. This dynamic is complicated in the US context, where incident-based physical violence is criminalized in all states, while coercive control is criminalized in only some states (Battered Women's Justice Project, 2021). Coercive control is not, however, criminalized in the research community.

## NAVIGATING THE VICTIM-OFFENDER BINARY

In 2000, I began navigating the victim-offender binary as a counselor at Jersey Battered Women's Service, Inc. (JBWS) in Morris County, New Jersey. I saw myself as working toward the larger movement goals of social justice, empowerment, self-determination, advocacy, and safety. I worked in the emergency shelter and in transitional housing. I counseled women living in the community who had been harmed by previous or current partners and men court ordered to the agency's BIP as a condition of probation. Similar to other agencies nationwide, our agency was affected by the state's 1991 mandatory arrest law. I witnessed the unintended consequences of that law and the practices that followed—for example, women with domestic and sexual violence survivorship histories were arrested for using self-defensive force against their partners. These women were left without traditional domestic violence support services because they did not fit the real victim stereotype; and increasingly, judges were court ordering them to BIPs created for and populated by men. It was not unusual to answer a call one week from a woman requesting supportive victim services, and then weeks later, the same woman would call to enroll in offender services to comply with a court order. Without services tailored to these women's needs, we could only offer letters of support, individual counseling, and apologies for not having the services they requested. Again and again, this strategy fell short.

Our agency was at a crossroads that included the following: justified concerns that creating such services would further stigmatize women;[17] funding limitations owing to VAWA restrictions for JBWS as a victim-support agency; judges who increasingly ordered women to enroll in BIPs alongside men; and women who continued to call and request supportive intervention and advocacy we did not offer. Believing the agency's inaction was causing further harm, JBWS leadership decided to create a formal program to serve women who had used force. The program aimed to address the women's diverse relationship needs while also attending to issues of race, class, economics, and national origin, for instance, considering the needs of women without US citizenship documentation who were, therefore, dependent on their husbands for residency. Working alongside colleagues and advocates,[18] I had the opportunity to cocreate, manage, and cofacilitate what became JBWS's Vista Program—one of the earliest formal programs in the United States to meet the needs of women who had used force. The first Vista group met in August 2002. We published our community-based curriculum framework, codesigned with the women in the group, in 2009 (Larance et al., 2009). This work put into motion my practice and research focused on understanding and addressing the complexity of women's use of force in the United States and abroad. Since that time, I have worked in community-based settings as a unit-of-service licensed clinical social worker, cofacilitated hundreds of intervention and support groups for women and battering intervention groups for men, and consulted for state coalitions against domestic and sexual violence, departments of correction, the Department of the Air Force Family Advocacy Program, and programs in Australia, China, and the United Kingdom.

In a direct practice setting, I strove to meet the women's emotional, intervention, and advocacy needs at a vulnerable time in their lives. As part of nongovernmental organizations receiving referrals from the legal system and CPS, I was also involved in a system that charged low-income women fees for their weekly court-ordered group sessions, closely surveilled their attendance, and did not provide transportation or childcare. I was also responsible for communication between probation officers, CPS caseworkers, and the AVI administration.

Over my years of practice, I have intentionally and creatively mitigated these challenges in various ways. But despite my best efforts, there is no question that I have unintentionally participated in the victim-offender binary that inflicts further injury on low-income court- ordered women in ways that this research brought to my attention, as well as in other ways I may never know. I believe that people deserve to be safe and that those who cause harm deserve appropriate intervention. I also believe that formal nongovernmental institutions can simultaneously promote justice and reduce harm. Indeed, I continue to contribute to such efforts. I recognize that in striving to do so, however, injustice and harm can result. This conundrum—promoting alternatives to harm and social justice through personal healing and systems change, while inadvertently causing harm—motivates my intersectional feminist social work and sociological research that critically integrates practice and theory, challenges the victim-offender binary, and attends to my reflexivity as a practitioner-researcher.

Although I came of age during the second wave of feminism, which often privileged gender at the expense of other identities, I identify with intersectional feminism, which emphasizes how interlocking categorical identities shape the way people experience power. I recognize that my personal identities shaped my professional opportunities, my practice, and my scholarship. I also believe that my place as both a practitioner and a researcher, a version of sociologist Patricia Hill Collins's (1986) "outsider within," provides a perspective that uniquely highlights systems harms, and therefore urges necessary systems change. This place is informed by my identities as a nondisabled, white, heterosexual, cisgender woman. From that place I also acknowledge that by writing about the experiences of many women of color with diverse sexual identities I risk reinforcing the same power differences I intend to challenge. Social activist bell hooks (1989) warns that, "when we write about the experiences of a group to which we do not belong, we should think about the ethics of our action, considering whether or not our work will be used to reinforce and perpetuate domination" (p. 43). Likewise, social scientist Chandra Mohanty (1991) acknowledges the difficult truth about feminist researchers navigating these power relations: "Feminist scholarly practices (whether reading, writing, critical, or textual) are inscribed in relations of power—relations which they counter, resist, or even perhaps implicitly support. There can, of course, be no apolitical scholarship" (p. 53). I heed hooks's warning and embrace Mohanty's acknowledgement. I have attempted to ameliorate these power differences by grounding my work in a Black feminist epistemological framework (Collins, 2009) and applying both standpoint (Harding, 1987; Hartsock, 1983) and intersectional theories (Collins, 2009; Combahee River Collective, 1977; Crenshaw, 1991). This theoretical grounding is consistent with a social work person-in-environment perspective, the movement's focus on the right to self-determination, and a trauma-informed lens that non-judgmentally recognizes and respects people as "feeling what they feel and knowing what they know" (van der Kolk, 2014, p. 127). Furthermore, I apply my rigorous training in intracategorical qualitative inquiry (McCall, 2005) and data analysis (see the appendix). When writing about women's experiences, I employ both Marjorie DeVault's (1990) and Kathleen Ferraro's (2006) approaches of presenting the women's words with little to no editing to capture the authenticity of their voices and language choices. In addition, I am reflexive throughout this work, which is particularly important given my place both in the movement and the women's lives. Thus, throughout *Broken*, I claim the place from which I speak, as it is for everyone, a place that is socially situated and ever changing (Bettie, 2014; Mann and Kelley, 1997).

I have also attended to the power dynamic between myself and those who participated in this work by foregrounding the women's voices rather than my own throughout the text. When applicable, I note my position in their narratives (see Morgaine, 2017), both in the text and the summary and reflection sections. Each woman's chosen pseudonym, self-identified racial and sexual identity, and age range are noted in table 1. This will be a useful reference when reading each chapter. By including aspects of the women's identities, my intention is to remind the reader that they are real people whose experiences of power are shaped by the bodies they inhabit and the identities of the people with whom they partner. Furthermore, each of the women's experiences are specific to a space and time and are not meant to capture the full range of their lives or define who they are as people.

TABLE 1 WOMEN'S INDIVIDUAL IDENTITIES AND PATHWAYS

| Name | Race | Sexual identity | Age | Disclosed domestic violence (DV) and sexual violence (SV) history | Antiviolence intervention referral source and legal system status | Entered a no contest plea ("plea deal") |
|---|---|---|---|---|---|---|
| Abby | White | Heterosexual | Mid-30s | DV and SV | Criminal court, two-year probation, DV conviction | Yes |
| Becky | White | Heterosexual | Mid-20s | DV | Criminal court, two-year probation, DV conviction | Yes |
| Benita | Black | Heterosexual | Early 20s | DV | Criminal court, two-year probation, DV conviction | Yes |
| Cherise | Black | Heterosexual | Late 20s | DV and SV | Criminal court, two-year probation, non-DV conviction, family court | Yes |
| Christine | White | Heterosexual | Early 30s | DV and SV | Criminal court, one-year probation, DV conviction | Yes |
| Darla | Black | Heterosexual | Late 20s | DV and SV | Criminal court, two-year probation, DV conviction | Yes |
| Devore | Black | Lesbian | Late 30s | Denies | Criminal court, two-year probation, DV conviction | Yes |
| Emersyn* | White | Heterosexual | Early 40s | DV and SV | Criminal court, five-year probation, non-DV conviction | Yes |

(Continued)

TABLE 1 (*continued*)

| Name | Race | Sexual identity | Age | Disclosed domestic violence (DV) and sexual violence (SV) history | Antiviolence intervention referral source and legal system status | Entered a no contest plea ("plea deal") |
|---|---|---|---|---|---|---|
| Essence | Black | Heterosexual | Early 40s | DV and SV | Criminal court, two-year probation, DV conviction | Yes |
| Ikeeylah | Black | Heterosexual | Late 20s | DV | Criminal court, two-year probation, DV conviction | Yes |
| Imani | Black | Bisexual | Late 30s | DV and SV | Criminal court, two-year probation, non-DV conviction | No |
| Jatara* | Black | Heterosexual | Mid-30s | DV and SV | Criminal court, two-year probation, DV conviction | No |
| Joy* | White | Heterosexual | Late 40s | DV and SV | Voluntary, there to learn | N/A |
| Lily* | White | Heterosexual | Mid-30s | DV | Criminal court, five-year probation, non-DV conviction, family court | Yes |
| Lola* | Black | Heterosexual | Early 40s | DV and SV | Criminal court, two-year probation, DV conviction | Yes (second charge) |
| Manuela* | White | Heterosexual | Early 50s | DV and SV | Criminal court, two-year probation, DV conviction | Yes |

| | | | | | | |
|---|---|---|---|---|---|---|
| Marcella | Latina** | Queer | Mid-20s | DV | Voluntary(ish), non-DV case pending | N/A |
| Moneesha* | Black | Heterosexual | Late 40s | DV and SV | Criminal court, two-year probation, non-DV conviction | Yes |
| Nikki* | White | Heterosexual | Late 30s | DV and SV | Criminal court, two-year probation, DV conviction | Yes |
| Olivia* | White | Heterosexual | Early 30s | DV and SV | Criminal court, two-year probation, DV conviction | Yes |
| Phoebe | Biracial: Native American/Black | Heterosexual | Early 20s | DV and SV | Criminal court, two-year probation, DV conviction | No |
| QuiShandra | Black | Heterosexual | Mid-20s | DV | Criminal court, two-year probation, DV conviction | Yes |
| Regina* | Biracial: White/Native American | Heterosexual | Early 50s | DV | Criminal court, two-year probation, non-DV conviction | Yes |
| Rosalee* | Native American | Heterosexual | Early 50s | DV | Criminal court, two-year probation, non-DV conviction | Yes |
| Rosemary | White | Bisexual | Mid-50s | DV and SV | Criminal court, two-year probation, DV conviction | Yes |
| RyAnn* | Black | Heterosexual | Mid-20s | DV and SV | Criminal court, two-year probation, DV conviction | Yes |

*(Continued)*

TABLE 1   (continued)

| Name | Race | Sexual identity | Age | Disclosed domestic violence (DV) and sexual violence (SV) history | Antiviolence intervention referral source and legal system status | Entered a no contest plea ("plea deal") |
|---|---|---|---|---|---|---|
| Sage* | Black | Heterosexual | Mid-30s | DV | Criminal court, two-year probation, DV conviction | Yes |
| Sheniqua | Black | Bisexual | Late 20s | DV and SV | Criminal court, two-year probation, DV conviction | Yes |
| Sissy | Latina** | Heterosexual | Mid-30s | DV and SV | Voluntary(ish), non-DV case pending | Yes |
| Suzie | White | Lesbian | Late 50s | DV and SV | Voluntary(ish) | N/A |
| Tiffany* | Asian-American | Heterosexual | Early 20s | DV | Criminal court, two-year probation, DV conviction | Yes |
| Tyra* | Black | Heterosexual | Late 20s | DV and SV | Family court | N/A |
| Valerie | White | Heterosexual | Early 20s | DV and SV | Criminal court, two-year probation, DV conviction, family court | Yes |

NOTE: The identities provided here are most relevant to the context in which the women's experiences are discussed.

* Denotes women with whom I had prior contact as a social work practitioner cofacilitating antiviolence intervention groups.

** Race is a socially constructed, ever-transforming category with no fixed meaning (Bettie, 2014). I made the choice to collapse Marcella's and Sissy's racial identities into the group labeled "Latina" owing to their common identity-based experiences and to promote their confidentiality.

## THIS PROJECT

*Broken* draws on my use of mixed qualitative methods over three years of fieldwork, building on my knowledge as an AVI practitioner who has developed, managed, and cofacilitated AVIs for more than 20 years. I conducted 51 in-depth trauma-informed life-history (Richie, 1996) interviews with 33 women who had AVI contact. Thirty-two of the 51 interviews were semi-ethnographic owing to the women inviting me into their space (e.g., homes, communities, workplaces). I often met their children and extended families, as well as their uninvited abusive partners. An additional six interviews were go-along interviews (Kusenbach, 2003) that took place in custody hearings, protection order hearings, healthcare institutions, and farmer's markets. Lastly, four more interviews were what I call middle position interviews, wherein I navigated a space between practice and research by providing formal advocacy that the women requested while also documenting the experience. I kept detailed fieldnotes from all interactions (see the appendix).

Most of the women I interviewed were low-income; the sample is roughly 50 percent Black; 25 percent Asian, Biracial, Indigenous, and Latina; and 25 percent white. Twenty-nine women's use of force or alleged use of force brought them to the attention of the CLS and CPS. Twenty of those women were criminal court ordered to AVI following a domestic violence conviction; five were criminal court ordered following a nondomestic violence conviction; one was family and criminal court ordered owing to a domestic violence conviction; two were family and criminal court ordered for nondomestic violence convictions; and one woman was family court ordered. None of the family court–ordered women disclosed having used force against their partners or children. Instead, their referrals were a result of their interactions with CPS workers and allegations of neglect. Four women attended AVI voluntarily. All the women disclosed a current or former partner's coercive control, and emotional, financial, physical, psychological, reproductive, sexual, and/or verbal abuse against them. Twenty-two women disclosed having also endured sexual violence perpetrated by friends, family members, strangers, and partners over their lifetimes.

## THEORETICAL FRAMING

As previously mentioned, this work is anchored in Black feminist epistemology (BFE) (Collins, 2009), as well as standpoint (Harding, 1987;

Hartsock, 1983), and intersectionality (Crenshaw, 1991) theories. BFE recognizes Black women as credible, their lived experiences as meaningful, and that knowledge is produced through dialogue, not isolation. It encourages an ethic of caring, which promotes individuality, emotion, and expressions of empathy, and holds individuals accountable for their knowledge claims. As this research amplifies the voices of women whose lives were affected by violence and the carceral system—voices often not recognized, heard, or listened to—*Broken's* theoretical framing includes diverse women marginalized by income inequality and systems identified as offenders.

Standpoint theory brings attention to an individual's perception of her location in social and institutional structures and how that location shapes her experience. Therefore, one's standpoint emerges from one's intersecting identities. Intersectionality theory pushes back against tendencies to essentialize one identity category—such as woman, heterosexual, victim, or offender—by focusing on how identities overlap and interlock to produce privilege and oppression (Crenshaw, 1991). Intersectionality is a critical tool in destabilizing binary thinking because it allows for viewing "the person in context," which is fundamental to the social work profession (Gringeri et al., 2010). Such a framework is essential to understanding how power relations dictate not only how people relate to each other, but who has certain advantages and who does not.

BFE, standpoint, and intersectionality theories provide the necessary framework to interrogate the victim-offender binary. This framing informed how I listened to the women and grew to understand how they defined themselves and their experiences. That process allowed a new concept to emerge—namely, that many of the women expressed feeling physically and emotionally broken by their experiences, rather than empowered by causing harm or devastated by their survivorship histories. Reconceptualizing them as broken—rather than only as victims or only as offenders—intentionally pushes beyond the binary by focusing on the women's experiences both before their systems contact and then within those systems. This reconceptualization centers the women's experiences, perspectives, and words. In doing this, *Broken* intentionally moves conversations beyond the more dominant focus on how systems authorities view and define women, making room for the necessary contradiction, ambiguity, and confusion that comprise their daily lives.

In no way does this reconceptualization suggest that domestic violence is gender neutral or that women and men in heterosexual

TABLE 2   WOMEN'S AGGREGATE DEMOGRAPHICS AND REFERRAL PATHWAYS, $N=33$

| Categories | N | Percentage* |
|---|---|---|
| **Race** | | |
| Asian American | 1 | 3% |
| Biracial | 2 | 3% |
| Black/African American | 15 | 45% |
| Latina | 2 | 6% |
| Native American | 1 | 3% |
| White | 12 | 39% |
| **Sexual identity** | | |
| Bisexual | 3 | 9% |
| Heterosexual | 27 | 82% |
| Lesbian | 2 | 6% |
| Queer | 1 | 3% |
| **Age Range** | | |
| 20–30 | 13 | 39% |
| 31–40 | 12 | 36% |
| 41–50 | 4 | 12% |
| 51–57 | 4 | 12% |
| *Mean* | *34* | |
| **Income in US Dollars** | | |
| 0–15,000 | 15 | 45% |
| 15,001–30,000 | 7 | 21% |
| 30,001–45,000 | 6 | 18% |
| 45,001–60,000 | 3 | 9% |
| 60,001–70,000 | 1 | 3% |
| 70k+ | 1 | 3% |
| **Number of children** | | |
| 0 | 8 | 24% |
| 1 | 3 | 9% |
| 2 | 10 | 30% |
| 3 | 5 | 15% |
| 4+ | 7 | 21% |
| **Housing** | | |
| Owns home | 11 | 33% |
| Rents | 11 | 33% |
| Lives with family | 9 | 27% |
| Lives in a shelter or hotel | 2 | 6% |
| **Education** | | |
| Some high school | 1 | 3% |
| High school diploma | 7 | 21% |
| General equivalency diploma | 3 | 9% |
| Some online college classes | 17 | 52% |
| College degree | 4 | 12% |
| Two master's degrees | 1 | 3% |

*(Continued)*

TABLE 2 *(Continued)*

| Categories | N | Percentage* |
|---|---|---|
| Mobility | | |
| Access to a car | 24 | 73% |
| Afford gas for a month | 9 | 38% |
| Disclosed domestic violence (DV) survivorship | 32 | 97% |
| Disclosed sexual violence (SV) survivorship | 22 | 67% |
| Referral pathway to antiviolence intervention (conviction) | | |
| Criminal court order (DV) | 20 | 61% |
| Criminal court order (non-DV) | 5 | 15% |
| Criminal (DV) and Family Court Orders | 1 | 3% |
| Criminal (non-DV) and family court orders | 2 | 6% |
| Family court order | 1 | 3% |
| Voluntary | 4 | 12% |

* Percentages for a given category do not always total 100 because of rounding conventions.

relationships are similarly affected by it. Men's violence against women is one of the most common human rights violations in the world (United Nations, 2015). Feminist scholars have long established that when analysis prioritizes relationship context—understanding the motivation, intent, and impact of partners' actions—women are more often physically harmed by the men in their lives; men more often hold the coercive power in heterosexual relationships; and sexual assault, strangulation, stalking, and murder are indicative of men's violence against women (Anderson, 2009; Armstrong et al., 2018; Bagwell-Gray, et al., 2015; DeKeseredy and Dragewicz, 2009; Dragiewicz and DeKeseredy, 2012; Dobash et al., 1992; Miller, 2005; Renzetti, 1999; Stark, 2007). Although there are women who do use violence or coercive control or both in their relationships, women's domestic and sexual violence survivorship histories are more often "a cause and consequence of inequality" (Armstrong et al., 2018, p. 100) with men. Instead, this reconceptualization demands that service providers have more thoughtful conversations foregrounding theoretical and practical innovations, challenging the overreliance on the carceral system, all while centering women's experiences. Everyone deserves a violence-free life. A better understanding of the experiences of women who have survived and caused harm will contribute to this goal.

## A VIEW BEYOND THE BINARY: BREAKAGE

The women's self-described *breakage* was physical and emotional, life-altering, integral to the fabric of their lives, and rooted in betrayal and shame.[19] In contrast to the "victim" or "offender" language often used across the CLS and CPS, the women's breakage existed in a complicated space that incorporated their historical, psychological, physical, and social experiences. These are the experiences some may associate with the language of "trauma," such as psychiatrists Judith Herman (1992, 2023), Maria Yellow Horse Brave Heart and others (2011), and Bessel van der Kolk (2014) explore. These early psychological and physical experiences comprise what social scientists call Adverse Childhood Experiences (Felitti et al., 1998), the understanding of which has become a cornerstone of clinical social work theory, practice, and scholarship (see Shapiro and Applegate, 2018). Indeed, some of the women spoke of this breakage as having been catalyzed by a particularly significant, even traumatic, event. Most, however, felt this breakage again and again—what Sage referred to as "thing on top of thing" —over the course of their lives, years before their systems contact.

Events that caused early breakage included witnessing violence between their caregivers; being raped as a young child, a teenager, or both; caregivers resorting to physical punishment; and watching their mothers, whose choices were constrained by their own breakage, seemingly choose abusive boyfriends over them. A closer look reveals that these harms also manifested in what did *not* happen, such as expecting relief of refuge in foster care but having uncaring foster parents; excitement to finally meet the biological father they never knew, who still did not show up; disclosing sexual assault as children, while adult caregivers disbelieved or dismissed them; and being detained in juvenile detention at 14 years old and family not visiting as further punishment. The breakage these early harms caused became deeper and more defined by these absences. And then there was the breakage of systemic oppression experienced by low-income women, women of color, disabled women, and those who identified beyond the confines of heterosexuality. Thus, this early breakage includes what sociologist Celeste Watkins-Hayes (2019) calls "injuries of inequality," involving what sociologist Elizabeth Comack (2018) explores as "the broader social contexts of people's lives," and what clinical social worker Resmaa Menakem (2017) describes as "soul wounds."[20] Then, abusive partners magnified this early breakage. Black feminist trauma psychologist Jennifer Gomez

(2023) points out that in addition to the physical abuse, ethnically and racially minoritized women who are harmed by similarly minoritized men—for example, Black women partnered with abusive Black men—also experience cultural betrayal. Sage explained that her partner and father of her children "helped me break way more than I was initially, but I was broken before he had any say so."

Although *Broken* builds on the theoretical contributions of others, the concept inductively evolved from the women's words in ways that do not separate intimate and systems-inflicted harms. Instead, *breakage* captures how the women's intimate and systems harms compounded in ways unbounded by arbitrarily demarcated lines of, for example, victim versus offender status, or psychological versus social harm. It was intertwined. Their self-described breakage was the result of surviving family, relationship, *and* systems abuse. Although systems actors viewed them as offenders, failed mothers, or both, these women endured intermingled interpersonal and institutional harms throughout their lives. They felt legal systems-specific events in public shaming—interactions with dismissive police officers, indelible police reports, bewildering court proceedings, intractable criminal records, strict probation officers, faithless CPS caseworkers, unaffordable AVI, and ongoing state surveillance. And again, in what did *not* happen—a responding police officer who witnessed injustice but said nothing; a partner who threatened them in front of their children, yet refused to acknowledge to responding officers the harm they had caused; police reports and criminal records that omitted what the women had endured; CPS caseworkers who judged the women for what they had not done, overlooking their protective parenting strategies; staff who promoted the AVI for court-ordered women as a safe space to share their feelings, but disregarded their inability to pay for those sessions; and state-sanctioned surveillance and referrals that singularly focused on the women as offenders, rather than the spectrum of their experiences. The system's disproportionate response and weaponization of their survivorship, and often their lack of financial resources, exacerbated this harm and amounted to what psychologists Carly Parnitzke Smith and Jennifer Freyd (2014) refer to as "institutional betrayal," when powerful systems entrusted with promoting safety and well-being instead cause further harm.[21] Some women felt the system, like their partners, had betrayed them. Others felt they had betrayed themselves. Many felt both.

The institutional betrayal catalyzed or added to shame, humiliation, and self-judgment, while also muting their voices and laying bare wounds inflicted in childhood and in their intimate relationships. These women not only felt this systems-inflicted "breakage" personally; they experienced it publicly in compounding events not possibly captured within the singular psychologizing, inward trauma focus practitioners have used to further pathologize marginalized women (DeGenna and Feske, 2013; Gilfus, 1999; Herman et al., 1989). Instead, the women's language and experiences of breakage were a multilayered merging of interpersonal relationship experiences with complex family histories, structural oppression, and systems abuse that occurred inside and across systems that were themselves broken.

## LEGAL SYSTEM CONTACT: HEARTBROKEN AND AT THEIR BREAKING POINT

Some women described the circumstances that led to their legal systems involvement as feeling *heartbroken* (e.g., systems misidentified as having caused harm), while others detailed how their heartbreak brought them to *their breaking point* (e.g., causing harm). The concepts of *heartbroken* and *at their breaking point* are fluid, derived from the women's words conveying their feelings about their legal systems involvement. These concepts move beyond victim and offender categories and attend to necessary complexities in language (see Tu and Penti, 2020). Across their experiences, these women spoke in terms of what Olivia called "heartbreak" and Tyra referred to as "heartache." It is this connection between an individual's heart and the physical as well as social harms that practice, theory, and policy often, if not always, overlook but that these systems-involved women feel deeply. In addition, although they were being held accountable by the state for their alleged harm, they readily admitted their actions and were largely unaware of how the CLS and CPS operated, making them more vulnerable. Although the *heartbroken* and those *at their breaking point* came to the system's attention for different reasons (see figure 1 for a visual comparison of *heartbroken* and *at their breaking point*), the low-income women of diverse identities were all under state surveillance, court ordered to AVI, and often lacked resource-rich social networks that could end their legal system's contact as offenders. The *heartbroken* described breakage by their intimate partners and others, as well as CLS and CPS personnel who did not believe they used actions that the CLS would typically define as "self-defensive."[22] Like Essence, some women described how they were physically and emotionally harmed and betrayed, first by their intimate partners and then by police officers who arrested them for protecting themselves. In some of these cases, police decisions to arrest were manipulated by partners' false accusations. Essence was devastated by how her former partner successfully leveraged her broken past to gaslight her—framing his scratch as evidence of her aggression, rather than self-protection. Having successfully convinced the police, Essence's former partner again broke her by casting her as a mother who failed to protect her children (see chapter 2). Likewise, Nikki physically protected herself against her abusive partner. Her self-protective actions went undetected by police, however, who instead weaponized her self-disclosure. As Nikki put it,

> He wouldn't admit to what he did, and I would admit to what I did . . . I would tell the truth, and he would lie, and the lie would win . . . I would tell them he threw me over the side of the stairs because I yelled at him or . . . he smashed my face into the ground because of whatever reason . . . and I ended up stabbing him because he locked me in the house for three days and wouldn't let me leave.

This aspect of *heartbroken* builds on scholarship regarding women's self-protective actions, often legally defined as "self-defense," toward physically abusive partners, as well as coercively controlling partners' false accusations or withholding of information from responding police officers (see, for similar findings, Ballan and Frye, 2012; Dasgupta, 2002; Gardner, 2009; Goodmark, 2008; Hamby, 2014; Larance and Miller, 2017; Larance and Rousson, 2016; Miller, 2005; Roy, 2012; Saunders, 2002). It also recognizes that some Black women, as Potter (2008) points out, see themselves as "dynamic resistors" who may be more likely than white women to fight back, as they view themselves as their children's protectors. The language and experiences of the *heartbroken* are derived from the women's descriptions.

In addition, the conceptualization of *heartbroken* moves practice, research, and policy conversations beyond a focus on women's self-protective actions against physically abusive intimate partners to actions against other people in their lives. It does so by acknowledging that early family of origin and relationship breakage can shape how women view the risk to their physical safety and the need to protect themselves across their relationships. Because of the combination of their actions and their intersectional identities, the CLS defines these women in ways that contrast with how they view themselves.

Imani's experiences illustrate this complexity. A self-described "outspoken low-income Black woman," Imani had a broad smile and a

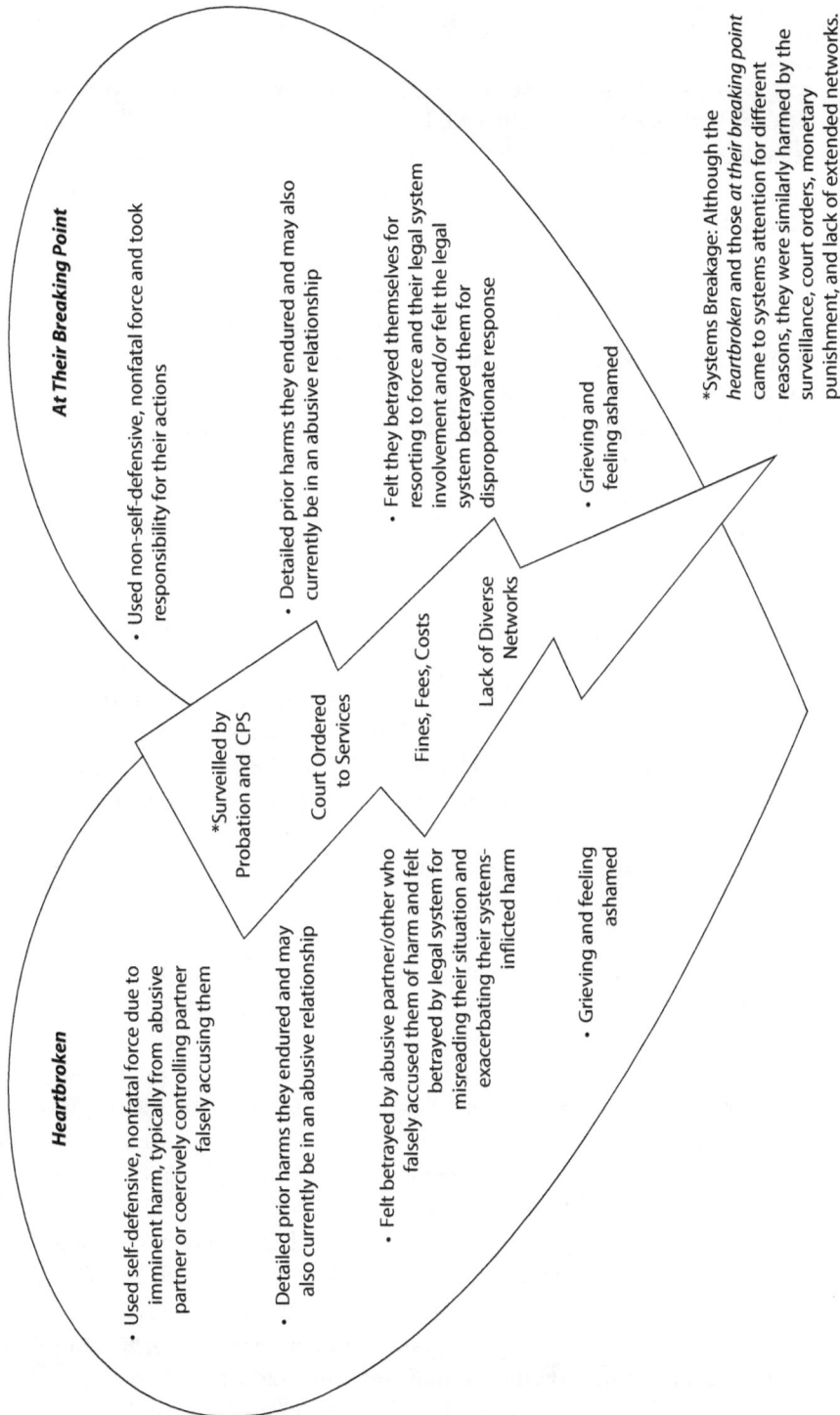

**Heartbroken**

- Used self-defensive, nonfatal force due to imminent harm, typically from abusive partner or coercively controlling partner falsely accusing them

- Detailed prior harms they endured and may also currently be in an abusive relationship

- Felt betrayed by abusive partner/other who falsely accused them of harm and felt betrayed by legal system for misreading their situation and exacerbating their systems-inflicted harm

  - Grieving and feeling ashamed

**At Their Breaking Point**

- Used non-self-defensive, nonfatal force and took responsibility for their actions

- Detailed prior harms they endured and may also currently be in an abusive relationship

- Felt they betrayed themselves for resorting to force and their legal system involvement and/or felt the legal system betrayed them for disproportionate response

  - Grieving and feeling ashamed

*Surveilled by Probation and CPS

Court Ordered to Services

Fines, Fees, Costs

Lack of Diverse Networks

*Systems Breakage: Although the *heartbroken* and those *at their breaking point* came to systems attention for different reasons, they were similarly harmed by the surveillance, court orders, monetary punishment, and lack of extended networks.

FIGURE I. Heartbroken and at their breaking point.

hearty laugh, but police read her as the "primary aggressor" after an incident with her former girlfriend. Imani explained that she physically defended herself. Not being believed by the police, the judge, and then her probation officer made her feel "literally broke down." As we talked, Imani's wounds from earlier breakage became visible. She described years of watching her mother being beaten by her brother's father and resenting her often absent mother for choosing a man "over your child." Imani decided that her mother "hates" her because she left her to find out about her "menstrual" on her own. And then there was the day Imani's mother dropped her off, without explanation, to live with her grandmother. That was where Imani's older uncle repeatedly "touched" her. He threatened to harm Imani if she told anyone about his sexual abuse and said they would not believe her anyway. "So," Imani explained, "I never, ever told anybody about it because I was young when it happened, and I was scared to get a whoopin'." Imani described her earlier relationship with her child's father as having informed her resolve that "I would never let a [man] put his hands on me [again]. I'm not about to sit up here and think you gonna eat my cooking, lay up next to me after you whoop my ass!" And the impact of those experiences? When she was younger, she "was ready to beat the bitches up because that's all [she] knew!" Despite how the CLS defined Imani, her history of intimate and systems harm shaped her hypervigilant response to others. Imani's identities and presentation as a masculine Black bisexual woman likely played a pivotal role in systems actors casting her as the offender.

Lastly, other women felt *heartbroken* from the harms CPS caseworker contact inflicted on nearly every aspect of their family lives—this was particularly true for low-income women and women of color.[23] CPS workers exacerbated the feeling of being *heartbroken* for some by making initial contact under the guise of being helpful, when their motivation was, in fact, coercive (see Fong, 2020). Similar to sociologist Kelly Fong's (2019) findings, this prompted already marginalized mothers to conceal their challenges rather than ask for needed support. Tyra (see chapter 2) details her "heartache" after her husband's violence against her "got to hospital stays, black eyes, and broken bones." What was worse, Tyra explained, was feeling "tricked and betrayed" by CPS caseworkers whose early "support" was actually a façade. After *he* assaulted her, CPS treated Tyra as a failed mother by removing her children from her care, ordering random referrals and carrying out sporadic checks. Now, Tyra explained, "I fear CPS more than him."

In contrast, women brought to the legal system's attention for using nonfatal, non-self-defensive physical force, such as Valerie, took responsibility for their actions that resulted in a CLS response. These women explained that their actions resulted from arriving *at their breaking point*—deciding they would no longer endure the indignity of their partner's treatment. These women did not use "self-defense" according to the law's definition. Nor did they abuse another person for the purpose of maintaining power and control. Instead, when they had "had enough," they resorted to what practitioners and researchers have called "defense of self" (Pence et al., 2011) and "asserting their dignity" (Larance and Miller, 2017). The women *at their breaking point* sought autonomy in ways consistent with the coping strategies clinical psychologist Sherry Hamby (2014) identifies among women who have disclosed histories of being harmed by their partners. It also brings into sharper focus the importance of the overlap or co-occurrence of intimate harms that Sherry Hamby and John Grych (2013) detail. Thus, the women's experiences of having endured and caused harm blur the "categorical boundaries between victimization and offending," similarly examined by sociologist Kathleen Ferraro (2006, p. 13). When we understand women at *their breaking point* as seeing themselves with limited relationship alternatives, we can more easily understand their forceful actions as strategies to overtly contradict their feelings of vulnerability by making themselves visibly active agents in their own lives. Women who were not currently in abusive relationships, but who had experienced harm in previous relationships and had not repaired that breakage, organized their current relationship dynamics around first protecting themselves. Unfortunately, these survival strategies put these women and others at risk of harm.

Abby's, Sheniqua's, Emersyn's, and QuiShandra's experiences provide necessary context to the conceptualization of women *at their breaking point*. With her hair pulled back in a ponytail, Abby explained that she and other women did not use force "because that's something we always do, . . . [but] because it's been done to us for so long or we've been hurt for so long we finally just hit a breaking point." What had Abby done before her arrest? She slapped her coercively controlling husband after learning he had cheated again. In response, he called the police—not because he sought protection but because he knew this was an effective way to punish Abby. Abby, who saw herself without other options, grew used to a predictable sequence of events. After he harmed her, threatened her, or, in this case, she learned of his infidelity, Abby slapped him. He called the police. Abby removed her shoelaces and put her cell phone away, knowing they were not allowed in jail. Then she sat on the curb and waited for the police to arrive. When they did, Abby introduced herself as the person they were looking for, placed her hands behind her back, and prepared to be handcuffed. Although Abby used physical force, her partner held the coercive power in his relationships with Abby *and* the police.

Although Abby reached her breaking point with her husband, she experienced years of intimate harm and institutional betrayal before their relationship. Her previous husband physically abused and coercively controlled her. She never responded with force. Abby explained that she called the police for help—once. The responding officers dismissed her. She never called again. Abby learned that the CLS did not take her survivorship seriously, instead punishing her for standing up for herself. Furthermore, Abby did not receive support to emotionally heal from earlier relationship experiences because they were now obscured by her CLS offender status. A closer look at Abby's unhealed wounds revealed her belief that she had no recourse other than physical force and submission to a routine sequence of events.

Similarly, other women who described themselves as *at their breaking point* had years of accumulated intimate and institutional betrayal that manifested itself in the harms they caused to their intimate partners and others in their lives. This was evident in Sheniqua's early heartbreak, only seeing her father twice, when she was eight years old and again when she was twelve. Sheniqua spent her childhood "going through things" with a mother who "didn't know how to discipline without . . . violence." Over time, Sheniqua's unresolved pain manifested in using non-self-defensive physical force to harm intimate partners whom she felt betrayed her.

The accumulated intimate betrayal Sage described earlier was also visible in how Emersyn described the early breakage and intimate betrayal that manifested in her response to an abusive former partner's marriage announcement. With her chihuahuas at her feet and having just served us both tea, Emersyn sat and explained how it felt like not so long ago that she had encouraged him to move in with her. He was jobless and "at a low point in his life." She believed she could help. Emersyn was mowing the lawn, working full-time, doing all that had to be done as a single mother when she learned, through his poorly concealed "sext," that he was seeking sex with other women. "Repulsed," Emersyn gathered her composure and told him to leave. The pain and betrayal were unbearable, but got worse when Emersyn realized she was pregnant. When she told him, he refused to support her. Only a few weeks later, a mutual friend told Emersyn he was getting married. She was devastated by the symbolic violence (Durfee, 2015) of his marrying so quickly, as well as on the same date they had long celebrated their anniversary and planned to one day have their wedding. Emersyn explained that she was "heartbroken," having just "lost a person I thought I'd be with for the rest of my life." Adding to her pain, he texted Emersyn on his wedding day and told her that he and his wife were getting a new place and starting over. Emersyn felt like she was "sinking" as a single parent in a flood of 50-hour work weeks, trying to put food on the table, and gas in the car. She had done all she could do to support him, despite his abusive behavior. Emersyn "started to break." One night she sat down and thought, "Okay, two can play at this game! I'm going to make him jealous how he always tried to do to me, and I'm going to annoy [his new wife] kind of thing. Malicious? Annoying? Yes. Did I ever think about the consequences? No." But Emersyn did think her behind-the-scenes edgework (Larance and Miller, 2017; Rajah, 2007) would "kind of stick it to" him, bringing her some satisfaction. In addition, Emersyn targeted his new wife with what Susan Miller and I (2017) refer to as "horizontal hostility," posting an online advertisement pretending to be his wife seeking sex. She intended for men to read the ad and call his wife on his wife's cell phone number Emersyn included in the advertisement. It would confuse his wife and make him jealous. Emersyn assumed that the new couple "would never know where it came from." Later that night, she thought about it and decided to delete the ad, thinking, "I probably shouldn't do that."

Emersyn made connections between how she enacted her feelings of betrayal for the combination of his abuse, infidelity, and new relationship and what she witnessed growing up. Emersyn's "big family secret" was that her "dad beat [her] mom pretty much daily. If a day went by [without him beating her] . . . you kind of wondered what was going on." Her dad also routinely cheated on Emersyn's mother. To make sense of it all, she theorized her experience as she explained, "I remember as a kid seeing [my mother] search through a phonebook to try and find the lady's name that she knew my dad was [having sex with] . . . I remember . . . [she would try to find her]. So, I do think some of my responses to the pain were learned . . . I learned that you react, and you lash out."

And then there was the sexual abuse Emersyn suffered by her uncle. There were layers of betrayal. The hardest part of the abuse was, "You're kind of a possession of your captor until you find . . . your bottom point, your break," she explained. Emersyn found her breaking point, coped with those feelings by attempting to "kind of stick it to him," and was then arrested for interfering with a telecommunications device.

Like Emersyn, QuiShandra was tired and found herself at her breaking point. Wearing a flawless brown suit with sparkling nail polish, QuiShandra explained how she, her partner, and their child lived with her partner's mother. QuiShandra worked long days to support them. Every day she drove 30 miles one way from home to work, "doing everything that I should have been doing as a mom, as a woman," while "he sat at home and did nothing." The evening of the incident, he once again falsely accused her of having an affair, and criticized how she dressed and the shoes she wore. They argued. He threatened her. She jumped in the car and tried to leave. But he caught up to her, reached through the open window, and punched her in the face. QuiShandra had had enough. Feeling angry and betrayed, she slammed on the brakes, got out of the car, grabbed a couple of bricks piled on the ground, and threw them at him and at his mother's house. He called the police. QuiShandra was arrested. Now she was alone. As she tearfully explained, once he had "kicked me to the curb, and dogged me, and did all these mean things to me, and pushed me away . . . nobody wants to deal with [me]."

Valerie's, Abby's, Sheniqua's, Emersyn's, and QuiShandra's stories illuminate the experiences of women *at their breaking point*. To be clear, they were not innocent of wrongdoing. Nor did they claim to be. Instead, they spoke up and spoke out in ways that publicly masked the complexity of their relationship histories. As a result, they risked being viewed through the victim-offender binary's lens as undeserving of legal protection and supportive intervention. In this context, the women in *Broken* encountered a carceral system that exacerbated their breakage and presented barriers to their healing and repair. Low-income women's lack of financial and social capital contributed to what often felt like the system's disproportionate response to holding them accountable for the harm they endured, the harm they caused, or both.

The concept of *breakage* is not meant to excuse or minimize the harm some of these women caused to others. Everyone should feel safe, and anyone affected by violence deserves support. It is not only possible but necessary to acknowledge the intimate and public harms they endured *and* to address the harm they caused. We must recognize that relationships are complicated. These women, regardless of how practitioners, scholars, and formal systems define them, are people who love and are loved by others. As readers we may be quick to judge them based on the language attached to their stories or our preconceived notions about who they *really* are. But when we are honest with ourselves, we may recognize our own breakage. We may also see that all of us have the capacity to do things we never thought we would do or unexpectedly exist in systems that define who we are. Thus, understanding their experiences of breakage encourages us to reconceptualize women who have caused harm in ways that do not simply pathologize them as mentally ill, vilify them for their actions, or evoke pity for their survivorship histories. Instead, it demands compassion for the human experience and thoughtful consideration for how we may innovatively address their circumstances. We currently exist in broken systems that seem designed to cause more heartbreak, especially in the lives of those made most vulnerable by income inequality, ableism, racism, sexism, and homophobia.

This view beyond the victim-offender binary centers the women's experiences in the community while complying with probation requirements, interacting with CPS caseworkers, making AVI contact, and living life after their formal systems contact ended. By focusing on these experiences—rather than the women's arrests and court interactions—I call the efficacy of community-based carceral approaches to intervention into question. Furthermore, I illuminate the breakage caused by community-based carceral approaches to promoting accountability that, although intended as less punitive than long-term incarceration or CPS involvement, are not only harmful in their own right but lack the same accountability they demand from others. With this view, I urge community-specific responses that reimagine intervention for those who have both survived and caused harm, grounded in a healing place philosophy, that intentionally move intervention beyond carceral systems of power.

*Broken* has two parts. Part 1 brings attention to the breakage caused by probation and CPS, as well as court-ordered AVI. Part 2 focuses on how the women engaged formal systems and informal alliances to mend their breakage. The final chapter is a call to action, providing considerations for healing and repair beyond the victim-offender binary.

## PART I. BREAKAGE
### Chapter 1. Probation

Central to this chapter is the concept of the *discretionary toolkit* (Watkins-Hayes, 2009), which explains how probation officers organized and deployed their power in shaping outcomes for those they supervised. The women on probation encountered a bureaucratic, routinized system with some probation officers leveraging their toolkits in ways that caused further breakage. The other women used their discretion to provide support. The misuse of discretionary power comes into sharp focus, as does the women's success in navigating that discretion.

## Chapter 2. Child Protective Services

The women discussed in this book experienced CPS caseworkers' discretionary power as replicating the abusive relationships they had with their coercively controlling partners. Thus, institutional harm replicated intimate harm through what I call a "failure to protect ideology." Whether or not there was a formal investigation, this ideology shaped CPS caseworkers' interactions with and discretion in monitoring women of marginalized identities with domestic and sexual violence survivorship histories. The women's stories became renarrated in the way CPS caseworkers portrayed them in official documents that followed them for years.

## Chapter 3. Antiviolence Intervention Administration

Although both are part of the same overall antiviolence intervention (AVI), I make the distinction between the antiviolence intervention administration (AVI-A) and the antiviolence intervention group (AVI-G). The women detailed vastly different experiences between a punishing administration (AVI-A) and a supportive group (AVI-G). The AVI-A's surveilled compulsory attendance, weekly group session fees, lack of childcare and transportation, and the expenditure of time to attend the group inflicted further harm on already marginalized criminal court–ordered women. Although family court–ordered women's attendance was financed by CPS, other costs were evident. For example, CPS could hold the women's reunification with their children in limbo until their AVI completion.

## PART 2. HEALING AND REPAIRING THE BREAKAGE

## Chapter 4. Antiviolence Intervention Group

The AVI-G was different from one-on-one probation reporting, CPS caseworker interactions, and AVI-A practices. Here, the women could interact with each other, discovering what Rosemary called a "common bond." In this space, the women engaged in a process QuiShandra described as "connecting a few dots" by exchanging information and discussing how to apply that information to their relationships. The shared insight provided opportunities to heal and repair their breakage by creating an AVI-G facilitated community.

## Chapter 5. After Antiviolence Intervention Group

This chapter begins by highlighting the women's voluntary connections made within, between, and after AVI-Gs. Some women used these informal connections to emotionally heal and repair the breakage from intimate and systems-inflicted harms. This chapter also attends to the experiences of the women who chose to have limited or no contact with other group members beyond the AVI for a variety of reasons. The chapter ends with a glimpse of the women's lives after their court-ordered obligations ended. By including the benefits some found in informal connections, choices not to have contact, and how the legal system affected their lives years later, this chapter encourages a more complex analysis of how carceral systems affect people in the community over years.

## Chapter 6. A Call to Action

The final chapter urges macro and micro approaches to work beyond the victim-offender binary that intentionally untether services from systems' harm. These goals can be accomplished in multiple ways that include but are not limited to extending the early battered women's movement's vision and engaging in reparative practices for those currently systems involved.

. . .

Thus, *Broken* tells the story of how the victim-offender binary persists in legal, child protection, and antiviolence intervention settings. By centering and problematizing the binary through women's stories, *Broken* challenges inclinations to vilify women for their violence or pity them for their survivorship, instead focusing on the complexity of their lives and the disproportionate consequences of their actions. In doing so, *Broken* demands an end to harmful community-based carceral practices and offers specific suggestions to encourage healing and repair across lives, institutions, and communities.

# PART ONE

# Breakage

# CHAPTER I

# Probation

"LITERALLY BROKE DOWN."
—IMANI

QuiShandra hoped her supervising probation officer would look out for her "best interests" and "want to see [her] succeed, and excel, and get better." The majority of the women in this project, also on probation for the first time, shared her hopes for probation-focused support. Most envisioned that "being on probation" would mean working with a supportive legal system liaison who would steward them through an unfamiliar process. Instead, they said, just like the warning QuiShandra eventually received, "Don't think your probation officer is your friend!" At odds with their initial hopes was probation officer-inflicted breakage, since they lacked the necessary probation-specific experiential capital (Watkins-Hayes, 2019) for success. This capital is the wisdom gained from prior experience that provides the tools to anticipate the reporting relationship dynamic and act in a manner that would keep them off, what Sheniqua referred to as the officer's "radar."

In this chapter, I detail the women's interactions with their supervising probation officers. I first review the goals of probation and present a general probationary framework. I then identify multiple complicating factors the women faced on their fraught paths to successful compliance: establishing a positive reporting relationship with their probation officer; complying with routine random drug testing and antiviolence intervention (AVI) contact; adjusting to probation officer turnover and recordkeeping changes; and navigating distinctly different probation officer supervisory styles. Their experiences demonstrate how their varying access to experiential, financial, social, and cultural capital largely determined their capacities to ease, but not entirely avoid, probation-specific breakage.[1]

## OVERVIEW: PROBATION

The general purposes of probation are to punish, deter, and rehabilitate. The specific purpose, according to the American Probation and Parole Association, "is to assist in reducing the incidence and impact of crime by probationers in the community" (American Probation and Parole Association, 1997). Probation is one of the possible court-ordered sanctions for a person convicted of committing a crime. Although it is not a sentencing option for all offenses, the court often offers probation as an alternative to or in combination with incarceration. For a court to grant probation, an individual must first agree to comply with the conditions ordered by a judge during court proceedings, which typically include obeying all laws, reporting to their probation officer, notifying their probation officer of any changes in address and employment, and remaining within the court's jurisdiction unless given approval to leave (Labrecque, 2017; Phelps and Ruhland, 2022). For people with domestic violence or domestic violence-related convictions, conditions may also require compliance with the court-ordered condition of no contact with the person that the criminal legal system (CLS) identifies as the victim; obtaining and maintaining legitimate gainful employment; completing community service;[2] complying with random drug and alcohol testing; paying court-ordered fines, fees, costs, and restitution; surrendering firearms; and attending AVI and substance use treatment groups. In some US cities, these conditions are met over a 22- to 24-month period of probation monitored by a probation officer.

The court then places a person who agrees to comply with these conditions under a probation officer's monitoring and supervision; that officer monitors their compliance with all court-ordered conditions and reports breaches in compliance to the court (American Probation and Parole Association, 2013). Probation officers' foundational practice principles are as follows: (1) case intervention is victim-focused; (2) abusive behavior is the responsibility of the offender; (3) unintended consequences should be considered; (4) evidence-based practices should be employed; and (5) practitioners and organizations should be held accountable (Crowe et al., 2009, pp. 54–55). If a person on probation violates or allegedly violates any conditions of probation, the probation officer must address the perceived violation with the person they are supervising (Labrecque, 2017). Probation officers have broad discretion in addressing violations, and may issue "technical violations" that do not require rearrest and incarceration (Campbell, 2016). When issuing technical violations, "Officers are often free to choose in which instances a probationer should receive a stern warning and those which warrant an officer to bring the probationer back before the court for a formalized hearing" (Labrecque, 2017, p. 6). If an alleged violation of probation is substantiated, the court may amend or revoke an individual's terms of probation (Allen et al., 2015). Therefore, people on probation tend to be highly motivated to comply with the court's initial terms (Latessa and Smith, 2015). If they do not comply, they may face a range of recommended sanctions including jail time. Thus, probation is both an alternative to jail and an opportunity to expand carceral involvement for marginalized people (Phelps and Ruhland, 2022).

Because probation is an alternative to jail, and typically not included in the analysis of mass incarceration, the public, members of the CLS, and scholars often view it as a "slap on the wrist" (Phelps, 2020). The majority of women under correctional control, however, are on probation (73 percent), with fewer being on parole (9 percent), in jail (7 percent), in state prison (1 percent), or in federal prison (1 percent) (Jones, 2018). Thus, for women, mass probation has outpaced mass imprisonment (Phelps, 2017; Kaebel and Cowhig, 2018; Sentencing Project, 2007). The burgeoning numbers of women on probation and the relentless victim-offender binary invite close scrutiny of how the reporting process may cause further breakage.

Twenty-seven of the 33 women in this project were on probation in one or more counties and attended the same AVI. A probation officer initially recommended the conditions of probation to the presiding judge, and then supervised the court-mandated tasks. Over the course of a typical two-year probation term, the women were required to regularly report to their probation officers and complete court-ordered tasks. Once on probation, women reported to their probation officers according to a regular schedule: they turned in pay stubs to show proof of formal employment; paying court fines, fees, and any restitution;[3] they attended any required court dates; they followed through with random drug and alcohol testing; and they paid for and attended AVI. After months of compliance, their probation officer may or may not have given them the option to report via email or text. Table 3, "Probation-involved women mentioned in chapter 1," brings attention

TABLE 3   PROBABION-INVOLVED WOMEN MENTIONED IN CHAPTER 1

| Name | System involvement | Race | Sexual identity | Education | Family | Income | Mobility | Housing |
|---|---|---|---|---|---|---|---|---|
| Benita | Criminal court, two-year probation, domestic violence (DV) conviction | Black | Bisexual | GED | Never married, single parent, one child | Less than 10K | Car, sometimes has enough gas for the month | Lives with her mother |
| Emersyn | Criminal court, five-year probation, non-DV conviction | White | Heterosexual | High school diploma | Never married, single parent, one child | 35k | Car, can afford enough gas for the month | Owns |
| Essence | Criminal court, two-year probation, DV conviction | Black | Heterosexual | Some nursing school | Never married, single parent, three children | 12k, disability and child support | Car, typically has enough gas for the month | Section 8 |
| Imani | Criminal court, two-year probation, non-DV conviction | Black | Bisexual | Some college | Never married, single parent, two children | Less than 10k | Car, can afford enough gas for a few days a month | Rents |
| Lily | Criminal court five-year probation, non-DV conviction family court | White | Heterosexual | Technical school | Never married, single parent, five children | Less than 10k | No car, borrows a car from a friend or takes the bus | Section 8 |
| Olivia | Criminal court, two-year probation, DV conviction | White | Heterosexual | Some college | Never married, single parent, one child | 25K | Car, can afford gas for most of the month | Rents |

| Name | Court | Race | Sexual orientation | Education | Marital status | Income | Transportation | Housing |
|---|---|---|---|---|---|---|---|---|
| Phoebe | Criminal court, two-year probation, DV conviction | Native American/ Black | Heterosexual | Some college | Never married, single parent, two children | Less than 10k | Car, can afford enough gas for the month | Lives with her grandparents |
| QuiShandra | Criminal court, two-year probation, DV conviction | Black | Heterosexual | Some college | Never married, single parent, two children | Less than 10k | No car, relies on her mother to drive her | Lives with her mother |
| Regina | Criminal court, two-year probation, non-DV conviction | White/ Native American | Heterosexual | High school diploma | Divorced, single parent three children | More than 70k | Car, can afford enough gas for the month | Owns |
| Rosemary | Criminal court, two-year probation, DV conviction | White | Bisexual | College degree | Married, stepparent, one child | 8k | Car, borrows gas money from employer | Owns |
| Sheniqua | Criminal court, two-year probation, DV conviction | Black | Bisexual | Some college | Never married, no children | 60k | Car, can afford enough gas for 20 days a month | Lives with grandmother |
| Valerie | Criminal court, two-year probation, DV conviction family court | White | Heterosexual | Some high school | Never married, single parent, four children | Less than 10k | Bus | Unhoused, living between motel rooms and shelters |

to the systems involvement, identities, families, income, mobility, and housing of women on probation discussed in this chapter. Table 1, "Women's individual identities and pathways," also provides necessary context for each woman's story.

## MANAGING PROBATION OFFICERS' BROAD DISCRETION

Probation officers had broad discretion in how they surveilled the women who largely came to their attention owing to domestic violence or domestic violence-related convictions (e.g., malicious destruction of property, shoplifting). Watkins-Hayes's (2009) "discretionary toolkit" provides a conceptual framework for understanding how individual probation officers exercised this discretion. For example, each "toolkit" contains "capabilities, perceptions, resources, and choices" (Watkins-Hayes, 2009, p. 56). Individual probation officers build their "toolkit" based on their interpretation of agency policies, procedures, practices, and ideologies, as well as on how they communicate with those they surveil and intervene in their lives. Among the "tools" in the probation officers' "kits" was the way they indirectly managed the women's time. Although often invisible, their access to broad discretion empowered probation officers to use time as a covert instrument of power (Lazarus-Black, 2007). With each interaction and decision, probation officers could contribute to systems-inflicted harms or ease those harms.

Women managed probation reporting by engaging in what sociologist Arlie Hochschild (1983) calls "emotion work," a kind of unpaid gendered labor meant to purposefully regulate or evoke others' emotions. The emotion work of women marginalized by race, class, sexual identity, or income status, is less explored by social scientists (Mirchandi, 2003). Because of how probation officers respond to their socially stigmatized identities, these women risk the additional likelihood that their probation officers will perceive them as difficult to work with or especially challenging. For these women, emotion work involves a significant, concerted effort to avoid any actual or perceived challenges to their probation officers' authority.

Olivia found the probation reporting process transactional—arrive, report, leave. Although she reported to her probation officer every week for two years, she recalled that she "didn't really get like that personal connection with [the probation officer]." Olivia attributed this dynamic to the probation officer's supervisory role and extensive caseload. But she knew that attending the weekly in-person meeting and presenting herself as pleasant and easy to work with were necessary for her to remain probation compliant.

For Benita, avoiding confrontation with her probation officer required her to hide the fact that her partner continued to physically abuse and coercively control her. Although systems-identified as the "offender," she reported she was defending herself when police first became involved. Despite suffering her partner's ongoing abuse, Benita was adamant that her probation officer learn nothing about it. Benita believed that because she "wasn't the victim on paperwork," (e.g., the police report, court documents), she would destroy her chances for successful probation completion. Her concern that her probation officer would view her as "difficult to work with" if she presented as anything other than an "offender" reflects the victim-offender binary's erasure of her experience and insidious control over CLS interactions.

QuiShandra believed her investment in emotion work was necessary to push back against her systems' label as an offender. She explained, "If you were placed as the . . . suspect [in the police report], I feel like you're getting looked at in a negative way. At this point, all I can do is rebuild my character for someone who doesn't really know [me], so that's all I try to strive to do as far as when I see a probation officer."

She viewed weekly probation reporting as an opportunity to "rebuild [her] character" in the eyes of her probation officer, who controlled a process she could not afford to go badly. QuiShandra described how she did "whatever" she had to do to maintain a positive probation reporting relationship: "I can't afford to be challenging . . . I don't really try to go in with tension or bad blood, bad vibes, negative energy. I like to try to make sure that we're all on one page. I'll communicate by phone if I need to—whatever it is that I can do to make sure that we are on a good note."

QuiShandra's tenuous finances were a constant worry. As a result of her criminal domestic violence conviction she was fired from her job. QuiShandra now pieced together small jobs to pay a $425 court fine and a 40-dollar monthly probation supervision fee. As a low-income, Black single mother, engaging in emotion work was one way she could try to ensure that she would not incur any further costs or that she would perhaps receive an understanding response from her officer, should she be unable to make future payments. QuiShandra declined sharing her probation officer's name or affiliation during her interviews, voicing concern about whether or not anything should ever "get back" to the probation officer.

Like QuiShandra, Rosemary also did her best to promote a positive reporting relationship with her probation officer. Rosemary modified her communication style during weekly check-ins, noting that at first, "I would talk his ear off because I felt comfortable with him." Seemingly in response, the officer "recommended" Rosemary attend AVI as a more appropriate venue to talk through her feelings. Now she had to pay for and attend AVI. Rosemary was convinced the probation officer made the referral to discourage her from talking during probation reporting. It worked. Following the referrals, Rosemary limited communication with her probation officer. "Now I check in, and he says, 'What's going on?' I tell him and that's it. You know, sign the papers and go on my way," she explained.

Low-income women's efforts to establish and maintain a positive rapport with probation officials presented extensive challenges. Those efforts were particularly onerous for the women whose first probation officer contact did not go well, however. Imani's first interaction went so poorly that she "hated" her probation officer. During their first meeting the officer asked Imani about her aspirations. Imani eagerly explained, "I'm going to school for criminal justice. I'm going to be a probation officer." The probation officer laughed dismissively at Imani. Shocked, Imani recalled, "That lady laughed in my face! . . . I hated that lady's guts. How dare you! Like you heard what I came from!" Imani added that when the probation officer, who was also a Black woman, asked about Imani's life story, Imani expected to be heard and respected: "I'm telling you my story because you're asking, and it's not many Black people out here anyway that had been through what I done been through or been where I came from that actually graduated or went back to school and got their GED, and went back to college . . . For you to laugh in my face?"

In sharing her ambitions, Imani hoped for some form of group solidarity (Watkins-Hayes, 2009).[4] Nonetheless, Imani knew that in order to challenge her own disadvantages and stereotypes, she had to engage in the emotion work necessary to report successfully and remain probation compliant. This emotion work was an ongoing investment of already marginalized women's energy and time, which was always tinged with the uncertainty that it may not even be worth the effort.

## ROUTINE RANDOM DRUG AND ALCOHOL TESTING: TIME, ENERGY, AND "ABUSE MYSELF AGAIN"

Routine random drug and alcohol testing also took extensive time and energy. The court ordered these tests for all the women on probation, regardless of their substance use histories. Probation officers monitored compliance, and typically administered tests during the first six months of a two-year probation term. The court could extend testing depending on a probation officer's recommendation and a woman's substance use history. Even in the absence of a substance use history, a probation officer could find a woman in violation of probation for having as little as one glass of wine or beer. A "clean" drug test meant a probationer would remain in compliance. "Dropping dirty" was the term the women used to describe a failed test. Those who failed a test could face additional community service or an extended probationary term.

The sentencing court typically ordered each person to complete her first drug test within 48 hours of initially reporting to probation. The drug testing was located at a different site from the probation reporting, and open weekdays from eight o'clock in the morning to four o'clock in the afternoon, an hour later twice a week, and occasional Saturdays and Sundays from nine o'clock until eleven thirty in the morning. For a majority of the women, the drug testing site was at least a 30- to 40-minute one-way car drive from their homes. The distance was often even farther from their places of employment. As Emersyn recalled, "A lot of times I was commuting to work so I had to make the choice if I was going to call in sick or say I had a flat tire." Because of the time commitment involved, there was often no way for the women to complete the testing *and* work a full day. The women who did not have access to a car asked others for rides or took the bus to the testing site. A bus ride from home to the testing site took a minimum of an hour, one way. Once at the site, women waited for 10 to 45 minutes before beginning the 10- to 15-minute procedure.

Day-to-day testing compliance involved an inflexible routine. During a woman's first meeting, the probation officer presented her with a sheet of paper listing a combination of letters, numbers, and colors. Each morning, she had to refer to the document when calling in to determine if those with her letter, number, and color combination were required to report for testing that day. The recorded message was available daily between seven o'clock in the morning and three o'clock in the afternoon. If identified for testing, she then had to complete the test between eight o'clock in the morning and four o'clock in the afternoon. If the testing site hours conflicted with her work hours, she had to weigh the risk of losing her job against an almost certain determination of probation noncompliance. Most probation officers cautioned the women that if they missed a compulsory test for any reason—including the inability to leave work or find childcare—they would be in violation of probation and risk additional sanctions. But because losing a job could also result in probation noncompliance, the drug testing scheme placed the women in an impossible double bind.

The call in process was, at best, confusing. For Emersyn, it felt like she and the other women had been "set up to fail." Each day Emersyn called in—whether or not it was her testing day—she would "write down all the letters, numbers, and colors so they would believe me in court" in the event she was falsely accused of missing a test. During Emersyn's interview, she showed me her tattered notepad with pages full of dates and accompanying letter, number, and color combinations. She maintained this detailed daily record as a form of protection. If there was ever a question as to when she tested, Emersyn could easily flip through her notebook and prove her diligence. "It's kind of a puzzle," she explained, "that's why I got in the habit of writing it because it's so confusing. I thought I had to have something to look back if they call me out." Although years had passed since she had had to call in for testing, Emersyn kept her notebook as protection.

Daily phone calls to determine if it was a test day and rearranging schedules were only a first step. If it was a woman's test day, she would travel to the test facility and pay 25 cents for a locker to store personal items. She would then have to pay for the test. Test fees varied according to the kind of test ordered, but generally, women paid 10 to 20 dollars in cash (other forms of payment were not accepted). Once called back for her urine test, she first had to take a breathalyzer test in the hallway in the middle of passersby. She then entered a more private room for the urine test. For Emersyn's drug test she was taken into "one large bathroom with a sink, a toilet, and almost like a full medical stand where [the drug test administrator] could put a clip board and the [specimen] bottle. It was just a big sterile blue room kind of empty to one side. So, it was just her and me."

According to Emersyn, the drug test administrator then "inspects you and watches you as you hold the cup down there. Sometimes I had a hard time going but she was still right there looking at you. You were not allowed to wipe or flush until she takes the specimen from you. She looks between your legs in the toilet and then you are allowed to wipe, flush, and wash your hands. Once they called you back it took maybe 10 minutes." The facility allowed the women 20 minutes to provide a urine sample that filled the bottle to the designated level. If a woman could not provide the sample within the allotted time, the facility sent a "failure to

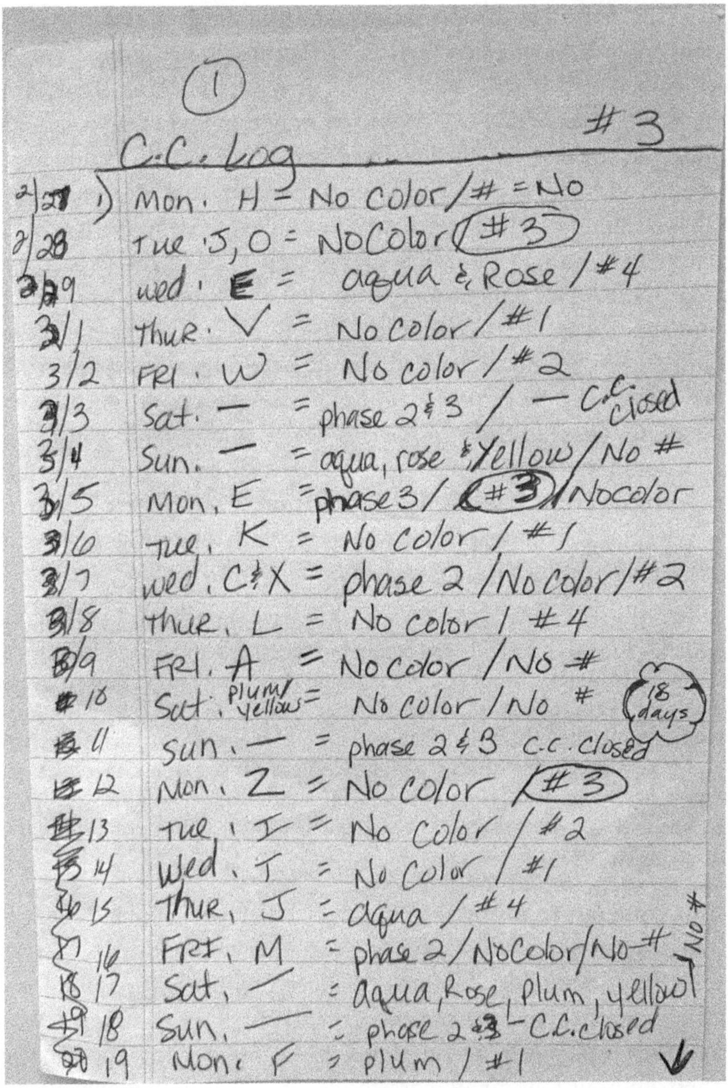

FIGURE 2. Emersyn's catalog of drug and alcohol testing codes upon call in.
Photo courtesy of the author.

provide sample" notice to her supervising probation officer. The first
time Emersyn provided a urine sample she barely had enough urine to
fill the bottle. The administrator told her it was, "okay, *this* time."

The second time Emersyn's letter, number, color combination came
up on the prerecorded testing site message she was menstruating. As

soon as she arrived at the test facility, she told the drug test administrator that she was having her "period . . . because I was going to have to touch myself and it was, well, yuck . . . it was uncomfortable." The administrator responded in a dismissive way that let Emersyn know she was used to the discomfort. But for Emersyn, who described herself as a "country girl who grew up with strict modesty," the idea of sitting on a toilet, holding her labia apart with her index and middle fingers, and urinating into a cup in front of a stranger, all while menstruating, made her very "nervous." Emersyn recalled that this time she "couldn't pee . . . for me it was very uncomfortable and messy." Because she could not urinate within the allotted 20 minutes, the administrator gave her a return pass. The pass provided Emersyn one opportunity to take "20 minutes to go to the lobby, drink water, and provide a urine sample." The administrator told her, "If you still can't [provide a urine sample] then you're in violation of probation." On the second attempt, Emersyn produced enough urine to comply with the testing process, but the experience left her feeling violated:

> My biggest takeaway [about the drug testing] was the trauma of it all. I was sexually abused as a child. The trauma of having to abuse myself again, that was very traumatic to me. I can't imagine that others don't have that issue. The fear of the whole situation but that specifically, in that whole experience, her standing there and making you pull yourself apart so she can view you is very degrading and very violating because you don't have a choice. I didn't have any power in the situation. I didn't have a choice. I own and accept that I made mistakes. I needed to be punished but I don't think it was done fairly.

This compulsory process weaponized Emersyn's sexual assault history and status as a low-income single mother without financial means or extensive community resources. The testing process required a significant investment of time and energy, anticipating when the test would be and then traveling to and completing the test. For low-income single mothers without low- or no-cost childcare, salaried employment complete with sick leave, and reliable transportation, the process was an especially onerous form of systems-inflicted harm.

## ENDURING ROUTINE RANDOM DRUG AND ALCOHOL TESTING: LILY, IMANI, AND EMERSYN

The testing process led many of the women to conclude that it was designed to cost them time, energy, money, and further harm rather than to deter substance use. As Regina reflected, "Telling someone that has no money, no home, no transportation, 'Oh, you've got to get down here to the police station to blow this breathalyzer because it's a condition of your [probation],' and just to be told, 'We don't care how you get there. We don't care how you pay for this. We don't care.' How does that make people better? . . . It doesn't."

Lily had a substance use history, and at one point, CPS removed her children as a result of her addiction. Although she understood why the court ordered drug testing, she viewed the sanction as wasting her time rather than supporting her sobriety. Lily resented the last-minute mandatory testing notification, which made it nearly impossible for her to figure out how to get across town to test and to care for her children when they were with her. Taking the bus was less expensive than driving, but it added delays associated with public transportation and the headache of wrangling five small children together. The test site did not provide childcare. As Lily recounted, "I couldn't take the [kids] back with me to pee, so then I had to find someone else to go with me. It was getting very difficult to find someone to go with me to sit with them so I could pee . . . Then, we had to take two carloads because we don't all fit in one car. It was really hard."

Lily had to test six days a week, then four, and finally, between three and four days a week for what seemed like "forever." Nevertheless, the time and expense invested in reporting for testing did not deter her substance use. Lily remembered that she "did drug tests because [probation and CPS] told me to. I even did those dirty . . . It took away from my drug money, so I wouldn't go to all of them, but I would still drop . . . [because] I had a chance of going to jail." Continued drug use, Lily explained, provided her the capacity to cope with the stress of legal involvement and losing her children. Her continued drug use showed the system that the drug testing regime was unhelpful. Exacerbating matters was the psychiatrist who did her CPS-ordered psychiatric evaluation. He told Lily she was a "failure" for her decisions and there was "no hope" for her future.

Unlike Lily, Imani did not have a substance use history. She did not understand why the court ordered drug testing, particularly given the inconvenience, transportation costs, and testing fees. She also became pregnant during her probation, which she believed should indicate to her probation officer that she would obviously not be using substances. Imani recalled,

> Every month I've got to drop. I'm like, "Okay, listen. What y'all wasting my time dropping for while I'm pregnant, too? I'm really not doing no drugs."

Even though I wasn't doing no drugs before, I never had a dirty drop. Not one time. So, what y'all keep wasting my time for making me come down there, pay ten dollars for parking . . . Then I've got to come upstairs and be out ten dollars for me to piss in a cup when I shouldn't even have to pee in the cup because you know it's going to come back clean. That's ridiculous.

As noted earlier, Emersyn, like Imani, did not have a substance use history. Emersyn found the testing process traumatic, and the time required to complete the testing made it impossible to keep her job. As a single parent, Emersyn took her young daughter to school each morning. That meant testing in the morning wouldn't work. Emersyn's shift ended at six o'clock in the evening. The testing site closed at four o'clock. As if still seeking a solution years later she asked, "How do you explain to an employer you have to leave [work early for a drug test]? . . . I can't run all the way across to the other side of town!"

Emersyn gave an example of how she tried to solve this puzzle one time. When her combination came up on the recorded message, Emersyn took the day off from work and completed the test. The following day her probation officer called her at work to inform her that although she had taken the urine test, she had submitted the results on the wrong form. What was the difference between the form Emersyn completed and the correct form? The title.

The probation officer told Emersyn she would have to return to the testing site, retest, pay for the retest, and resubmit the results on the correct substance testing form the following day. Emersyn explained that given the limited testing hours she would have to delay retesting until she could get permission to leave work again—or risk losing her job. Her probation officer responded, "Well, you'll have to make that choice! I have to have the urine sample done . . . or that puts you in a violation status."

The next day Emersyn attempted to retest during her lunch hour, hoping to "race over there," complete the drug test, and return to work. Unfortunately, there were already "about 40 people in line." Nearly two hours passed before she made it back to work. She managed her late return by fabricating a story about tire problems. Emersyn successfully retested, resubmitted the correct test documentation, and avoided a probation violation. Two weeks later, however, she was laid off from her job because of her multiple absences and "extended lunch hours." Now without gainful employment, Emersyn again risked violating the terms of probation.

## PROBATION OFFICER TURNOVER AND
## RECORDKEEPING CHANGES

Probation reporting and drug and alcohol testing became routinized: report, drop, repeat. Imani's, Emersyn's, and Lily's experiences demonstrate what happened when probation officer turnover and changes in the county's recordkeeping upended this routine.

Imani only learned that she had a new probation officer when she called multiple times to report for probation, could not reach her officer, and then called the probation office's main desk. The receptionist explained that Imani's officer was no longer working there. Just before the receptionist hung up, Imani asked for her new officer's name and number. She was concerned that no one was documenting her attempts to contact her probation officer and that she would therefore be falsely accused of violating probation. Imani explained, "I'm calling this lady and leaving her messages to the point where her voicemail was full. I'm calling her and leaving her messages, emailing her . . . I ain't want to violate because I'm scared the bitch is going to try to lock me up, so I ain't going to violate. I kept calling and calling."

Imani eventually learned from a friend, not the probation office, that an arrest warrant was issued for her alleged probation violation for failing to report. Although it was beyond her means, Imani retained an attorney to contact probation and set up a court date when she could present her case.

While Imani was relatively new to probation when this complication arose, Emersyn had reached the final six months of her five-year probation term when her probation officer went on leave. Emersyn continued to report to the new officer by email, following the same reporting procedure as she had done during the previous four and a half years. After two months of reporting to the new officer, Emersyn received the following email, "Miss [Emersyn] . . . these correspondences cannot be sent via email as you are on probation for a computer crime. I'll need to look into this. This may also be another violation." Emersyn felt sick. The warning confirmed her suspicions that probation was engineered to keep her in debt and mired in the CLS. "It was like starting over," Emersyn sighed.

At the time of Lily's first interview, she had successfully completed probation five years earlier. After paying $1,200 in court fines, she and her children moved to a different state to begin a new life. After the move she secured gainful employment. During the early days of her employment, however, she was stunned to learn the results of the agency's interstate background check: an arrest warrant for an unspecified probation violation. After repeated unsuccessful attempts to reach her former probation officer, Lily learned that the officer was on medical leave. She also learned that, since her discharge from probation, the court's recordkeeping had transitioned to a fully digital system. The court's records showed no evidence of Lily's $1,200 payment. In the transition from paper to electronic records, Lily's payment history was lost. Probation refused to reach out to Lily's former officer to verify prior payment and promised Lily that they would pursue the active warrant until she (re)paid the $1,200.

When Imani went to court to respond to the alleged violation for not reporting to the new probation officer, she armed herself with an attorney, phone records, and audio recordings. As Imani pointed out, "Documentation is everything!" Although her lawyer "had to go through loops and leaps and bounds" to talk to her new probation officer, and "leave a threatening voicemail on [the probation officer's] voicemail," he made a court appearance happen. At court the attorney provided Imani background guidance. His presence was also physical proof to the court that Imani had formal CLS support. It was Imani, however, who compiled and brought the cell phone billing statements and recordings of every dead-end automated voicemail message. She had a feeling of what was coming, and Imani "ain't no damn dummy!"

Emersyn kept every paper copy and digital email correspondence between her and her first probation officer. She had learned "You have to protect yourself." Emersyn responded to the new probation officer's threats by forwarding the prior four and a half years' worth of email correspondence to her. She also noted that she would retain an attorney if the new officer followed through with placing her in violation for continuing with a reporting routine she had followed over the past four and a half years. Emersyn did not get a response from the new officer. Four months later, she received an automated email notifying her that she was finished with probation. The email stated that although she was released from probation, she was not allowed to pick up her completion paperwork in person. Emersyn would have to wait "two to four weeks" to receive proof of completion in the mail.

Although it was not Lily's habit, she had decided to discard the paperwork proving she had completed probation and paid her fees in full. Throwing it out meant finishing that chapter of her life. All this time, she believed she was "good with everything." Now Lily blamed herself for not holding on to the paperwork, which meant that she now had to spend money repaying fees that she and her five children could have used for their basic needs. When Lily described this "mistake" she pointed out that "I was so upset, but there was nothing I could do. It wasn't worth arguing because I didn't have proof, but I know I had paid." She then explained that although she had to "repay all that . . . luckily they did a payment plan with me, so it was good." Lily was grateful for any flexibility on probation's part, even if this flexibility meant reconciling their mistake at her expense. Lily's gratitude was intertwined with her relief that she was finally able to leave her abusive partner by leaving the state. She felt safe. In a way, Lily considered the $1,200 repayment, although an unfair economic burden, a cost worth paying for her safety and her freedom. But the irony was not lost on Lily. A system focused on holding offenders accountable seemed accountable to no one.

## DISTINCT SUPERVISION STYLES: OFFICER PHOENIX AND OFFICER RIGOR

The women's day-to-day experiences regarding probation varied based on their officers' supervision style. Officer Phoenix and Officer Rigor, for example, worked in the same county, but were responsible for people sentenced by different judges from separate courts.[5] Most of the women in this project were supervised by Officer Phoenix or Officer Rigor. Comparing their distinct supervision styles demonstrates differences between what scholars have identified as a gender-responsive approach and a law enforcement approach (Bloom et al., 2004; Clear and Latessa, 1993; Morash, 2010; Morash et al., 2019).[6] A gender-responsive approach is grounded in the recognition that women on probation have gender-specific challenges with drugs, alcohol, mental illness, parenting, and maintaining child custody (Morash, 2010). Rather than only foregrounding gender, Officer Phoenix saw and responded—nonjudgmentally, even kindly—to the women's complex intersectional needs across survivorship histories, caregiving responsibilities, employment demands, and resource needs. The main tool in Officer Phoenix's discretionary toolkit (Watkins-Hayes, 2009) was therefore what I refer to as his holistically responsive supervisory approach. It encourages accessible supervision through kindness and flexibility, in tandem with explicit support and sharing of resources tailored to each person's diverse needs, with consideration for mental and physical well-being and the social factors that may undermine both. In contrast, the women experienced Officer Rigor's supervision style as a punitive, law enforcement approach. The tools in Officer Rigor's discretionary toolkit were shaped by her strict interpretation of and adherence to probation rules and regulations, dismissing the context of the women's circumstances. Officer Rigor's approach was generally inflexible, and her main goal seemed to be enforcing supervision's legal requirements. The officers' different approaches broadly affected the women's emotional, financial, and physical well-being, causing ripple effects across their daily lives, relationships, and communities.

*Officer Phoenix: Phoebe, Essence, Valerie, and Abby*

Phoebe "still burned" from the warrant issued for her arrest that was based on her child's father's false allegation that she kicked him. Even so, she liked Officer Phoenix for a range of reasons. Phoebe recalled, "It seems like he's coming from a place of really just trying to be supportive and helpful, you know. He's not looking at me like a criminal . . . He's just looking at it like it's a situation that happened, and you need help emotionally for what you've been through."

She explained that what made Officer Phoenix "a good probation officer" was that "he's able to pick up a vibe and also look at information and put two and two together, and then base his judgement off of that." Because of this ability, Phoebe "didn't feel judged or anything."

Essence also liked Officer Phoenix. She smiled and explained, "I don't mind being on probation . . . [Officer Phoenix] is very helpful, . . . [but] I hate that it's on my [permanent criminal] record." She also reported that although she had had many concerns over her first few weeks of probation, Officer Phoenix addressed them all. When she texted him with questions, he got right back to her. This was an interaction style, Essence pointed out, that Officer Phoenix encouraged among all those he supervised.

Valerie also had a positive impression of Officer Phoenix. She appreciated that although he was responsible for monitoring her probation compliance, he recognized her survivorship history. Valerie explained, "He knows I didn't deserve to be on probation. Even he said it. He's like, 'You have one domestic against a man who beat you for three and a half years, and you've never been in trouble in your life.'"

Valerie smiled and said, "I love him . . . I thought I was going to die being on probation . . . [but] he's made it so easy for me." She then explained that Officer Phoenix is "a really good person. He would come and see me when I was supposed to be going to see him . . . I was supposed to be at my last court date, and he actually made it to where I was excused because I was getting [to see my] kids [at the same time scheduled for court]." She attributed the relative ease of her probation to Officer Phoenix considering her complex relationship history and tailoring the terms of her in-person reporting to her circumstances.

Abby expressed a similar level of fondness for Officer Phoenix. She remembered one occasion when he saw her crying at the courthouse before a scheduled appearance. Abby recalled, "I was sitting there crying [in court], and [Officer Phoenix] came over to see what was wrong. I said, 'I'm afraid I'm going to jail.'"

He assured Abby that she would not be going to jail, and he asked if she had any further questions. Officer Phoenix stayed by Abby's side until she felt that he had fully explained what was going to happen in the courtroom and after. Abby remembered that in their brief exchange Phoenix kindly addressed her concerns. Given his accessible and flexible supervisory style, Officer Phoenix was able to simultaneously meet the women's individual needs and monitor their compliance. It also seemed that this approach encouraged compliance and resulted in successful discharge.

*Officer Rigor: Sheniqua, Emersyn, and Regina*

The women's experiences with Officer Rigor contrasted sharply with those of Officer Phoenix. The women typically referred to Officer Rigor only as "Rigor," in a tone and manner suggesting her name was synonymous with a tyrannical form of power. Sheniqua was on probation for assaulting her intimate partner. Her retelling of her first meeting with "Rigor" captured not only Rigor's no-nonsense approach to supervision but Sheniqua's well-cultivated, identity-based, probation-specific experiential capital (Watkins-Hayes, 2019), which she used to navigate their interactions. During Sheniqua's first probation check-in Officer Rigor warned her, "Look, you fail one more time, I'm going to send your butt to the slammer!" Sheniqua had been "in trouble" before. She knew what probation involved and received Rigor's warning "for what it was. I was in trouble, so I had to correct it." Despite Rigor also being a woman of color, Sheniqua described her own awareness that she had to exercise additional care as a highly visible "Black big boy dyke" who weighed more than 250 pounds, wore all black clothes, "big sweatpants

[,] . . . a backwards hat . . . [, and] had scratches all over [her] face from fighting all the time." She understood that her personal appearance influenced how she moved through the world and navigated interactions. Sheniqua already felt like she attracted attention because of her personal appearance and did not want to bring any more attention to herself by challenging Officer Rigor or by even being *perceived* as challenging her. Therefore, Sheniqua heeded Officer Rigor's warning, followed the rules, and moved through Officer Rigor's strict, law enforcement-style of supervision while seeking to "remain below her radar."

Like Sheniqua, Emersyn and Regina were also supervised by Officer Rigor. Unlike Sheniqua, Emersyn and Regina had no prior criminal history and lacked Sheniqua's probation-specific experiential capital (Watkins-Hayes, 2019). Emersyn and Regina had no framework to assist in navigating probation, let alone Office Rigor's particularly strict supervisory style. Moreover, as white-passing, heterosexual, single mothers with high school diplomas Emersyn and Regina's identities differed markedly from Sheniqua's. Neither Emersyn nor Regina reported an awareness of possibly needing to tailor their physical presentation to promote personal safety or avoid being perceived as "difficult." But although Emersyn and Regina had similar identities, the women had vastly different financial and social resources. Emersyn had a modest income, with limited social networks. Regina had extensive financial and social capital. Furthermore, with the combination of her wealth and identities, Regina carried herself in a confident and aloof manner that Emersyn did not. Their probation experiences illustrate how their differing access to capital shaped the women's capacity to navigate Officer Rigor's law-enforcement probation monitoring style.

Emersyn explained that her first interaction with Officer Rigor was at the courthouse immediately after a judge sentenced her to five years of probation. Emersyn remembered, in the chaos and shock of it all, "spilling and telling [Rigor] everything" about her case. By sharing "everything," Emersyn hoped that Rigor would empathize with her situation, but she did not understand Officer Rigor's supervisory style. On reflection, Emersyn believed that the details she disclosed aggravated Rigor's punitive approach in the years that followed. Emersyn now regretted telling Officer Rigor anything. She realized she should have been more self-protective, as Rigor would hold any disclosure against her. Although Emersyn knew her story mattered, Rigor used it to punish her disproportionately. The terms of Emersyn's probation were to complete a psychiatric evaluation ($364), 40 hours of commu-

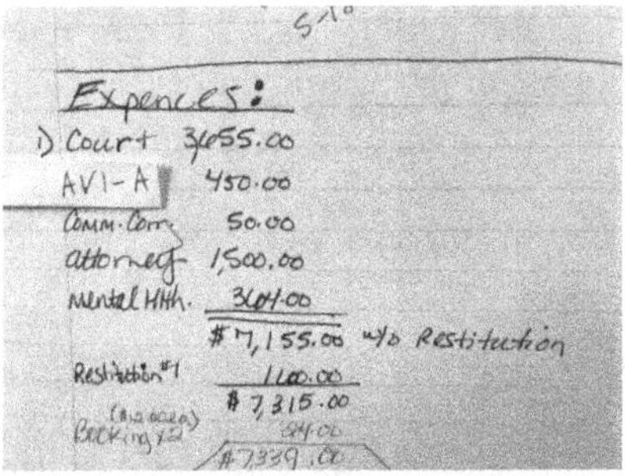

FIGURE 3. Emersyn's total cost list.
Photo courtesy of the author.

nity service, 26 weeks of AVI (20 miles one way),[7] and random drug testing (16 miles one way)—all at her own expense. Emersyn explained, "I think it's pretty clear I don't have a mental health issue. I had a broken heart and bad choices." As a low-income single mother with a full-time job and scarce childcare, Emersyn did her best to complete her community service on 10 consecutive weekends, attend and pay 15 dollars per AVI session, submit to random drug testing at 10 dollars a test, and pay for extra gas to travel from here to there. As figure 3 shows, Emersyn's probation and court costs amounted to more than $7,300—a financial burden for someone in her situation. Furthermore, because Emersyn was ashamed of her CLS involvement, she initially did not share her situation with her close family and friends. Although this helped limit family "gossip," it also meant she had less support.

During Emersyn's first three months on probation, she did all she could to "follow the rules" and engage in a submissive form of emotion work to encourage a positive reporting relationship. Emersyn recounted how she gradually moved from a collegial to a deferential tone when she met with or emailed Rigor. With the Christmas holiday growing closer, however, Emersyn realized she would not have enough money to afford gifts for her daughter, probation costs, drug testing, gas to drive to her multiple probation requirements, and the weekly AVI fee. She was also afraid she was going to lose another job because of the time she missed to make court appearances. When Emersyn shared her predicament with Officer Rigor, she asked for permission to "take a break" from AVI for the month of December, explaining that she needed the 60 dollars for December's fees to buy her daughter Christmas gifts. Officer Rigor responded, "Well, you've known Christmas is coming for a year. This is court-ordered. You're going to have to borrow it or figure out a way."

When recalling this interaction, Emersyn pointed out that the year before she had no idea that she would be on probation, and even if she had known, how could she have possibly planned for how it would affect her finances? Among her family and friends of modest income, she had always been the one from whom everyone else borrowed. Not only did they not have the financial means to help her; she was too ashamed to tell them. To whom could she go? No one. "You can't bleed a dead horse," Emersyn explained. She reasoned that, for Officer Rigor, the inability to come up with such a small amount for an entire month was "out of her realm of reasoning because maybe she hasn't been in that spot in a long time or ever." To manage in the short term, Emersyn delayed business school ($79.16 per month), borrowed from her daughter's piggy bank ($37.39), and skipped the December AVI sessions. Now she would have the money to buy Christmas gifts. She hoped Rigor would have mercy on her. But there was no mercy. In January, Rigor placed Emersyn in violation of probation, and recommended that the court sentence her to 80 hours of community service and 21 days of jail time spread out over consecutive weekends. If Emersyn did not meet the new terms, she would face more jail time and an extension of her time on probation.

Where the victim-offender binary left Emersyn with few options owing to her limited resources, Regina's privilege enabled her to effectively navigate the binary. From the beginning of Regina's probation relationship with Officer Rigor, she remembered being very frustrated that she was convicted and on probation at all, as she had no prior criminal record—"not even . . . a traffic ticket!" The terms of Regina's probation included completion of 30 sessions of AVI (one group a week, 20 miles one way, 50 dollars per group), and random drug testing (16 miles one way, 20 dollars per test) at her expense. Similar to other women on Rigor's caseload, Regina felt Officer Rigor was "rooting against" her, wanted her to "fail," wanted to see her arrested, and was "just waiting" for her to make a mistake. But in contrast to the less capital-rich women, including Emersyn, Regina did not enact the kind of emotion work necessary to cultivate a positive probation reporting relationship with Rigor. Instead, Regina recalled,

> I was not cooperative at all. I was incensed that I was even there . . . but being true to myself, I didn't care . . . I probably had an attitude with her. I'm sure that when she was serving it, I was serving it back. I'm sure I wasn't acting like a respectful angel with her. . . . It got to be so insulting. It was just like she acted like I put a gun to someone's head or something. It's like really? It was preposterous.

After a brief time on probation, Regina's assault "victim" alleged that Regina had stalked him and left him afraid.[8] In response, Officer Rigor recommended to the judge that Regina be found in violation of probation, and ordered to complete community service, jail time, pay additional fees, and have her time on probation extended.

## Managing the Systems-Inflicted Breakage: Emersyn and Regina

Emersyn's response to Officer Rigor placing her in violation of probation for not attending AVI for December was, after much deliberation, to hire an attorney she could not afford. She felt she was "being railroaded" and had to do something to protect herself. The attorney cost Emersyn fifteen hundred dollars. Although he was unable to get rid of the four weekends in jail, he had Officer Rigor's community service recommendation reduced from 80 to 40 hours. By the time the first six months of her five-year probation had passed, Emersyn had spent a weekend in jail, completed 80 hours of community service, paid for and attended 14 AVI sessions, completed multiple random drug tests, and returned to jail for the violation. She had also disclosed her CLS involvement, but only to her mother. She felt forced into the disclosure. Emersyn needed someone she trusted to care for her daughter while she was completing her community service and spending weekends in jail.

Through this five-year process, Emersyn experienced what sociologist Alexes Harris (2016) refers to as the CLS's monetary "punishment culture"—the financial penalties levied on systems-identified offenders. She lost three full-time jobs, could no longer pay her mortgage, and filed for bankruptcy. As noted earlier, Emersyn lost her jobs because she missed work for compulsory probation reporting, court appearances, and substance use testing. Because her health insurance was employer-provided, Emersyn lost coverage and had to apply for medical benefits and then food stamps for the first time. "When you're running to all the appointments and you have no money coming in, food stamps saved us there for a little bit," she explained. Emersyn saw a bankruptcy filing as her only option. She will forever remember her "$7,339.00" debt—the total for her psychiatric evaluation, jail booking fees, probation fines, AVI fees, attorney's fees, and restitution. Emersyn added that the debt did not include lost wages, gas money, and childcare costs. She tearfully blamed herself: "It just disappoints me how much I took from my family that wasn't there to give." It took Emersyn three years after completing her five-year probation to "get back where I was when I started" before the conviction.

Years later, Emersyn still had all of her probation and court documents from those five years. She organized them as: "receipts," "notices to appear in court," "miscellaneous notes of mine," "client notices/probation," "social media shutdown," "monthly probation reports," "community work program," "misc. backup," "community corrections," "attorney stuff," "community service," "ordered psych eval.," "search warrant/seizure," "[AVI] and poems," and "misc. sentencing documents." Emersyn kept the documents for a range of reasons: they were a visible deterrent to responding in a similar way in the future, physical proof that she made it through a difficult time, and a means of future "protection." Emersyn explained the documents were "some sort of protection because I felt like they were after me. So, it makes you crazy. I feel like it occupies your mind." When reflecting on her experiences, Emersyn recalled,

> My domestic partner at the time and the legal system [betrayed me]. Going into it, I would have 100 percent described that [betrayal] as my partner . . . Coming out of it, the betrayal more feels like the legal system than him. If I think about it right now where I feel betrayed, he isn't even a thing that comes to my mind. Isn't that weird? . . . I mean, that was a healable wound . . . a superficial kind of thing . . . [but the legal system betrayal] was financial, emotional, it affected my family, my job, my housing, everything . . . those wounds were much deeper.

For Emersyn, the initial betrayal by her former partner and then, later, that of the CLS were like physical wounds, the deepest left by the CLS.

Unlike Emersyn, Regina did not feel betrayed or wounded. She had extensive social networks from years of professional and familial contacts. When Regina's children were small she had the financial means and social support necessary to volunteer her time in a range of community organizations. She also had the funds to start her own business, which gave her additional income and flexibility to develop professional and community relationships. Both explain Regina's diverse network ties (Granovetter, 1973; Small, 2009). In contrast, as a single parent with fewer resources, Emersyn did not have the flexibility to volunteer or start her own business. Although she had rich friendship and family networks, she did not have the diverse social ties that can be vital bridges to information and resource sharing across the community. Regina's ties gave her confidence that was especially evident when she smiled, threw her head back, and asserted, "I know everybody, of course!" Although Regina recalled that it was initially embarrassing to be publicly labeled "a probationer," each affiliation gradually acted as a

FIGURE 4. Emersyn's document pile. Photo courtesy of the author.

buffer—rather than a form of public shaming—against the indignities Emersyn experienced. Regina explained, "Everybody knew" her conviction and probation sentence "was so ridiculous." When Regina appeared for her first drug test, the breathalyzer operator was one of her friends. Regina believed she could have blown "anything" and her friend "would have just zeroed it out." She also knew the person conducting the residential weapons inspection. When the inspector arrived at her home, Regina recalled, "He walked in my house, he's like, 'Oh, you have a beautiful home, [Regina]. I'm not going through your stuff. . . . and I'm not looking around. I'm not doing that."

Already supported by diverse social networks, then, Regina's response to her alleged probation violation was swift and reflected her rich financial and social capital. She had readily accessible means to quickly hire the county's most prominent criminal defense attorney, who was also a personal friend. She also disclosed her situation to an influential uncle, ultimately asking both him and the criminal defense attorney to accompany her to court. Before the court appearance Regina's uncle—whom she described as "so rogue, he wasn't the type of person that would have thought, 'Well, I might need to make an appointment with the judge'"—simply walked into the judge's chambers and explained his perspective. According to Regina, her uncle and the judge, who "knew each other socially," "laughed it out," recognizing that the "victim" was in a public place when he saw Regina and was obviously trying to manipulate the system, Regina, and her family. For Regina, this marked the end of Officer Rigor's "witch hunt": "That's where it ended, and I think that she realized after that judge and [the defense attorney] really making a strong face down . . . okay, now we're really going to start resisting you. If anything negative would have happened that day, we were going to take it a step further and would have filed actions against her as well because it was just a witch hunt."

The proposed sanctions for Regina's alleged violation were dropped. She received no community service, no jail time, and no additional fees. Regina was back on the initially established two-year probation trajectory of court fines and costs, AVI participation and fees, and random drug testing. She easily paid for them all. She was protected against further monetary sanctions and armed with extensive networks. Regina acknowledged that her access to financial resources, her well-connected uncle, and a powerful attorney friend meant she had the power to make sure Officer Rigor's "gig [*sic*] was up." With a tone of disgust, Regina recalled that she would "guarantee there's people out there that got railroaded by [Rigor]." Regina knew that Rigor had "done even worse things to other people," and "got away with it" because they, unlike her, lacked resources. Regina not only acknowledged her privilege; she was passionate in her belief that Rigor's treatment of other less well-resourced women was unfair. They deserved better. Regina explained,

> I never deserved that entitlement. I was in a different situation. I had money; I had resources. I had all the tools to do it. I didn't deserve any of that entitlement by no means. But all the other people that I met there? They deserved better than they got treated for sure . . . they get some probation officer like [Rigor], who is . . . power-hungry . . . instead of taking her power and doing good with it, she was just miserable . . . You have to show [people] respect and dignity even if they don't have anything.

As Regina pointed out, Officer Rigor's probationers did not feel respected; nor were they able to maintain their dignity while on her caseload. Because Emersyn did not have access to financial and extensive social capital, the probation process left her emotionally and financially broken. Emersyn's shame prevented her from reaching out. Regina, in contrast, leveraged her reputation and resources, taking control of the public portrayal of her situation. She felt emboldened in her perspective that it was all "ridiculous." Whereas Emersyn and Lily blamed themselves, Regina felt justified that it was only a "witch hunt" and that she was blameless.

This dramatic difference in experiences with the same probation officer demonstrates how social class and access to resources can act as protective mechanisms. As sociologist Michelle Phelps (2018) points out, probation for the disadvantaged can be a "conveyor belt" to further CLS involvement; for the privileged, it is an "off-ramp" to life beyond the CLS. This was evident years later (see chapter 5) when Emersyn still felt the impact of her probation involvement, while the same involvement was only a distant memory for Regina.

## SUMMARY AND REFLECTIONS

This contextual view of these women's daily struggles to comply with probation affords a closer look at intimate and systems harms caused by a process that is clearly far more than a "slap on the wrist" (Phelps, 2020). Contrary to its stated purpose, probation contact perpetuated rather than reduced harm by draining women already marginalized by race, class, and poverty of money, time, and energy, while posing risks to their mental and physical health. Regardless of how the women became CLS-involved, probation-inflicted harms exacerbated their self-described breakage as they complied with random drug and alcohol testing, rectified bureaucratic failures, and enacted emotion work in attempts to manage probation officers' broad discretion.

As a researcher, I learned how the victim-offender binary impeded my view of the women's probation interactions years prior as an AVI practitioner—making their probation-inflicted breakage nearly invisible. The binary dictated that the women protect themselves through lack of disclosure, cutting them off from social networks and resources. The interviews now situated me within the women's probation contact and their ongoing efforts to tailor that contact to best suit their needs. For example, when Benita, whom I had not met before, arrived for her interview, her right hand was red, bloody, and swollen. She was late, she explained, because she had just had a fight with her abusive former partner and her hand was "probably broken." Although there was a no contact order in place against her identifying him as the "victim," he had called and asked her to drop by his apartment and pick up her clothes on the way to this interview. Benita was eager to get her things. When she got to his place, he tried to rape her. He knew that she was not going to call the police and report his attempt because contact with him would violate her probation. He was right. Benita explained that after he attacked her, she "hit him in the face" in a successful effort to escape. I encouraged her to delay the interview and seek medical attention. Benita explained that she had been looking forward to the opportunity to tell her story and did not want to wait any longer. Throughout our conversation she asked me to "please" not say anything to her probation officer. She worried how the "terms" could change if she seemed "challenging." Benita's case was unusual only in how recent the violence had taken place relative to her interview. Many of the women lived complex lives where they had survived or were actively surviving harm in their intimate relationships while systems-identified as "offenders on probation."

As a practitioner who managed the AVI when Emersyn and Regina were court ordered to attend, I knew both women. At that time, however, I did not have the view of their probation officer interactions that this research made possible. Although I did have a front row seat to the women's conversations about probation while I cofacilitated AVI sessions, I did not know the extent to which they had to, in Emersyn's words, "abuse myself," to be probation "compliant." As a practitioner-researcher who now has this view, I am acutely aware of the power I held in that position. As the person who documented their AVI contact that was then accessible to their probation officer, I could inadvertently cause or reduce harm at any point. This dynamic became especially evident when, during this research, I learned from Emersyn how probation had devastated her life. If she had told me all those years ago that she needed the month of December to be payment-free so she could afford gifts for her daughter, I could have approached the issue in a range of ways. Not knowing whom she could trust, she tried to not make things worse for herself. Emersyn acknowledged the "mistake" she made that resulted in her CLS involvement, but that was not enough. She had to navigate and pay a system of power that further harmed her. The end result of her probation contact was that she felt more betrayed by the system than by the former partner she had retaliated against. Emersyn was not alone.

In this broad discretion and lack of transparency, probation, as part of the system of carceral power, gained and kept its momentum in causing breakage. Only those with ample experiential, financial, and social capital could mitigate the harm. Of course, individual probation officers can be agents of change. For example, Essence, like other women, found Officer Phoenix's holistically responsive supervision style "very helpful" because of how he spoke to and supported her with community resources. This additional access to resources was what social scientists Rueben Miller and Forrest Stuart (2017) have called the "(perverse) benefits" of "carceral citizenship."[9] For Essence, this "benefit" occurred at the cost of wrongful arrest and a misdemeanor domestic violence conviction on her criminal record.[10] As scholars Michelle Phelps and Ebony Ruhland (2022) point out, despite the limited supportive aspects of probation for marginalized people, probation involves stigma, lack of liberty, risk of poor treatment by the probation officer, and investment of time and energy. A view beyond the victim-offender binary must be grounded in the recognition that community monitoring places people minoritized by a range of factors, such as their disability, race, sexuality, gender, income, and class, in especially precarious circumstances, making them feel, in Imani's words, "literally broke down."

# CHAPTER 2

# Child Protective Services

"THE SYSTEM LOVES BROKENNESS . . ."
—JATARA

Despite a woman's circumstances at the time of law enforcement's response to a domestic violence incident, if children are present, responding officers must contact Child Protective Services (CPS) personnel. Most states identify police officers as mandatory reporters, tethering CPS intervention to police involvement. I begin this chapter with a broad overview of this legislation and CPS, and then transition to CPS's connection with domestic violence and failure to protect statutes. Next, I provide an overview of how failure to protect statutes differentially affect mothers based on gender, race, income, and broad CPS caseworker discretion. I then detail Essence's, Valerie's, and Tyra's interactions with CPS caseworkers. Their experiences illuminate CPS-inflicted breakage in its early stages, when it recurs, and over the years.

## OVERVIEW: CHILD PROTECTIVE SERVICES

CPS is the central component of the US child welfare system (Walfogel, 2009). CPS caseworkers staff offices in each state and respond to reports of child abuse and neglect. The 1974 Federal Child Abuse and Prevention Treatment Act (CAPTA) was pivotal in defining child abuse and neglect, and required all states receiving federal funding to support the enforcement of child abuse and neglect laws, establish mandatory reporting laws, and have CPS offices that process abuse and neglect allegations.

CAPTA (P.L. 93–247, enacted in 1974; last amended in 2016 as P.L. 114–98) defines child maltreatment as "at a minimum, any recent act or *failure* to act on the part of a parent or caretaker, which results in death, serious physical or emotional harm, sexual abuse or exploitation, or an act or *failure* to act which presents an imminent risk of serious harm" (CAPTA, 2010; emphasis added). When police arrive at the scene of a violent incident where children are present, they are required to report the children's suspected exposure to the violence to the state's child welfare agency. This mandate, which formally links law enforcement and CPS, is included in the original 1974 CAPTA legislation as a condition with which states must comply to receive federal funding for child welfare services. The original CAPTA legislation says that states must "provide for the cooperation of law enforcement officials, courts of competent jurisdiction, and appropriate State agencies providing human services" (CAPTA [P.L. 93–247, enacted in 1974; Section F]). Thus, although CAPTA further encourages cross-reporting between law enforcement and CPS, the mandated reporting laws solidify this relationship.

In carrying out the stated CPS goal of protecting children, each CPS office has state-specific procedures guiding responses to child abuse and neglect allegations. According to Child Maltreatment (2020), during federal fiscal year 2020, child welfare agencies in all fifty states, as well as in the Commonwealth and the District of Columbia, received a total of 3.9 million referrals with 2.1 million of those referrals "screened in." When a report is "screened in," CPS caseworkers assess the reported family's circumstances and determine if opening a formal investigation is warranted. Short of a formal investigation, caseworkers may provide a range of services through community-based agencies, or they may open a formal investigation. Caseworkers in the research community may refer CPS-involved parents or caregivers to parenting, budgeting, or healthy eating classes, psychiatric evaluations, domestic violence survivor support groups, and antiviolence intervention groups (AVI-Gs).

*Overview: CPS, Domestic Violence, and Failure to Protect*

Social scientists Jennifer Lawson (2019) and Bryan Victor and others (2019) estimate that domestic violence between caregivers is present in one- to two-thirds of all child abuse and neglect cases. Undoubtedly, domestic violence influences parenting (see Sousa et al., 2022). Failure to protect (FTP) statutes inform CPS caseworkers' responses to allegations of child abuse and neglect. Although FTP does not have a specific legal definition, US federal and state statutes allow FTP to be interpreted as a form of maltreatment (Henry et al., 2020). A general federal definition includes "*failure* to act . . ." (CAPTA, 2010; emphasis added) language. State statutes often include FTP as a neglect subtype.[1] Under CAPTA, parents and caregivers whose actions fall under the state's definition of "child abuse and neglect" may be charged with FTP (Mahoney, 2019).[2] CPS caseworkers may respond by removing the offending caregiver's children and placing them with family or in foster care. There is significant racial disproportionality in these removals. For example, Black children comprised 14 percent of the child population in 2021 but represented 22 percent of all children placed in foster care nationwide (Annie E. Casey Foundation, 2023).

## Failure to Protect Ideology

Once CPS enters the life of heterosexual cisgender caregivers where a man is perpetrating violence against a woman, CPS assesses her "success" by determining whether or not his violence against her ends or she leaves him. In other words, "ending the abuse becomes the woman's responsibility" (Magen, 1999, p. 132). This perspective endures despite research that an abused woman is in the greatest danger soon after she has left the man who is abusing her (Campbell, 1995). Advocate and social work professor Mimi Kim (2013) attributes this to the legal system's "fetishization of safety," whereby the dichotomous victim-offender binary and safety-danger frameworks establish separation as the ideal and identify any victim/woman not ready to leave as irrational.

Social scientists Alisa Bierra and Colby Lenz (2019) observe that FTP prosecutions are a consequence of the "no-win" contradictions that define the ideology of mothering (see Glenn, 1994). FTP prosecutions are particularly flexible in a manner that unfairly and arbitrarily holds mothers accountable for their own abuse, for example:

> Survivors have been found guilty if they do not escape and if they try to escape, if they take their child to receive medical help and if they try to tend to their children themselves, if judges believe they are genuinely victims of domestic violence and if judges believe that they are lying about the abuse. Any scenario can be manipulated back into ideological alignment in order to blame mothers for their abusers' actions (Bierra and Lenz, 2019, p. 95).

Although FTP statutes use gender-neutral language, in practice they provide courts license to disproportionately criminalize mothers who have been abused by their partners for their "participation" in the violence perpetrated against them (Bierra and Lenz, 2019; Henry et al., 2020; Mahoney, 2019; Miller and Manzur, 2021; Roberts, 2002). Even if a child is not physically abused by their mother, if the child witnessed their mother being abused by a partner, many FTP statutes provide CPS justification to remove the child from the mother's care (Mahoney, 2019). Social scientists Elizabeth Marie Armstrong and Emily Bosk (2020) refer to this approach as a "punitive framework" that conflicts with more supportive approaches. Bryan Victor and others (2021), however, note counterexamples from Iowa and Oregon in which policy frameworks serve to protect abused women from additional CPS abuse.

According to sociologist, law professor, and social justice advocate Dorothy Roberts (2002), because states have such broad statutory definitions of failure to protect and do not require actual proof that harm has occurred, the initial decision to open an abuse investigation is entirely within CPS's discretion. Further complicating matters, CPS caseworkers often have inadequate training and are encouraged to rely on "gut instincts" or "hunches" when deciding whether or not to move forward with formal investigations. Most states use a preponderance of evidence threshold to substantiate allegations of mistreatment, which requires evidence that alleged maltreatment most likely occurred. Only after a caseworker has determined whether or not an allegation is valid and what actions are necessary do details from their investigations face judicial review. Many caseworkers operate from the assumption that a white, middle-class family with married heterosexual cisgender parents is the ideal family structure. This bias places Black families at a disadvantage, according to Roberts (2002), as many are headed by unmarried mothers and embrace cultural practices different from those normalized by white families. The compounding effects of sexism, racism, poverty, vague FTP statutes, and caseworker discretion provide a basis for criminalizing a mother's domestic violence survivorship, while overlooking her child-focused protective strategies.

In their critique of FTP prosecutions, Bierra and Lenz (2019) propose "battering court syndrome" (BCS), a phenomenon whereby courts criminalize the person who was abused, thereby colluding with her abusive partner.[3] In this chapter, I build on this BCS phenomenon, focusing on CPS caseworker interactions with women struggling to parent their children in the midst of their former partners' abuse. I identify CPS caseworkers' inadvertent collusion with women's abusive former partners as an FTP ideology. The ideology, regardless of whether or not there is a formal FTP conviction, influences how caseworkers perceive and interact with the women, viewing them as failures, and misunderstanding or disregarding the protective strategies they use in the care and concern for their children and their own dignity. As a result, some CPS caseworkers enlist punitive, shaming interaction styles and consequences that reproduce the intimate harm women suffer from their former partners. In this collusion, CPS caseworkers hold abused mothers to a higher standard for parenting than the children's fathers.

## CPS CASEWORKER INTERACTIONS AND BREAKAGE

Federal and state governments enacted FTP statutes to protect children from their caregivers' abuse and neglect. This research details, however, how mothers surviving relationship abuse experience FTP as an ideological and legal justification for CPS caseworkers to replicate the abuse women's partners perpetrate against them. Of the 33 women who participated in this project, 16 had contact with CPS at some point during their legal systems journey. Table 4, "Child protective services (CPS) contact," details each woman's CPS referral source and the most recent CPS action at the time of the last interview.

Fifteen of those women experienced FTP ideology in their interactions with CPS caseworkers. Although CPS contact varied, the women's CPS contact typically aggravated systems-inflicted harm for the women who were also on probation. In contrast to situations involving arrest, where police officers entered and exited an individual's life within hours, or probation, where a monitoring term was court ordered, CPS caseworkers seemed to intervene in the women's lives at any time. They could also remain in family members' lives for weeks, months, or years. Once involved, CPS caseworkers could control child-rearing and place extensive conditions on the women's involvement with their children, which could change without notice or explanation. They required the women to complete multiple obligations in the community that involved extensive time and energy with no clear indication of expected outcomes. As Nikki explained, this uncertainty caused many of the women to feel "overwhelmed and stressed out [and] . . . a lot of tension." All of this made the women's CPS contact confusing and more difficult to navigate than other aspects of the legal system.

Essence's, Valerie's, and Tyra's CPS caseworker interactions expose these challenges. Although a formal CPS investigation precipitated by her arrest had been closed, Essence experienced ongoing interactions

TABLE 4  CHILD PROTECTIVE SERVICES (CPS) CONTACT

|  | CPS referral source | CPS action at time of last contact |
|---|---|---|
| Abby | Police responded to domestic violence (DV) incident and contacted CPS. | Investigation initiated. Investigation dropped for undisclosed reason. |
| Becky | Police responded to DV incident and contacted CPS. | CPS removed her children from her care, placed children in foster care; ongoing case. |
| Benita | Police responded to DV incident and contacted CPS. | CPS placed children in her grand-mother's care; ongoing case. |
| Cherise | School guidance counselor made a CPS report after her child disclosed a DV incident at school. | CPS removed her children from her care, placed children in foster care; ongoing case. |
| Christine | Police responded to DV incident but did not contact CPS. | N/A |
| Darla | No children. No police contact. | N/A |
| Devore | No children. No police contact. | N/A |
| Emersyn | No CPS contact. | N/A |
| Essence | Police responded to DV incident and contacted CPS. | Ongoing CPS caseworker contact. Although she has custody, father has the child and refuses to let child see Essence. |
| Ikeeylah | No children. No CPS contact. | N/A |
| Imani | No CPS contact. | N/A |
| Jatara | Former partner made allegations to CPS. | CPS investigated and found the allegations to be false. Case closed. |
| Joy | No CPS contact. | N/A |
| Lily | Police responded to incident of drug misuse and contacted CPS. | Children placed in foster care. CPS compliance. Children returned to her custody. Case closed. |
| Lola | Police responded to DV incident and contacted CPS. | CPS investigation. Case closed. |
| Manuela | No children. No CPS contact. | N/A |
| Marcella | No children. No CPS contact. | N/A |
| Moneesha | Former partner made allegations to CPS. | CPS investigated and found the allegations to be false. Case closed. |
| Nikki | Police responded to DV incident and contacted CPS. | CPS investigation. Case closed. |
| Olivia | Police responded to DV incident but did not contact CPS. | N/A |
| Phoebe | Former partner made allegations to CPS. | CPS investigated and found the allegations to be false. Case closed. |

*(Continued)*

TABLE 4  *(Continued)*

| | CPS referral source | CPS action at time of last contact |
| --- | --- | --- |
| QuiShandra | Children were not present during police response to DV incident. No referral made. | N/A |
| Regina | Adult children. No CPS contact. | N/A |
| Rosalee | Adult children. No CPS contact. | N/A |
| Rosemary | Former partner made allegations to CPS. | CPS investigation ongoing. |
| RyAnn | No children. No CPS contact. | N/A |
| Sage | Police responded to DV incident and contacted CPS. | CPS investigation. Case closed. |
| Sheniqua | No children. No CPS contact. | N/A |
| Sissy | She contacted CPS after learning her youngest child's father was listed on the sex offender registry and was also given unsupervised parenting time. | CPS is working with Sissy to investigate child's father. |
| Suzie | Adult children. No CPS contact. | N/A |
| Tiffany | No children. No CPS contact. | N/A |
| Tyra | Police responded to DV incident and contacted CPS. | Children placed in foster care. CPS compliance. Children returned to her care. |
| Valerie | Police responded to DV incident and contacted CPS. Hospital staff contacted CPS during Valerie's hospitalization. | CPS removed children from her care twice. Children were in and out of her care at the time of multiple interviews. |

with a CPS caseworker as an extension of her former partner's coercive control. Similarly, Valerie's CPS case was also closed; however, she lost custody of her children to CPS soon after achieving reunification with them despite employing child-focused protective strategies. Tyra's CPS contact spanned more than three years, with multiple interactions that demonstrate how CPS caseworkers' FTP ideology made her feel "tricked and betrayed" again and again.

*Essence*

After Essence entered a no-contest plea, the judge placed her on probation. Simultaneously, Essence was quickly becoming entangled with CPS because her former partner was using CPS to strategically compromise her agency by gradually and purposefully manipulating the investigating caseworker. This process demonstrates how a CPS caseworker's FTP ideology became an extension of Essence's former partner's coercive control.

After the domestic violence incident but before the police arrived, Essence's former partner took the children outside while Essence waited inside for the police to respond to her call for help. She assumed that he went outside to give her some space. She did not know that once outside he encouraged their daughter to call 911 and report that Essence was suicidal. Essence also did not know that their daughter's call and the police response activated a CPS investigation. She learned this a week after the incident, when a CPS caseworker called Essence and told her that she was there moments after the incident. At that time, the CPS caseworker interviewed Essence's former partner, who claimed Essence's children were not safe in her care. As Essence recalled, "I never saw her. She never got my side of the story at all."

Essence credits the relationship her former partner and the CPS caseworker built after the incident—but days before the CPS caseworker spoke to Essence—to the way in which interactions between Essence and the caseworker unfolded. Essence reasoned that "They got a good rapport that day that they were outside. Maybe he told her I was unstable. I don't know. She's been very harsh [to me since then]." When the CPS caseworker interviewed Essence the week after the incident, Essence recalled that the worker threatened her:

> At first, she was going to charge me with something . . . I don't know what . . . She said I could like never work in a daycare. I could never do certain things with children if she did charge me . . . But after she talked it over with her supervisor, she wasn't going to charge me with anything . . . So, she didn't charge anything and she closed that case, but she still kept coming around . . . She still stayed in the situation because [my former partner] would always call her.

Although the CPS case was closed, Essence's former partner continued to contact the caseworker and report false allegations concerning Essence's caregiving. With each contact, he strategically used their daughter and others in her life to portray Essence as a failed mother.

About a month after Essence's arrest, her former partner told their daughter that when Essence learned she was pregnant with her, she wanted to abort her. When their daughter confronted Essence, she explained that was not the case. In fact, her former partner had insisted Essence abort the pregnancy and gave her money for the procedure.

Essence told their daughter that she wanted the pregnancy and used the money for baby clothes. Their daughter did not believe Essence and tearfully asked to see her father who had surreptitiously invited her for an overnight visit. Essence had sole custody of their teenage daughter; but, owing to the recent incident, there was a no contact order in place that prevented Essence from contacting him. Nonetheless, Essence believed it was "the right thing" for her to let their daughter go for the overnight visit with her father. Although Essence knew he engineered the stay by creating a false narrative about her pregnancy, she was trying to be consistent in her parenting philosophy that "what happens between me and him is between me and him."

She agreed to let their daughter go to his house. But, not wanting "to violate anything," Essence had one of her older children drop the teenager off at her father's house. Essence recalled that their daughter was barefoot, in pajamas, and not wearing a coat. After all, the visit was "only supposed to be an overnight type of thing. . . . I thought I was doing the right thing, so of course she's not going to have all of her clothes. Of course, she's not going to have outfits and bags because I thought she was coming home, but she never did."

Their daughter did not return to Essence's home the next day as planned. Instead, shortly after their daughter was dropped off, Essence's former partner called CPS, alleging that Essence was a neglectful parent for having her dropped off without shoes or a coat on a cold evening. He then refused to return their daughter to Essence's care, claiming this proved she was an unfit parent.

Their teen daughter's "overnight" turned into weeks at Essence's former partner's house. Because he blocked Essence's emails and calls from the cell phone he bought their daughter, Essence could not communicate with her. Within days of the "overnight," Essence received a court summons. Her former partner had petitioned the court for custody of all three of Essence's children. Essence recalled,

> When we went before the judge because he was [trying to take] custody, his reasons for me losing my children were I had other boyfriends, I never allowed them to learn [about his religion], I assaulted him . . . It's not true what he's saying, but yet he's getting gratification from me having to go to court, from me worrying because he knows I'm worrying. He knows that's the only way he can hurt me is through my kids, so he's getting gratification from dragging me into court.

His attempt to win custody was unsuccessful. The judge ordered her former partner to return their daughter to Essence's care. Essence was relieved to leave the courtroom with documentation proving her sole legal and physical custody. But she also felt that the whole process culminated in what criminologists Susan Miller and Nicole Smolter (2011) call "paper abuse," which involves overwhelming the legal system with frivolous lawsuits, making false allegations to CPS, and otherwise manipulating the formal legal process with the end goal of burdening the ex-partner.[4] His abusive tactics "paid off for him," because of the time and energy she expended going to court and the rapport he built with the CPS caseworker. Even after the court ruling, he kept their daughter and blocked all contact with Essence. The CPS caseworker refused to intervene on Essence's behalf.

Without other options, but with the judge's order in hand, Essence drove across town to her daughter's school to speak with her. After entering the building, Essence stopped at the main office, introduced herself, and asked to see her daughter: "I'm sitting at the reception desk and I see police walk by. I see Child Protective Services, I see the principals, the counselors . . . they were all coming for me." Although Essence had sole legal custody, her former partner had preemptively convinced school administrators that Essence was a threat; if she attempted to contact their daughter, they should call the police and CPS.

The principals, the police officer, and the CPS caseworker initially refused to honor Essence's request to see her daughter. Instead, they falsely accused Essence of being drunk and insisted she take a breathalyzer test in the school hallway. She agreed and "tested 0.0." Essence then presented her court documents and noted that she had legal custody of her daughter. Essence recalled the police officer's response: "Well, what does *legal* mean?" As Essence put it, "The police officer act like he couldn't even comprehend what the order said." Then two principals, the police officer, and the CPS caseworker spoke with Essence in a private room. They told Essence her daughter did not want to speak with her. Essence recalled: "I said, 'Okay. Can I write her a letter? I just want her to know that her mom loves her no matter what.' Child Protective Services said, 'You have the other two [children] to worry about. [Your daughter] is with her dad. It's not like she's with some boy.'"

Essence explained that she could not dismiss her concerns about her daughter's safety just because she had two other children. She also noted that her former partner was blocking all of Essence's attempts to communicate with their daughter. Therefore, coming by the school was not only her last option but her legal right. The CPS caseworker responded by shouting, "If you keep pursuing [your daughter], I'm going to take *all* of your kids away from you!" In disbelief, Essence tried to clarify what was implied by the CPS caseworker's threat: "So, you put me in an impossible situation. You are telling me to walk away from my daughter to save my other two?" Essence remembered that she "started crying and . . . asked the CPS caseworker, 'Why would you do that?'" The caseworker shouted, "Because that's what the 'f' I do!" Essence ran out of the school. She tearfully explained, "I had to get out of there. I really did because that is horrible for somebody to have to choose [between her children] . . . My whole thing about this is I had a court order. That day [at the high school] and [my daughter] was supposed to come home with me based on what the judge ordered. I had it in my hand."

Even in the absence of an investigation, Essence was under attack by CPS. She yielded to the CPS caseworker's threats, believing, "if I took [my daughter], I would have lost all my kids." The CPS caseworker, police officer, school administrators, and counselor were unable to see or even consider the wider pattern of abuse and control deployed by Essence's former partner. Instead, they only saw Essence as the problem.

*Valerie*

Valerie, who was arrested for assaulting her abusive partner in front of police officers, also had an extensive history of enduring harm. Like Essence, she found Probation Officer Phoenix supportive and flexible. Unlike Phoenix, however, her CPS caseworker was unsupportive and inflexible. CPS did not address her pleas for institutional support and instead ordered her to complete what felt like "random" referrals that were "a waste of time." Additionally, CPS imposed a monitoring process that set her up to have her children once again removed from her care, enacting breakage in ways that felt similar to how her former partner had abused her.

After initially removing Valerie's three children from her care, CPS placed the children in two different foster homes. Two months later, CPS moved the children to one home. The placement lasted 13 months. As long as Valerie attended her CPS-ordered community obligations, she was allowed to visit her children twice a week. She earned those visits by attending parenting classes, domestic violence support groups, appointments with a psychiatrist, and completing AVI-G sessions. Valerie did not think the parenting classes were helpful. As she explained the matter, "The parenting classes were just worksheets and stuff telling you how to basically . . . cope with tantrums. Show you how to and how not to punish your child and stuff like that . . . It was stuff that, you know, a typical parent would already know. At least a decent parent would already know unless they was doped out or something, you know."

Valerie also reported that she gained little from the domestic violence survivor support classes. She recalled,

I'm not really screwed up from the domestic violence. I mean it's how I grew up, so I've learned to cope with it, and I've learned how to grow past it. That's what they fail to realize, so they think it screws my head up more that I went through it because they knew I went through it as a kid, but that's why [CPS] didn't want to give them back to me right away because [CPS] was like, "Oh, she went through so much as a kid and now she went through the domestic with him" . . . It wasn't that at all.

Valerie did not need caregiving instructions. She already had the skills to cope with domestic violence. What Valerie needed most was a job that paid a livable wage, transportation she could rely on, housing that was safe and affordable, and childcare at no or low cost. Lacking all of those, Valerie's last resort was to rely on her abusive partner, who would at least stay with the children while she earned money for the family.

Valerie completed her CPS-ordered classes and the supervised parenting time visits in 15 months. She also reported her abusive partner to the police for the last time he harmed her. He went to jail and Valerie was reunified with her children. At the time of their reunification, her three children moved into the Motel 6 with Valerie and her new partner. She remained on a waiting list for space in what she described as "a family homeless shelter." While waiting for a more permanent residence, they avoided motel eviction policies by cycling between budget motels. Her new partner cared for Valerie's children while she worked at a fast-food restaurant across town. Valerie was also eight months pregnant and hoped to find housing before the baby arrived. After CPS closed her case, they referred her to a local nonprofit for help securing permanent housing. For Valerie, the nonprofit worker's assistance was "pointless" because she and her children still did not have a place to live.

Although CPS closed her case after reunification, they continued to monitor Valerie and her children. When her baby was one month old, CPS scheduled a "family team meeting" in which Valerie, the baby, and her three small children under five years old met with caseworkers at the CPS office. The stated purpose of the meeting was to confirm her children's well-being. As Valerie recalled, exasperatedly, "It was cold and I was supposed to travel with four kids on a city bus with a newborn to come to this meeting." Instead, Valerie skipped the meeting, believing it was irresponsible to take her infant on a bus in the freezing cold.

Later that day, her new partner cared for the children in the motel room while Valerie took the bus across town to work the afternoon shift. Valerie explained that before she left for work, she had a "sinking feeling" that CPS might try to take her kids. She recalled, "We was like, 'Should I go to work? Should I not go to work?' But we couldn't really afford me not to go to work, so I went to work." Valerie comforted herself that because she did not have an open case, there was no basis for CPS to take emergency custody. Because she needed the money and was constantly worried about losing her job, Valerie went to work. After all, she pointed out, "Nobody's going to want me to work for them when I have to do meetings on Tuesdays, and a visit on Mondays, and a visit on Thursdays, and a court date here and there. It's a lot for some employers, so it's just really stressful."

As Valerie got off the bus at work her new partner called and shouted, "They're here taking the kids!" Valerie immediately tried to find a ride back across town. But, she explained,

> they took them. Fully took them while I was gone because it took me so long to get back. I . . . was already on the other side of town, so I had to wait. While I was arranging transportation to get back, [CPS and the police] had already been [at the motel room] for 10 or 15 minutes so they was rushing to take them . . . One of the cops was trying to be nice and wait until I got there, but it took too long and they have other calls to do.

Her new partner kept her on the phone while she asked people at the fast-food restaurant for a ride back to the motel. When that failed, she ran to the bus stop and tried to get a bus back. Valerie described the removal as follows:

> I was on the phone the whole time with [my new partner]. I guess he was sitting on the bed listening to his headphones. The [children] were laying down watching TV . . . [CPS and the police] had a key card and opened the door. We had the latch thing on so they couldn't open it regardless . . . I guess [my new partner] didn't hear them because his headphones were in . . . [My five-year-old was] like, "The police are at the door!" She thought the police were going to take her . . . I told him, "Don't make it worse! Don't make it worse on the kids! Just open the door!" . . . The whole time they was in the room, [the youngest child] was like . . . glued to [my new partner's] leg. She would not let go. She would scream any time somebody tried to grab her, so he had to take her out to the [police] car himself. Yeah, I wasn't there when they got taken. I had just missed it.

When Valerie finally returned to the motel room, she called CPS to ask why they had taken her children. They told her they removed the children because Valerie missed the scheduled "family team meeting" earlier that day. Valerie repeated, "We had an investigation going on—not an open case," as though she were still trying to make sense of what had happened. She had had the children back in her custody for less than three months and now she would have to start the reunification process all over again. FTP ideology framed Valerie as a neglectful parent from CPS's first contact with her. That ideology continued to shape Valerie's CPS interactions despite her efforts to strategically protect and parent her children and her pleas for the necessary institutional supports to do so.

## Tyra

Tyra's formative relationship with her husband and her interactions with CPS illuminate both intimate and institutional breakage. When Tyra met her soon-to-be husband, she was 14 and he was 17. She had just been released from juvenile detention and was recovering from being sexually assaulted by a family member. By "doing things" for her and "taking care" of her needs, her soon-to-be husband quickly became Tyra's "prince." As she put it, "I stuck to [him] like glue. I literally lost myself in him. I did. I thought [him], I woke up [him], I prayed [him]. I was all [him] . . . he was my knight in shining armor. That's what he was—my prince. He made me feel like I was important. He made me feel like I was beautiful. He made me feel like I was loved."

When Tyra became pregnant at 15, they got married. Being married made Tyra feel as though she had escaped the stigma of being "a statistic"—a low-income, Black, single, pregnant teenager. Tyra explained, "I was married. What teenager in high school, Black on top of that, is married to the father of her child in high school? Girls my age back then—that never happened. I was so excited just to be married in high school to the father of my child, and the second child, and the third child, so it was kind of like I had already accomplished something."

Over the course of their relationship, Tyra's husband started physically and emotionally abusing her. She thinks her neighbor called the police at one point and reported him for beating her. The responding officers contacted CPS. Tyra managed the CPS caseworker's investigation at that time by lying. What happened to her mouth? She bit it chewing on something. What happened to her hand? She was opening boxes with a knife and cut herself. Tyra lied because she was afraid of how much angrier a CPS allegation would make her husband and she knew that CPS intervention would tear her family apart.

When his abuse "got out of hand . . . to hospital stays, and black eyes, and broken bones," Tyra contacted the local domestic violence shelter for help. The shelter provided a safe place where Tyra could consider her next steps. When it was time to leave the shelter, staff offered Tyra and her children agency-sponsored transitional housing, which gave her an avenue for gradual independence and, ideally, safety. Tyra continued to long for an intact nuclear family, however. Tyra remembered,

> I just had started to get things back under control with [living in] transitional housing. I was trying to do the right thing [by keeping him away] . . . and then he sweet-talked me again. Promised he would change . . . He wouldn't hit me. He'd keep his hands off me. He was going to go to church. He found God. He's a new person now. He just was a good con artist . . . so I always forgave him.

In hopes that he was "a new person" Tyra allowed her husband to move into her transitional housing, making the family whole. Not long thereafter, Tyra walked into their apartment after having breakfast with friends. She did not remember much about what happened next, but she was able to recall this: "He was mad. I can't remember why. I just know he smacked me over the head with something. I can't remember what it was. I fell to the floor. He grabbed the knife and cut me right through the hand."

One of their children ran to the neighbor's house for help and the neighbor reported the incident to the police. The police arrested and jailed Tyra's husband, and Tyra and her children were removed from transitional housing and returned to the shelter. After she had worked so long to secure housing, Tyra "was embarrassed all over again" to return to the shelter, but she had nowhere else to go. She was estranged from her family because of her husband's violence. The domestic violence agency then informed Tyra that they "no longer wanted to work with me because they felt unsafe." With transitional housing no longer an option, Tyra remained in the shelter until her husband's criminal prosecution was complete.

After the violent incident, Tyra and her children were settling into a new room at the shelter when she received a call from CPS. A caseworker asked Tyra and the children to meet her outside because she wanted "to check on the welfare of the kids." Tyra explained that she "thought it was normal" for caseworkers to drop by and check in on people they were worried about, and she remembered appreciating the caseworker's concern. When Tyra stepped outside the shelter with her children, a police officer approached her, clutching "official-looking papers" and in the company of two CPS caseworkers. Although years had passed since this happened, tears rolled down Tyra's face as she recalled how "intimidating" it was "because people don't question the police. This is not something we're told is okay. If a police officer tells you to do something, you do it. He asked me to hand him my baby. That's what I did."

Tyra did not fully comprehend what was taking place:

> I didn't realize they were taking the kids until [one of the CPS caseworkers] asked me if I had all their belongings in the shelter with me—what I had with me or what was at the house, what could I give her. That's when I realized, okay, she's taking my kids . . . [I] cried. That's all I could do. It was like really hard because I thought she was supposed to help me, and that was not what I felt afterwards. I did not feel that way at all.

Tyra explained that, feeling "blindsided" by CPS caseworkers and the police officer, she voluntarily "gave my kids so easily without asking questions"—a handover "that just tore my life up." She recalled that she "felt tricked and . . . betrayed" by the sequence of events because the CPS caseworker had said she was only dropping by to check on their welfare. CPS's deception effectively coupled "assistance" with coercive authority (Fong, 2020). Tyra did not have a chance to ask questions or say goodbye to her children. Years later, Tyra still felt the breakage of institutional betrayal. She remembered, "When I first met [the CPS caseworker], she acted like she wanted to help me, like she was my friend. I could tell her anything and she would help me." Instead, CPS's coercive approach left Tyra feeling "stripped of everything." Tyra explained, "It was heartaching because, as a mom, you don't want somebody to tell you how to take care of what belongs to you, like what you brought on this Earth, especially if you think that that person is supposed to help you get better."

Tyra was especially bitter when she learned months later that she had no obligation to give CPS her children. Legally, Tyra had the right to a court hearing where a judge "could have made the decision if he felt like they needed to be removed." But all Tyra knew at that time was that a uniformed police officer was walking toward her with two CPS caseworkers. The police officer holding what looked like official papers, the caseworkers' authoritative stance, and the police cruiser convinced Tyra that she had no option. She did not have networks of supportive friends and family to rely on. She did not have the money to retain a private attorney to assert and defend her rights. From Tyra's perspective, CPS's decision to remove her children was based on the assumption that living arrangements and relationship status were the only factors in determining risk. Tyra pointed out that CPS ignored the significant dangers children face in foster care. Furthermore, how would her children be affected by losing regular contact with their mother and each other? How would they cope with disrupted school schedules and other changes in their routine? Tyra's experience reflects the unfortunate reality that many Black women face in their interactions with CPS. As Roberts (2002) has argued, "Once Black children are removed from their homes, they "remain in foster care longer, are moved more often, receive fewer services, and are less likely to be either returned home or adopted than other children" (p. vi).

Because Tyra's children witnessed their father beating and stabbing their mother, and because Tyra let him back in their home, CPS alleged that Tyra failed to protect her children. From CPS's perspective, Tyra's "failure to protect" was evidence of neglect. As Tyra recalled the matter, "When I had went to court, the judge had said that CPS felt like I couldn't distinguish a healthy relationship, and they felt like it was endangering the welfare of my children, so that was the allegation for the termination of my parental rights. So it just spiraled from there."

Tyra did not understand how her dream of a nuclear family, her efforts at forgiveness, her struggle to reunite with her husband, and his violence supported a court's determination that meant *she* was neglectful. Tyra pointed out that when she thought of "real" child abuse and neglect, she thought

> of the pictures you see of the kids with the black eyes, purple, bruised faces, they're skinny, their clothes have holes in them, they can't read, they can't write, they have imaginary friends at 10 and 14 years old beyond what statistics says. I think of kids like that. I think of kids that come, and they have bruises, and you can't explain them. I think about the kids that are sexually assaulted by dads and uncles. That's what I think of when I think of child abuse and neglect.

CPS held Tyra responsible for her husband's abuse and punished her for attempting to maintain an intact family. Missing from CPS's consideration was the wider pattern of abuse and control her husband had exerted. Without that pattern in view, CPS inadvertently replicated the physical and emotional abuse Tyra had suffered.

Tyra tried to mend her relationship with her first CPS caseworker by apologizing for lying about her husband's abusive behavior. Although Tyra acknowledged it was odd that she felt compelled to apologize for behaviors she used to protect her family, she knew it was necessary to improve the relationship. But engaging in the emotion work (Hochschild, 1983) of an apology did not change anything. Instead, Tyra recollected, "even after I admitted that I lied about stuff, even after I apologized, and even after I started to become more open and honest, I feel like she just never gave me a chance because of the way things started. I feel like she literally had a closed off opinion of me."

Tyra gradually learned that the precarious relationship with her CPS caseworker was not only about the lies. Her low-income status, her prior CLS involvement, and her husband's claims that she was "mutually violent" shaped the caseworker's judgments about Tyra. The caseworker then provided or withheld services based on those judgments.

> I felt like because I was on welfare, I felt like [the first caseworker] treated me a certain way. "Well, Tyra, we don't have funding to do this or to do that," and I wouldn't even be asking her anything like that. I would be asking for advice like, "Do you know anybody I can call to help me get clothes for [my children]?" She doesn't want to tell me that schools offer a voucher during the cold seasons. I didn't get that information from her. I just got, "Oh, CPS can't pay for everything." That's not what I asked you. I told you that I need help . . . you're assigned to help my family, and I don't feel like that's what she did.

In addition to identifying her as low-income, Tyra's first caseworker learned she spent time in juvenile detention following a felony conviction. The caseworker, Tyra explained, "kind of just ran with that, too. It was kind of like I was labeled and that's pretty much how they dealt with me." Furthermore, the same caseworker documented Tyra's husband's characterization of the abuse as "mutual." There were no formal CPS assessments of him or Tyra and no conversations with her about his claim. The caseworker took his word as fact, making it part of Tyra's permanent file. She pointed out, "What is on the paper is not always accurate . . . I wasn't the aggressor, [he] was." The CPS caseworker created a false narrative about who Tyra was and the services she and her children needed, a false narrative that followed her for years.

Without family willing to support Tyra, CPS placed her children in three separate foster homes. She was assigned a CPS caseworker who recommended to the family court judge that she complete multiple services, including individual therapy, family therapy, parenting classes, healthy eating classes, and budgeting classes. At one point during the service referral process, Tyra became frustrated with the number of CPS-ordered obligations and yelled at her caseworker. The consequence was a sixth referral: completion of 30 two-hour AVI-G sessions.

In exchange for consistent attendance in all six services, Tyra received separate supervised parenting time with each of her three children once a week. Although relieved to finally have contact with them, she was also exhausted. Taking public transportation an hour each way to all obligated services was exceptionally time-consuming and draining. Tyra explained, "I did parenting time and I did parenting classes [on the same day], so I would go to a parenting class at [a social services agency], and then I would catch the bus to [the CPS office on the other side of town], and they would let me do like an hour visit with each kid on a different day."

Although CPS covered the fees associated with the various services, Tyra found little benefit. She did not like sitting and listening to the parenting class instructors, who provided handouts and expected her to take notes on their presentations. She wondered why the instructors did not discuss the handouts with participants, giving them a chance to learn from each other. Instead, they told participants to remain quiet, take the handouts home, and read the content on their own. For Tyra, "parenting class . . . was like the most boring class on Earth. It just was a lot of pamphlets, a lot of videos, a lot of paperwork that said answer yes or no . . . I was kind of by myself. It was kind of just a director telling us to read this, watch that, and go home."

In addition to feeling unstimulated by the class instructors, overwhelmed with handouts, and disconnected from the other people in the room, Tyra felt her assigned CPS caseworkers were "always recycled." In other words, her caseworkers often changed roles arbitrarily without warning or explanation. Tyra found the process overwhelming and confusing. She explained,

> One minute [Joan] was the *guardian ad litem*[5] for the kids, and [Margaret] was the CPS worker, and then it switched. [Margaret] was the *guardian ad litem* for the kids, and then [Joan] was the CPS worker coming to my house and doing the checks. At one point they wanted reunification, and then at another point this CPS worker didn't agree with the reunification because she felt like I didn't complete this parenting class correctly or I didn't benefit from this therapist. They wanted to get a second opinion, or they wanted to get somebody to mentally evaluate me.

Because of this dynamic, Tyra believed CPS was working to terminate her parental rights rather than prioritizing and supporting family reunification.

Tyra attended all her community-based programming and gradually earned more parenting time with her children, graduating from one hour of agency-based supervised visitation to longer periods of supervised parenting time in a designated CPS space. Later, CPS allowed Tyra to visit her children at a McDonald's Play Place and other indoor children's play areas. Eventually, Tyra was allowed caseworker-monitored parenting time at her apartment. They established a routine where the CPS caseworker sat on the couch while Tyra and the kids "were on the computer, and then came back into the living room. The [kids] went into the bathroom. They got their baths, they got their pajamas on, they ate dinner. We did homework, and then CPS would gather everybody up and leave." The new routine of time at home together, although monitored, gave Tyra hope that there may be an end to CPS's oversight. Then everything changed because of how her CPS caseworker responded to something Tyra's four-year-old son had said.

Out of nowhere Tyra received a call one morning from her CPS caseworker. Her home visits with her children were over, effective immediately. There would be a family court hearing in one week. Despite Tyra's pleas, the worker refused to share any further information indicating the reason for the termination. Tyra had to wait for court.

At the hearing, Tyra listened as her CPS caseworker told the judge that on the evening of her children's last home visit, Tyra's four-year-old claimed that "Daddy was hiding in the [linen] closet." The caseworker concluded that while she monitored the child's siblings playing in the front room, Tyra had knowingly allowed her abusive husband to see the boy by hiding out in the bedroom linen closet. Without considering that the child may have been fantasizing about seeing his father, or even whether or not the claim was realistic given the closet's size compared to that of the child's father, the caseworker accepted the four-year-old's claim as true. The caseworker then recommended that the judge end Tyra's home visits with her children until further notice. The judge accepted the recommendation and Tyra's supervised parenting visits were thereafter restricted to a designated CPS space. She left court feeling defeated and angry.

A few hours after her court appearance, Tyra's caseworker knocked on her door and announced that she was going to check the linen closet for the child's father. Tyra was dumbfounded. What right did the caseworker have to enter her home now?

I said, "You just want to do a check? What kind of check? You want to walk through the house?" She's like, "Yeah, I want to check the closet specifically." "Hold on, wait. You want to go in my room, and you want to check my closet because of something [my four-year-old child] said happened a week ago?" She's like, "Yeah." So, I told her no. I told her "No, you can leave!" Aw, man. That must have really set them off because they just assumed he was in the closet. I'm thinking in my head this little-bitty-ass closet and this man that stands damn near six foot tall, 200 pounds, is hiding in a little-bitty linen closet. Are you kidding me? You want to check the closet? You just took away my home visit because of an allegation from what you said was a four-year-old kid! Are you kidding me? I was so upset. I was so angry, and I had to start all over again.

Tyra was furious. She had not seen or talked to her husband for more than a year. Through no fault of her own, Tyra had to restart the reunification process. Tyra felt CPS's actions were calculated to turn her children against her rather than reunite her family. In hindsight, Tyra understood that refusing to let the caseworker in her house significantly extended the time it would take for her to earn back her parenting time. Nonetheless, it was a self-protective strategy deployed in an untenable situation that left Tyra feeling she had no other recourse.

When supervised home visits finally resumed, Tyra's CPS caseworker would check the entire house before the children entered. Tyra was obligated to then present the caseworker with a full plan for the evening. As Tyra recollected,

[The CPS caseworker] would go through the underwear drawers, and I'm like where the hell is he hiding in the drawer? Come on now! This is insane. I would have to have a plan of what the evening was going to be before the kids came, like we just couldn't be normal. Oh, like I had to tell her what I was cooking for dinner, or we're going to do homework at nine o'clock and then after that we're going to do this, and then we'll do baths at this time . . . it was just really like scripted, and it drove me insane.

Tyra believed the checks and plan were a performative façade engineered to make it look like CPS was promoting the children's safety. Tyra felt undermined by the home visit requirements. She thought they were designed to strategically prod her into expressing her powerlessness through physical or verbal demonstrations of anger. Over time she recognized that giving into expressing that anger would provide CPS evidence to ruin her chances for reunification. Tyra felt her caseworkers were focused only on her failings, and wondered why they did not recognize what it took for her to survive and still parent her children despite being abused before their removal. Why did they not see how hard she worked toward reunification? Instead, CPS caseworkers appeared intent on replicating the abuse and control she long suffered in her marriage. Tyra recalled how her CPS caseworkers repeatedly criticized her failed marriage and told Tyra she could not recognize a "healthy relationship": "I would always tell them back, 'Yeah, I do, because I know that you and I don't work well together. This is a bad relationship.' They would think that I was trying to be funny, and I'm like no, this is an unhealthy relationship, too."

With unhelpful yet obligatory referrals, recycled and judgmental caseworkers, inaccurate documentation, inconsistent messaging, and arbitrary surveillance, CPS created a coercive power dynamic similar to the one inherent in Tyra's husband's relationship with her. But Tyra explained, "I fear CPS more than him." Why? Because CPS could manufacture reasons to take her children and end her right to parent them—and with the state's full support.

## MANAGING THE BREAKAGE

CPS caseworkers misunderstood Essence's, Valerie's, and Tyra's strategies to maintain their dignity while parenting their children as these women being uncooperative and therefore deserving of further punishment. Highlighting how Essence and Valerie continued to manage CPS monitoring at our last contact, and how Tyra eventually became free from CPS scrutiny, encourages researchers and practitioners to consider systems-involved women's often seemingly invisible fortitude.

### Essence

When I last spoke with Essence she was in the early stages of CPS contact initiated by her former partner and the CPS caseworker who colluded with him. At this point, Essence felt she did not have a choice about "every little thing" because of her former partner's ongoing coercively controlling tactics in his interactions with their daughter, the CPS caseworker, police, school administrators, and the court system. Her extended family lived out of state. She had few friends because she had become isolated owing to his abuse, and she barely supported herself on her combined child support and disability income. Yet Essence continued to survive and persist as a means of resisting CPS. For example, Essence got up every day, used child-focused protective strategies to check on her daughter, armed herself with documentation of her legal rights, and directly confronted the CPS caseworker and administrators. But Essence's survival and persistence were the same attributes that the CPS caseworker used against her, threatening to remove *all* her children if Essence did not retreat. As a low-income Black mother, Essence knew she was likely held to a different standard than a wealthy white woman would be in similar circumstances. She identified her systems-inflicted harms as originating with her arrest and culminating with CPS caseworker contact: "My arrest benefitted [my former partner]—He got to turn everybody against me. He got my daughter." And to whom could she report the CPS-inflicted breakage and receive just recourse? No one. Although her psychologist encouraged her to contact the CPS caseworker's supervisor and formally complain, Essence explained, "I have *not* [contacted her supervisor] . . . I am terrified [of the caseworker]!"

## Valerie

Similarly, Valerie felt CPS caseworkers did not listen to her pleas for institutional support or consider her child-focused protective strategies to parent her children. Instead, they misunderstood why she would not leave her partner, they enforced mandated obligations that wasted her time, and they monitored her movements in ways that diminished her agency and ability to parent. The combination of CPS's ongoing surveillance and Valerie's inability to meet her daily needs meant she continued to suffer CPS-inflicted harm.

## Tyra

From Tyra's perspective, lying to CPS caseworkers about the abuse she endured was her only defense against a system that could tear her family apart. By encouraging her to leave her husband to maintain custody of her children, caseworkers overlooked her strategic choice of favoring known over unknown dangers. Her husband's abuse was the known danger. The unknown danger was what would happen if her family "broke up" because she disclosed his abuse. Once CPS was involved, Tyra was caught in the system and often felt she would never get free.

Everything changed when Tyra met Gloria, however, a CPS caseworker who did not enlist an FTP ideology. Instead, Gloria listened to Tyra and seemed invested in learning the full context of her situation.

Gloria then made meaningful, supportive referrals for Tyra and her children. As Tyra explained,

> Things felt different with her. I felt like I could talk to her. I felt like I could be honest with her because I wasn't afraid to share something with her. I felt like she was there for us . . . I felt like she took the time to look into different resources versus I felt like [the first caseworker] was kind of like just go do this class, but I felt like with [Gloria] it was like, okay, let me see if [Tyra] could benefit from this. Let me think about her strengths and let me think about her.

In addition to listening and making meaningful referrals, Gloria provided Tyra with a path beyond CPS surveillance. As Tyra put it, "She was the first CPS worker that I actually felt was there to help us . . . She would tell me, and I use this all the time with the kids, 'This is the problem; this is the way that it needs to be corrected; this is the time frame to correct it; this is the consequence.' The whole layout. She gave me everything." For Tyra, managing and then eventually healing from and repairing CPS-inflicted breakage involved a holistically responsive CPS caseworker who listened, contextualized her experience, made meaningful referrals, and provided "the whole layout" for a way forward.

## SUMMARY AND REFLECTIONS

Tyra was the only woman in this chapter I knew from cofacilitating her AVI-G years previously. Ironically, I met Tyra's husband before I met her. Her husband participated in a BIP group I cofacilitated at the time. As Tyra's AVI-G cofacilitator I had heard her mention CPS caseworker interactions now and then, but I did not know the extent of her CPS-inflicted breakage. As a researcher, it was evident from the women's stories that Essence's, Valerie's, and Tyra's efforts to proactively parent their children in the midst of their former partners' abuse resulted in their CPS punishment, while the abuse and coercive control they experienced remained largely invisible. Thus, the women's punishment grew out of an FTP ideology that shaped their CPS caseworkers' interactions and discretion in monitoring the women. By threatening Essence, by removing Valerie's children again, and by perpetually treating Tyra as a failed mother, CPS caseworkers became state-sanctioned proxies for each woman's abuser. With limited access to resource-rich social networks and finances, all three women had little recourse in formally separating themselves from CPS. Instead, they enlisted a range of situation-specific strategies (e.g.,

Essence carrying court documents while attempting to see her daughter; Valerie deciding to keep her children warm and at home instead of taking a bus in cold weather to a CPS meeting; and Tyra lying to and later preventing a CPS caseworker from entering her home) to emotionally and practically manage their CPS breakage. In doing so, however, the caseworkers and court officials viewed the women as challenging CPS's authority, and therefore as being deserving of further punishment. Luckily for Tyra, Gloria operated independently from FTP ideology.

The women experienced this punishment as sanctioned by some authorities who were complicit in CPS-inflicted harm. Uniformed but silent police officers stood next to CPS caseworkers—at a school, at a motel, in a domestic violence shelter parking lot—symbolizing impenetrable, coercive state power. Intimidated by all these things, the women believed they had no choice but to submit to the caseworkers' demands. Given the troubled relationships between police officers and communities of color—again brought to the public's attention by the #BlackLivesMatter and #SayHerName social justice movements—police presence paired with CPS intervention is problematic. Police presence may be especially traumatizing given community experiences with carceral grief (Sewell and Ray, 2020). The combination of CPS caseworkers' interaction styles and alliances with law enforcement prompted Rise Magazine (2020), an online resource for CPS-involved parents, to follow Roberts's (2020) lead in referring to CPS as the "family policing system" rather than "child protection" or "child welfare" systems. Whereas "child protection" and "child welfare" terminology imply CPS is focused on protecting children, some CPS caseworkers seem, instead, to be focused on regulating and policing already marginalized families.

Although CPS was tasked with protecting the welfare of the women's children owing to the possibility of domestic violence exposure, the women in this chapter experienced most CPS caseworker interactions as further destabilizing their families' safety and well-being. The caseworkers used coercive tactics that reflected an apparent lack of awareness according to which protecting abused mothers' welfare is synonymous with protecting and caring for the children. Jatara, whose family was involved with criminal and family courts, made the connection between this CPS breakage and individual breakage when she pointed out that CPS caseworkers purposefully made matters in her family worse. As she put it, "I feel the system loves brokenness. It loves it. If everybody was doing the best for . . . the child's sake . . . they wouldn't have a job."

# CHAPTER 3

# Antiviolence Intervention Administration

"GETTING STRANGLED TO DEATH . . ."
—RYANN

In this chapter, I detail how the women of *Broken* experienced community-based antiviolence intervention (AVI). The AVI was designed to meet the complex needs of the women who had used force in their relationships. The women I interviewed made a distinction between AVI *administration* (AVI-A) and AVI *group* (AVI-G), describing vastly different experiences between a punishing administration, including the fees and monitoring (the AVI-A), and a supportive, interactive group (the AVI-G). I open this chapter with a brief historical overview of AVI for women in the United States. Next, I explain the research site's AVI-A intake assessment process, attendance management, and service fees. I then explain how aspects of this framework affected low-income criminal court–ordered women, those who were family court–ordered, and women who voluntarily sought services. By attending to the referral pathways, I demonstrate how the combination of low-income women's court-ordered probation, CPS, and AVI contact caused what one of the women I interviewed, Sage, called "thing-on-top-of-thing" breakage. This cumulative harm, illustrated in figure 5, compromised their financial, physical, and emotional well-being. Throughout this chapter I also bring attention to how the women of *Broken* navigated these layers despite the considerable harm it inflicted on them.

**PROBATION**

- Emotional labor
- Probation officer discretion
- Drug and alcohol testing
- Bureaucratic failures
- Fees
- Time
- Multiple referrals
- Monitoring

**AVI**

- Emotional labor
- Fees
- Monitoring
- Time
- No transportation
- No childcare
- Mental and physical burden

**CPS**

- Emotional labor
- Failure to protect ideology
- CPS caseworker discretion
- Separation from children
- Time
- Multiple referrals
- Monitoring

Court-ordered women

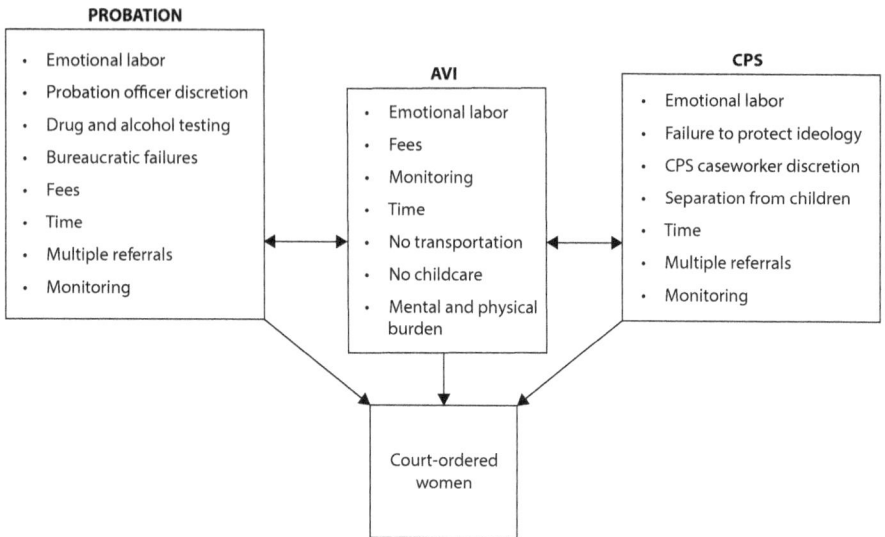

FIGURE 5. Probation's, AVI-A's, and CPS's cumulative harm.

## OVERVIEW: US-BASED ANTIVIOLENCE INTERVENTION FOR WOMEN

When someone in the United States is convicted of domestic violence, a general legal systems pathway involves placing the person under court supervision. Once under the court's supervision, that person must comply with probation officer-supervised orders. In the 1970s, battering intervention programs (BIPs) for men using physical violence and coercive control became a component of these court-ordered consequences (Edelson and Tolman, 1992; Gondolf, 2012; Saunders, 2008). BIPs were designed to address men's "power and entitlement to master and control their intimate partners in society" (Dasgupta, 2002, p. 1368). According to activist, practitioner, and scholar Shamita Das Dasgupta (2002),

> The significance of battering as well as the philosophy underlying many batterer's programs is based on the politics of gender roles and history of intergender interactions in society. Many researchers and activists tend to define battering as a pattern of intimidation, coercive control, and oppression . . . Although batterers use physical assault to consolidate a pattern of domination, they may not always rely on actual beatings. Battering behavior is supported by historical and social entitlements afforded to the male gender role. (p. 1367)

With the rise in arrests of women owing to mandatory arrest policies (Durfee, 2012) came judicial demand for suitable consequences. In the 1980s, communities largely met this need through informal means with more formal practices evolving in the late 1990s (Larance et al., 2019b). In the mid-2000s, formal AVI curricula grounded in a contextual understanding of the experiences of women who resorted to using nonfatal force became available (Larance et al., 2009; Pence et al., 2011; Van Dieten et al., 2014). Although these programs were an important resource, feminist practitioners and researchers warned that the very existence of these court-ordered interventions could undermine justice for systems-involved women (Dasgupta, 2002; Gardner, 2009; Worcester, 2002). This warning was owing, in part, to concerns that practitioners operating along the victim-offender binary would use a one-size-fits all approach to intervention by placing "women offenders" in BIPs (Larance et al., 2022; Miller et al., 2005). Feminist practitioners and researchers pointed out that, because these women typically have extensive domestic and sexual violence survivorship histories, appropriate interventions must move beyond the victim-offender binary. Doing so involves intersectional, trauma-informed approaches that address the social and historical contexts of diverse women's lived experiences (Larance et al., 2022). Community responses to women's use of force continue to take many forms. Some are for women only, but they are based on BIP frameworks designed to address heterosexual men's coercive control; others are women-only interventions developed specifically for cisgender women in heterosexual relationships; others place women of diverse sexual identities in groups with men and follow a gender-neutral curriculum; and still others are various combinations of the aforementioned. I explore AVI approaches in more detail in chapter 6.

## THE RESEARCH SITE'S ANTIVIOLENCE INTERVENTION ADMINISTRATION (AVI-A)

A woman's entry into the research site's AVI began with an hour-long, 60 dollar individual intake assessment, during which a staff member asked her a range of questions about her relationship history, general information about the incident that resulted in her referral, and access to supportive services. A staff member then established a criminal court–ordered or voluntary per-session group fee using her proof of income on the agency's sliding scale. For those who expressed difficulty paying, individual payment plans offered lower or zero payment options for a designated period, allowing those ordered by the criminal court to remain probation compliant. A woman's per-session fee would continue to accrue with each attendance. Should she complete the required number of criminal court–ordered sessions with a balance, the system placed her official completion on hold until she paid in full. AVI completion required attending 30 two-hour, in-person group sessions. The referring criminal and family courts also ordered the women to complete the number of sessions they determined necessary for compliance, however, which could be more or less than the AVI's 30 sessions.

During the intake assessment, a staff person also asked court-ordered women to sign an information release consenting to communication between the AVI-A and the referring entity. For criminal court–ordered women this communication pertained to attendance and payment status. For family court–ordered women the contact regarded their attendance. Although signing the form was voluntary, not signing the form meant their participation would not be reported to probation or CPS or both, leaving them in violation of the court order and at risk for noncompliant status. Signing the form meant a staff person logged their attendance into a password-protected online system within 24 hours of each group session, which was available to probation officers, CPS caseworkers, and referring entities 24 hours a day, seven days a week. An absence, lateness, or missed payment in the online system would signal a woman's noncompliance to referring entities.

While criminal court–ordered women were responsible for paying their AVI-A fees, CPS paid the AVI-A fees for family court–ordered women's assessment and weekly group attendance directly to the agency. The women who voluntarily sought services were responsible for paying all AVI-A-related fees, but their payment and attendance status were not communicated to an outside entity unless they provided written consent.

Within approximately a week of completing the intake assessment, each woman joined the two-hour, women-only AVI-G. The discussion-focused psychoeducational support and intervention groups engaged a range of curriculum topics designed to address the complex circumstances of women who have often both survived and caused harm in their intimate relationships (see Larance et al., 2009; Pence et al., 2011). Depending on the number of referrals, the AVI-A held approximately two groups each week, a morning group and an evening group. The women had the option of attending one or both of the two groups. Court-ordered women were expected to attend at least one group per week to be court-compliant. As long as voluntary group members paid for services, however, they could come and go as they pleased. The AVI-A did not provide transportation, transportation assistance, childcare, or childcare support. As this chapter will show, low-income, criminal court–ordered women experienced the AVI-A fees and surveillance as financially and mentally harmful.[1]

## MANAGING THE AVI-A: LOW-INCOME CRIMINAL COURT–ORDERED WOMEN

Money for food, gas, bus rides, rent, utilities, laundry, phone, internet, and toiletries is already scarce for low-income single mothers of young children. They also have additional costs for childcare, clothes, shoes, and school supplies. And, with or without children, how could low-income women budget for the unexpected obligations of being on probation? There was already little, if any, room to afford gifts for family birthdays, holidays, or any "extras" outside those necessities. But, as detailed in chapter 1, the women on probation now had to do all these things: pay court fines, fees, and costs; a monthly "probation fee"; a booking fee if they were jailed at any point; random drug and alcohol testing fees; a locker fee at drug and alcohol testing; at least one court-ordered psychiatric evaluation; and budget for the extra gas money or bus fare necessary to get to court-ordered programming, including AVI, and then get back home or to work.

Like those in Susan Miller's (2005) research, the women in *Broken* were shocked by the additional AVI costs. At their first meeting with their probation officer, they received the AVI service name and agency telephone number and were told to call and set up an intake assessment within the week. Often, the probation officer provided no further program detail. During their first call to schedule their assessment, the women learned they would have to pay 60 dollars for the assessment in addition to weekly session fees. They also had to manage childcare during their in-person group attendance. The additional fees, the expenditure of time, and the lack of childcare—on top of other probation obligations, fines, fees, and costs—were overwhelming. When QuiShandra learned about this additional burden, she remembered thinking, "This is like bullcrap!"

Many women struggled to keep or find a job, aggravating their financial burden. Typically, the women had been in contact with the AVI and on probation for a month when their employers first informed them that they had lost their jobs owing to their convictions. These were the same jobs that had allowed most women to barely balance their obligations in the first place, the same jobs they needed to remain "probation compliant."

Sage referred to this process as the "domino effect," which made her feel that her "life was ruined."

This situation placed the women in a double bind. With a criminal record that marked them as "carceral citizens" (Miller and Stuart, 2017, p. 6) they had great difficulty finding and keeping employment. Any arrests or charges, whether or not they resulted in convictions, were documented on their criminal record. Prospective employers use background checks to learn whether someone had a documented criminal history, often using this record as a proxy for evaluating trustworthiness and employability. QuiShandra looked for jobs without any luck. In a state of utter exasperation, she explained, "Even like temp jobs turned me down . . . I got turned down like seriously from four different jobs at one temp agency in one day . . . they were like, 'Okay, we'll talk to a supervisor about you' . . . and they still turned me down!"

Furthermore, sectors in which the women typically worked before the incident—healthcare and education—would no longer employ them. Sage "ended up losing a really good job" in healthcare making $14.50 per hour. She resigned herself to applying for a 10-dollar-an-hour job bagging groceries but could not believe it when her application was denied because of the conviction. The inability to secure even a low-paying job that some people have described as low-skilled "was humiliating," explained Emersyn.

In addition to the financial costs, there was the mental burden. QuiShandra described it as

> a mental thing for me . . . it just kind of brings me down every time I think about the fact that like this is my reality; this is my life. I have to like live like this. I have to move around like this. I have to try to network like this. I have to occupy my time, and my day, and my weeks around this . . . correcting my wrong.

This "mental thing" also affected how QuiShandra interacted with her family members. Her uncle had recently passed away and, although to do so was unlike the way she would normally mourn a loved one, she decided not to attend the funeral. QuiShandra explained that particular situation in this way:

> I'm trying to balance and keep myself [mentally] above water, and just going to a funeral would just totally break me all the way down. I don't want to have a setback. I want to continue moving forward in this process, and at the point that I'm at, I just can't afford to keep going back . . . [I] just hope that my family still knows that I care and I love [my uncle].

The financial and mental breakage of compulsory, probation-monitored AVI-A manifested in anxiety. For Abby the anxiety was two-fold. She was "behind in paying" and often could not hear the group discussions because of a hearing impairment. As she put it,

> It's hard in group because . . . I can't hear people when they're talking . . . The one girl who was sitting across from me, she talks so quietly anyway, and she doesn't really move her lips when she talks, so I gave up [trying to read her lips]. I just sat there and acted like I was listening. Nodding every now and then . . . It's very frustrating.

Although Abby found Probation Officer Phoenix supportive, she was concerned that disclosing the extent of her hearing loss, as well as her challenges participating in the AVI, would make her seem difficult to supervise. She did not consider telling the AVI staff or Officer Phoenix about her disability. She just wanted to "get through it." It was easier to sit in the group, deal with her anxiety, and push through to be "compliant" with the court order than risk further consequences. But, she noticed, it was also damaging her physical health: "I'm always sick lately—my ears, my kidneys. I've always got something going on.[2] I'd rather just be home." Abby was not alone. The women who mentioned the emotional and physical stressors related to AVI-A contact believed that it would be easier to push through and be compliant than for their probation officers to perceive them as "being difficult." Their experiences illustrate how the victim-offender binary is embodied for systems-involved people, taking a toll on their physical and emotional well-being, not unlike what they endured in their abusive intimate relationships.

To mitigate the cumulative effects of the financial burden, some women "took a break" from or dropped out of college degree programs and got a second job. Others vacated their apartments and moved in with extended family—whether or not to do so was emotionally and physically safe. Some sent their children to live with the biological fathers or extended family, giving themselves room to stabilize their finances. Others picked up a shift at the local factory, sold their car, worked "under the table" cleaning houses, slept in their car, borrowed from friends, grew hot house vegetables and crocheted mittens and scarves to sell at area farmer's markets, asked abusive partners or former partners for money, engaged in sex work, deposited bottles and cans for refunds, donated blood plasma, started in-home businesses selling make-up or jewelry, bought clothes and household items wholesale and sold them at retail prices on eBay, or borrowed from their young child's piggy bank. They also did not pay anything they did not *have to* pay immediately, leaving car insurance, car registration fees, parking tickets, and so on unpaid.

There were also times when the women pitched in directly to ease each other's mental burden by helping other group members pay their AVI-A fees, even leaving a bit of a cushion. Imani remembered being "second or third" in line while waiting to pay her AVI-A fee. She was talking to other group members when she overheard the first woman in line tell the AVI-A staff person that she did not have the money to pay her session fee, had not eaten all day, and did not have bus money to get home. Imani jumped in to fill the gap. She also initiated a process of collective action. Imani explained,

> I ain't rich, you know, but I'm not bad off either, so I gave her a couple of dollars like, "Here. At least go get you something to eat. It's not much, but it will help." I think I gave her like 15 bucks or something like that. When I did that, it made like everybody else . . . gave her like two dollars here or a dollar here or whatever. By the time she left, she had about a good 20 dollars, 30 dollars. You know, that's enough to get on the bus and get you something to eat.

As they managed to fill in the financial gaps for themselves, the women eased the emotional harm with a patchwork of solutions. Some, like Christine and Lily, chose religiously focused coping strategies (Knickmeyer et al., 2003), choosing to see it all as "a blessing" and by "relying on prayer." Others, like Abby, "just [tried] to get through it." Many saved documents; and most eventually confided in those from the group. Their incremental, time-intensive efforts to ease the systems-inflicted harms for themselves and others illuminates not only how deeply embedded in context these efforts were, but what often goes unseen when women surviving "breakage" gradually work toward repairing their intimate and structural harms.

A closer view of the financial and emotional impact of growing probation and AVI-A costs, as well as the ways in which individual women mitigated them, is evident in Olivia's, Sheniqua's, Becky's, and Phoebe's experiences. Their stories illuminate the probation- and AVI-A-inflicted breakage in the pressure to pay probation and AVI-A fees, manage their daily lives, and struggle to be court-compliant.

## Olivia

Olivia was wrongfully arrested after her former partner and the father of her child convinced responding officers that she had stabbed him—

claiming her blood on his abdomen as his own, when, in reality, she had held up a kitchen knife, clutching it with both hands, as self-protection after he verbally threatened her and before he physically came after her. As she put it,

> I came in that night [from work] . . . and he went to put his hands on me again. I honestly thought that he was going to hurt me, you know, because he'd just go into these rages . . . I mean even though he had never closed-fist beat me or anything like that, but he had been on top of me before. He had pushed me down before. He had threatened me that he was going to kill me multiple times. You know, put his hands around my neck. I mean I remember being held up against the wall . . . I didn't really put anything past him . . . I grabbed a knife, and I told him, "Don't put your hands on me again . . . Do not come near me!" He told me, "Oh, you did it now, bitch! I'm calling the cops . . . You're never going to see your son again!"

Because she dared to hold up a knife, he promised she would never see their child again. With his six foot two, 200 pound body, he wrestled the five foot four, 115 pound Olivia for the knife, cutting her hand in the process. She managed to push by him—her bloody hand brushing against his naked abdomen—and lock herself in their bathroom. Olivia "was freaked out in there." He had "broken down at least two doors" when coming after her in the past. Her mother had always told her to never get the police involved. With her cellphone, which she had shoved into her pocket before escaping to the bathroom, Olivia called her cousin and her father for help. She waited, hoping they would arrive before the police did. The police arrived first, responding to her then-partner's call. Olivia was still in the bathroom but could hear him telling responding officers that she had attacked him. He claimed she had "just gone crazy" with a knife and he was afraid she would hurt him. He knowingly and intentionally retold the entire incident to protect himself, portraying Olivia as violent and insane.

For Olivia, there were multiple collateral consequences. First, her economic situation changed. Olivia became a single, low-income mother who struggled to support her young child, to finish her university degree, and to remain court compliant. Owing to her domestic violence conviction, she was ineligible to work in her chosen healthcare-related field. Based on the AVI-A sliding fee scale, her per-session group fee was 20 dollars for the weekly two-hour session. She explained, "It was 20 bucks, but shoot, that was 20 bucks! I had [waitressing] shifts where all I made was 20 bucks." Olivia drove an old SUV 60 miles from home to attend the AVI-G, paid for after-hours childcare, and rushed to evening college classes nearly 75 miles away (in the opposite direction) after group. To make up for the added expenditures, she waited tables on the weekends. Olivia did not ask for an individual payment plan because she worried about going into debt. She recalled, "If I worked all day Saturday and Sunday I could still survive." In other words, in addition to her 40 dollar per month probation supervision fee, gas for group cost Olivia approximately 30 dollars round trip, and four hours of childcare was at least 40 dollars depending on whom she was able to get as a caregiver. This meant the actual cost of her AVI-A contact was more than 100 dollars each week. Furthermore, the time necessary to attend the AVI-G meant that she was also "struggling with finding enough time to devote to . . . studying." Her academic advisor went from lauding her for "doing so well" and encouraging her to take more classes to suggesting she change her major to something "less demanding." Over time it became too much: "I'm like 'everything's crumbling,' and eventually I had to take time off of school. I'm like 'I just can't.'" Olivia decided she had to drop out of school to have the time and money necessary to meet her court-ordered obligations.

## Sheniqua

Sheniqua continued to manage Officer Rigor with ease, given her experiential capital (Watkins-Hayes, 2019). But the financial burden was especially punishing. She explained the matter as follows:

> Until I'm done paying this probation stuff off, I'm always gonna be broke. Just last paycheck or the last paycheck I got a call from [Officer Rigor] saying, "That's your last garnishment." I was like "getting my checks garnished. Well, portions." It wasn't like a ton, but to me, 20 dollars, that's a lot . . . They were taking like 100 dollars a month garnishing that from my checks, so I was kind of happy to not have that happen.

The AVI-A costs made it all even more difficult, with Sheniqua "just trying to get through." Although she did not have the caregiving responsibilities and school obligations that Oliva had, she had her own challenges that made paying the weekly group session fees impossible. After Sheniqua explained to an AVI-A staff person that she lost her well-paying job because of her domestic violence convictions, the staff person offered her a payment plan. Sheniqua accepted. Even so, any relief Sheniqua felt for being able to attend the AVI and remain probation-compliant, despite her inability to pay, was undermined by her accruing

AVI-A debt. After almost three months of attendance and delayed payments, Sheniqua owed the AVI-A 335 dollars. She knew she could not be released from probation until that amount was paid. Searching for ways to save money, Sheniqua moved out of her apartment and in with her grandmother where she could live for free. She picked up a second job and borrowed "lump sums" of cash from friends and "associates" to pay down the balance. But the repayment process was anything but smooth. She quickly learned that she could not rely on AVI-A staff to accurately track her payments. As she put it,

> If you pay in cash, you better keep on to your receipt because they don't know nothing unless you got your receipt. Me, I was paying on my debit card, so when they told me that I had only paid a certain amount, I was like, "Oh no, I have my bank statements. I paid you guys 90 dollars cash, and I paid 20 dollars cash one day." That equals up. You have to keep proof of everything!

When AVI-A staff told her they had no record of her payments, Sheniqua "was flipping out," digging for "a little white rectangular piece of paper" in the dumpster behind her apartment building in the pouring rain. It was her only hope of proving her cash payment. Sheniqua found the paper but knew that if she had not, "they would have told me I owed 90 dollars on top of what I already had paid. I was happy to have found it, but I was kind of stressed out because of it, too." Sheniqua wiped her brow with the back of her hand, as if clearing away perspiration.

### Becky

Becky was using her boyfriend's phone and "talking to another guy." It felt like respite from her boyfriend's abuse. When her boyfriend found out about her phone conversation, his verbal and emotional abuse escalated. He "hollered really loud" and spat at her. Becky explained,

> He was scaring me . . . the only thing that was running through my mind was what he just said . . . I was just thinking to myself like "why, why, why?" I got mad, so I picked up a brick, and I went to his back sliding door, and I threw a brick through the sliding door, and it shattered . . . my goal was like "that window was going to get broken even if I wanted to stop." I was so hurt . . . I was just so outraged!

He called the police. Becky took responsibility. When she got out of jail, "I broke the no contact order right away . . . I broke down to him." He was "the first person I called . . . I don't know no one else." Despite "catching a case" for "a domestic," Becky said, "I love this man with all my heart. [Without him] I don't have anybody." After she was arrested, his abuse got worse. She called the local domestic violence shelter for refuge but they "denied me," she recalled. She guessed it was because "I'm the one that got the charges."

After her arrest, Becky and her boyfriend were evicted. Now they cycled between low-budget hotel rooms and emergency shelters. He was on disability. She worked in fast food. Having had her first baby at 17, she did not have her family's support to get through high school or to get a driver's license. But her boyfriend drove her to work and helped her see her two kids every other weekend. He seemed to understand how much Becky wanted them back. For now, the children were living with extended family while Becky was "trying to get on [her] feet." Being on probation for "the domestic" was an unbearable financial load. She explained, "I have to pay probation every month. Every week, every chance that I get, I have to pay, and I'm behind, and they're on me. If I don't pay, I'm violating." The AVI-A added to her burden. Becky tearfully shared,

> I'm just trying to balance out paying probation and paying [the AVI-A] off . . . [but] I need necessities. I need things for myself, as well, you know. I'm trying. I am. I waitress. I get paid $3.38 [per hour], plus I get to keep tips . . . I get paid every two weeks. I don't get paid much, but you know, the tip money I bring home, I'm living. I have to live off of that. I have to have food.

Becky exhaled. "It's just stressful." And the financial stress continued. "I still owe $1,300 to court," Becky explained, "and I owe 500 dollars to [the AVI-A], so I'm looking at about . . . two thousand dollars . . . I have until next year to pay that." "Next year" meant seven more months before it was all due. Becky was feeling the pressure through reminders from the staff. She described the process as follows:

> Like, if you start from day one and go to [the AVI] group and don't pay . . . [an AVI-A staff person will] eventually talk to you like, "Listen, you've got to start paying. It's not looking good on your probation officer." . . . He sees if you're compliant, if you paid, if you didn't pay. He sees everything. You know, just like [an AVI-A staff person] told me recently, "You know, you've got to start paying . . .," [an AVI-A staff person said], "I know your situation. If it was me, you can come whenever, but your PO does look at this, and they are going to start cracking down on people." [An AVI-A staff person said,] "I'll let him know if anything happens . . . You come to group. You're one of the good ones. You try, but if they don't see you making an effort, your PO's just going to violate you automatically."

To complicate the pressure to pay, Becky did not feel like she was getting her money's worth. She explained that recently she "couldn't wait to get to the group to let that out [and talk] . . . it just sucks that things are so expensive. I pay 30 dollars to talk for two minutes." Becky was frustrated. She was court ordered to a space where she had to pay to share her feelings, but still did not get that opportunity. Although staff would "work with you" on payment, it seemed to Becky like making money, rather than supporting her, was the legal system's goal. She reflected, "You know, a lot of these things are really just about money. [The AVI-G] is helpful. Don't get me wrong, but you know, probation officers and all them, that's all they really care about, just like he told me. He said just worry about going to [the AVI-G] and pay me your money. That's money both ways."

Becky described herself as having emotionally "come to a breaking point plenty of times." The other day," she explained, "I was like, you know, I'm done with this job. I'm done with everything. I'm giving up." But instead, Becky took a break, smoked a cigarette, and thought, "Get it together!" She shifted her perspective by breathing and praying: "I prayed really hard God would just keep me strong, give me strength because I need it." Becky was strong and resilient, but she was also tired of having to be strong and resilient. She knew she still had a long way to go to repair the emotional and financial harm she experienced. While wiping her tears, Becky explained, "I want to be able to pay my own bills and feel good about myself for doing that . . . You know, I've had enough time to mess up and to think [about] what I've done wrong. I'm ready just to be happy." Becky took a deep breath and looked away.

*Phoebe*

Phoebe was a student at the local university. She was earning a "good income" and caring for her baby. She was also frustrated that her partner, the father of her baby, would not pitch in. Phoebe noticed that he was "trying to be a family guy" when they were together but when she left for work, he "hit the streets" to sell drugs. She understood he had limited options in their neighborhood. But it was not the life she wanted for herself or her children. Phoebe knew she had to "start making moves" out of the relationship, the neighborhood, and all that came with both. She also wanted to show herself and her children that she was capable of "breaking a cycle" of domestic violence that she

witnessed between her parents.[3] She decided to have "the conversation," to tell him that the relationship was over, that she was leaving.
After the conversation Phoebe walked out, but "he ran outside, picked
me up, brought me back in . . . pin[ned] me on the bed. I was like fighting him trying to get up and get out of the house, and I actually have
like a permanent scar right here by my neck because some glass had
broke."

As they "wrestled," he held a piece of broken glass to her neck,
threatening to cut her if she left. She got free, filed domestic violence
charges, and stayed in the relationship to avoid another violent attack.
It was not the first time he had hurt her. Phoebe knew it would not be
the last. Eventually she moved out and ended the relationship, but then,

> it got to the point where he was just destroying my property since he couldn't
> get to me . . . I would get a new car, and he would come take the tag off my
> car or he would like bust my tire . . . He took a rock and would bust
> my window open . . . He would just mess up anything that I would get.
> That's why . . . my kids [and I] live on the third floor because I knew if I had
> like an apartment on the first or second, it's no telling what would have
> happened.

One afternoon he called Phoebe and asked her to stop by his aunt's
house to discuss a more formal parenting schedule. Tired of fighting, she
agreed. The conversation "got heated," but that was nothing unusual.
Not long after, Phoebe "got a call out of the blue" from a police officer
notifying her of a warrant for her arrest on domestic violence charges. Her
former partner had called the police and falsely accused her of kicking
him, harming his aunt, and assaulting their child during their discussion.

Although the public defender encouraged her to take a plea deal that
would include a delayed sentence, Phoebe thought, "Oh, hell no!" She
knew she was innocent, and she wanted a bench trial—where a judge
rather than a jury would decide the outcome—as soon as possible to
prove her case. Phoebe recalled the issue as follows:

> I thought that I would be successful in the trial because I thought that they
> would see past the lies . . . I really had no legal direction. I didn't know what
> I was doing. I was just like I want to address this today . . . because this is
> not about to happen like this . . . I feel like I just need to do this right now
> . . . He's trying to take everything. He's trying to take my [child], trying to
> make sure I don't work . . . That's where my mind was. Instead of being
> more cautious and calm about it, and kind of just taking a breath and really
> thinking it through, I kind of just went off adrenaline.

The judge found Phoebe guilty. She was convicted of domestic violence for kicking her former partner. The other charges were dropped. She blamed herself for rushing into a trial without legal counsel.

To afford all of her probation and AVI-A fees, she had "taken a break" from university, sent her children to live with their biological fathers' families, and moved in with her grandparents. She was grateful to have a free place to live but there were costs she could not quantify. When she had lived with her grandparents as a child, a family friend had sexually abused her. She had disclosed the incident to her grandmother, but her grandmother refused to believe her because she "didn't see it happen." Since then, Phoebe felt she had "basically no [emotional] support" from her extended family. The probation and AVI-A costs and time involved hit Phoebe hard. Officer Phoenix was helpful, but Phoenix was still a probation officer monitoring her compliance. She described the AVI-A as having "consume[d] my life." Phoebe explained,

> Just having to schedule times to get there around work and then on top of that, having to keep up with the payments . . . . paying 30 dollars each session, and having to incorporate that into any fees or finances that I had to pay and everything . . . I just had to like incorporate that into my daily life every week . . . the financial aspect of it was extremely hard . . . Thirty dollars might not be a lot to some people, but it's like I have two kids, and bills, and a lot of stuff going on. It was like something else I have to take care of, and then on top of it having that thought in the back of your mind like I can still go to jail if I don't pay even though I'm coming.

Phoebe paused and then stressed: "It's like that money that I would put in the gas tank, it's like I'm putting that money towards this class."

Although she initially held off asking for an individual payment plan, she eventually had no choice. Staff "worked with" Phoebe to allow temporary 10 dollar per-session payments rather than the assessed 30 dollar fee. The remainder accrued. Gradually she "got past that" and was able to get "caught up with all my fees." The plan helped at the time, but she felt betrayed later. Phoebe learned during informal conversations in the parking lot after group that another woman was paying only 11 dollars per session *without* a payment plan. She thought to herself, "Well, how did that happen?!" It did not seem fair, "But hey," Phoebe laughed, "I was just like, look, the whole situation hasn't been fair so I couldn't even get upset. I'm like, [Phoebe], just try to get through it because this whole thing hasn't been fair anyways!" Exhausted and exasperated, Phoebe slowly shrugged her shoulders.

MANAGING THE AVI-A: LOW-INCOME
FAMILY COURT–ORDERED WOMEN

Surveilled attendance and lack of childcare especially affected low-income single mothers—Valerie, Cherise, Lily, and Tyra—who were family court ordered. Were these women to achieve their goal of reuniting with their children, attending the family court–ordered AVI became significantly more challenging, if not impossible.

*Valerie*

Valerie (see the introduction and chapter 2) was criminal and family court ordered to AVI. Her children were returned to her care after eight AVI-G sessions, making her unable to continue the group without childcare. As Valerie put it, "I'm technically supposed to be still doing groups. My [CPS] worker . . . asked me about them the other day. She was like, 'Are you doing your groups?' I was like, 'Seriously? Are you going to come get my kids while I go to this two-hour class? I want to, but I can't.'" Without childcare, she risked noncompliance and once again having her children removed from her care. She hoped the courts understood her conundrum.

Although CPS paid for family court–ordered women's assessments and group sessions, there were other costs. CPS caseworkers constantly reminded the women that CPS was paying the bill. Tyra (see chapter 2) recalled that one of her CPS caseworkers would preemptively tell her that "CPS can't pay for *everything*," before she made general inquiries about access to community supports. The most significant "cost" was CPS caseworkers' ability to hold the women's reunification with their children in limbo until their AVI completion. Cherise's, Lily's, and Tyra's experiences bring visibility to the cumulative harm caused by CPS and AVI-A obligations.

*Cherise*

Cherise was on probation for non-DV "animal cruelty charges" related to her family court order to the AVI-A. Her neighbor had asked Cherise to "babysit" her dogs when she was out of town. During that time, Cherise was hospitalized for a stillbirth. Her partner, who was also her children's father, was home with the dogs but refused to take care of them. As Cherise explained,

He didn't want to care for them while I was [hospitalized], and he just let them loose. It was really cold. It snowed out there at the time, and it was causing a lot of noise because [he] had left them outside . . . Someone called the police . . . the police got to the house . . . [another neighbor] said that they seen him on the couch . . . but he still wouldn't answer the door.

At court she blamed herself: "I was telling them that it was my responsibility because . . . I was dog sitting. I didn't know that I was going to have to go into the hospital because that's when I had the stillborn last year . . . I didn't . . . say that he was there. I'm always covering for him."

Covering for him typically kept her safe from his abuse. Around that time, one of their children disclosed an argument between Cherise and her partner to a school guidance counselor. As a mandatory reporter, the counselor, who made the call to CPS, initiated an investigation. CPS assessed Cherise as a neglectful, disengaged parent, and removed her children from her care. Cherise described her parenting style differently, more as withdrawn from everyone and everything to manage her abusive partner while raising their children: "I kind of just withdrawed myself from everybody because he made me think that he was all that I needed . . . so when I started having kids, I just withdrawed from everything." In addition to family court ordering her to the AVI, which confused Cherise because she had not used force, her CPS "treatment plan" included individual therapy, group therapy, parenting classes, Al-Anon, domestic violence survivor counseling, and full-time employment. She was coping by working at night to pay the rent, keep the utilities on, and make sure there was food in the cupboards and gas in the car. Her partner was out of the house now but he was usually unemployed and had never provided financial support. Cherise worked around the clock to meet all of her court-ordered obligations and financially support herself, while hoping for reunification with her children. When arriving for her 10:00 a.m. interview for this project Cherise explained,

I actually just got off work this morning at 6:00 a.m. . . . I picked the midnight schedule because of the different things I have to do throughout the day for my children . . . different appointments that they have that [CPS] would like me to attend because I know the most about them, so to answer questions or even just the different things like counseling and stuff that I have to do . . . throughout the day. I'd rather get no sleep and get this stuff done so that it can be over with soon.

Cherise described a typical day: "Going to work at 6:00 p.m., getting off work at 6:00 a.m., going home to shower, be at the [domestic violence] shelter for counseling in the morning, going to court dates, meeting with the reunification program counselor in the afternoon, and then back to work. There will be no time for a nap."

The multiple trips for mandated referrals demanded more gas than usual and money was especially tight. Cherise rarely made it through a whole month with enough money to keep her gas tank full *and* have groceries in the house. This meant, according to Cherise, that "I have actually had to take the bus [rather] than take my own vehicle most of the time." She could afford the bus, but it took much longer. Saving money on transportation to be court compliant meant fewer hours in the day to achieve that compliance.

*Lily*

CPS removed Lily's children from her care because of her substance use. She did not remember much about the incident that brought her to the police's attention—she was too high. But she did remember the police officer pulling her over:

> I had heroin in the car with the kids in the car . . . I had been trying to get clean, so instead of trying to hide it from the cops, I just told them I was [high]. They couldn't get a hold of anyone to take the kids, so . . . CPS took them, and then they went into foster care because I didn't have anyone to take care of them.

Lily would describe the incident more than 10 years later as all starting "because of addiction." At the time she was living with her boyfriend who was the father of one of her children. She described him as "a dope dealer . . . [who] beat me." Lily remembered how difficult it was to manage her court-ordered obligations without reliable transportation, the necessary supports to address her substance use, or safety from her abusive partner. She had an initial psychiatric evaluation and random routine drug and alcohol tests. Every week for at least 33 weeks she had to complete AVI, Alcoholics Anonymous meetings, therapeutic counseling, a budgeting class, a domestic violence survivor support group, a healthy eating class, a parenting class, and a substance use treatment group—all at separate locations. She knew that each office reported her weekly attendance to her CPS caseworker. This meant that any absences would be considered CPS violations, immediately interrupting her reunification goal. It all seemed impossible. And why was she ordered to AVI in the first place? She had not used force against a partner or her children or anyone else. Lily explained, in a manner that suggested she was still confused about the referral, "I think it was just my tone [with my caseworker] . . . I don't think it was specifically anything I said. I think it was just my tone . . . It was just crazy. I was just angry."

Even though her interview for this project took place years later, one thing still bothered Lily. It was what the psychiatrist said, the psychiatrist she saw for the CPS-ordered evaluation soon after CPS removed her children. At the end of the evaluation he told Lily she was a "failure" and "there was no hope" for her. Lily laughed nervously with tears in her eyes as she slowly repeated what he had said to her—"failure," "no hope"—at the most vulnerable time of her life. In contrast, the AVI-G became a supportive space for Lily, one she describes as "a blessing." She now preferred to see all of what had happened to her as a blessing. But she also emphasized that she would not have had the opportunity to attend AVI-Gs if CPS had not paid because "I wouldn't have been able to afford it." Of course, Lily was talking about the financial support offered by CPS, for which she expressed gratitude. But what about the other costs? The costs to her mental and physical health with the onerous referrals, the psychiatrist's "evaluation," and her lack of control over the process?

*Tyra*

Tyra was also family court ordered to complete 30 AVI-G sessions after yelling at her CPS caseworker. She also had to complete a one-time psychiatric evaluation, and weekly therapeutic counseling sessions, budgeting classes, domestic violence survivor support group sessions, healthy eating classes, and parenting classes—all of which, again, were housed at separate locations. Like Lily, Tyra also described the AVI-G as a supportive and meaningful space that she was grateful to access through the AVI-A. If, however, CPS had not paid for AVI, Tyra explained, "I wouldn't have went [to the AVI-Gs]. It was too expensive. There is no way I would have been able to afford that on my own. No way . . . It probably would have took a long time for me to get my kids back because that was a requirement and I could not afford to pay that on my own."

CPS payment meant she was granted access she later appreciated, but the hidden costs of the referral seemed insurmountable at times. Furthermore, although the AVI-G was meant for women who had come to systems attention for causing harm, neither Cherise, nor Lily, nor Tyra fit that description. Thus, the referral provided an additional avenue for the legal system to intervene in their private lives while draining them of already scarce mental and physical energy.

## STRATEGIC AVI-G ATTENDANCE: VOLUNTARY AND VOLUNTARY-ISH PARTICIPATION

Joy and Marcella voluntarily self-referred and attended AVI-Gs. Joy and Marcella sought AVI to learn more about their feelings and expressions of rage and anger.[4] Sissy and Suzie were "voluntary-ish"—that is, although the courts had not formally ordered them, they strategically used their contact to attain legal and relationship goals. Payment requirements and access to a payment plan were the same for voluntary women, but if they stopped attending at any point, there were no formal sanctions. They were free to come and go as they saw fit. Highlighting Sissy's and Suzie's circumstances brings visibility to the control voluntarily referred women had over their AVI experience.

### Sissy

Sissy came to the United States as a teenager seeking opportunities that she found and created. But without US citizenship documentation, her daily life and future in the country were precarious. Adding to her troubles was her youngest child's father who abused her. Sissy was "so used to" his abuse that she described it as "like furniture"—something that she lived with but did not have time to think much about. He used Sissy's undocumented status to control her by demanding she engage in illegal activities. If she resisted, he threatened to disclose her status to the authorities. Most recently at the time of her interview, she had been charged with stealing a pair of work boots for him. But as Sissy put it, "I didn't have any other choice than do what he wanted."

Sissy sought out the AVI as a tool "to prove what I was going through." She reasoned that by taking her AVI-G attendance record and letters of advocacy to the court, she could show, "[shoplifting] wasn't something I decide to do. [I didn't] wake up in the morning, and say I'm going to go steal in the store." Instead, he coerced her into doing it. Sissy hoped AVI documentation would offer written proof of two things: (1) that she took responsibility for the crime, and (2) the context about how her child's father coerced her into committing the crime in the first place. Because Sissy came to AVI on her own she could attend when it suited her, taking months off during the most demanding season for her work. For now, the AVI met her needs.

## Suzie

On the way to a family party Suzie assaulted her wife. She described the assault as follows:

> [My wife] . . . would not stop arguing with me about, of all things, cat litter . . . and it just escalated . . . We were riding in a car . . . and she would not stop [the car], so I just got very upset. I hit her in the head three times . . . with my hand, my open hand . . . Then, I grabbed her arm and broke skin when I grabbed her arm . . . Still in the car going down the expressway at 70 miles an hour, . . . I balled up my fist and was threatening to punch her . . . she finally pulled alongside the road and told me to get out, which I didn't do. I told her that I wasn't going to get out. [She] went home . . . I went to the . . . party.

Once at home, Suzie's wife called the police. She reported the assault and expressed her fear that Suzie would hurt her when she returned home from the party. When Suzie arrived at the party, she answered a cell phone call from a police officer. The officer "wanted to talk to me to see my side of the story." Suzie responded by telling the officer "it wasn't a good time to talk," that she was busy. The officer said he would call her back later.

After the party Suzie went home and started to drink. She was angry that her wife had involved the police. At some point she noticed she had a voicemail from the officer she had spoken to earlier. His message said that she would be arrested for hitting her wife. With this news, Suzie began yelling and calling her wife names. She also became physically threatening by pounding on the light switch and breaking plates. Her wife ran to the couple's car, locked herself in, and called the police again. She wanted immediate police protection. The police responded by coming to the couple's home and interviewing both women separately. They asked Suzie to leave but she said she could not because she had been drinking, so they told her wife to leave. When Suzie texted her wife the next day, she did not respond. Two days later, Suzie was served with a Personal Protection Order (PPO) her wife had filed, which obligated Suzie to vacate their home. Suzie did not have any further police contact. She lived with her mother for eight months and waited for the police "to pull up at any time to arrest me, but fortunately it never happened." The delayed police response remained a mystery. Although Suzie assaulted her wife in June, a police officer called Suzie's wife the following May. Almost a year later he asked if she still wanted to press charges. She said she did not, so the case was dropped.

Long after the assault Suzie's wife continued to involuntarily show her fear of Suzie. As Suzie put it, "This past weekend I saw her flinch . . . when I was raising my hand to get something . . . I've never seen that before . . . We weren't fighting or anything. I just saw it." Suzie took responsibility for her actions and inadvertently disclosed her own sexual assault history as a teenager. Although her wife called the police, it seemed clear they did not take the situation between two middle-aged white lesbians seriously. Although Suzie was not court ordered to AVI, her wife gave her an ultimatum: attend AVI or their marriage would be over.

By moving in with her mother, Suzie had additional income to pay her assessed AVI fee of 50 dollars a week. She recalled, "I did have the money, but that's a lot." She attended "14 straight weeks and never missed at all," but then the holidays came. She needed to "free up cash" to buy gifts for her grandchildren. She also believed she had gotten what she needed from AVI. Just before Christmas Suzie left the AVI without informing staff and without any systems' consequences. Her situation simultaneously demonstrates the benefits of voluntary services and the injustice of the carceral system. As a "voluntary-ish" AVI member, she could walk away at any time and not suffer formal consequences. Even though she had harmed her partner, who still feared her, her identities as a white, middle-class, middle-aged lesbian seemed to protect her from arrest. Whereas low-income court-ordered women suffered immense emotional and financial breakage, Suzie walked away freely.

## SUMMARY AND REFLECTIONS

Whatever the turn of events that brought low-income criminal court–ordered women to the AVI, their compulsory attendance, weekly group session fees, lack of childcare, and time required to attend the group inflicted further harm. These obligations meant that Olivia, for example, had to leave college. The AVI-A fees, although low, were significant given her limited income. For other women, the individualized payment plans facilitated both attendance and debt. The AVI's inaccurate record-keeping not only placed the women in precarious systems circumstances, but caused significant economic harm and tremendous anxiety, which

QuiShandra described as a "mental thing" and Sheniqua characterized as "flipping out." These pressures were particularly burdensome for Abby, for whom the stress of getting "through it" despite not being able to hear resulted in physical symptoms. Although it may be heartening to learn that Imani and others mitigated some of this harm through their collective efforts, these women should not have been placed in situations where they felt compelled to make up for systems failures.

The women's stories illuminate how the AVI served as an instrument of carceral power by tethering court-ordered women to widening systems of surveillance. This reality is evident in the weekly reports made to probation and CPS, AVI-G cofacilitators warning group members of probation officers checking their payment statuses, and CPS caseworkers using the AVI as punishment for yelling at them. Lily and Tyra, both of whom were family court ordered, expressed gratitude that CPS paid for AVI services because it was a necessary gateway to their supportive AVI-G interactions; however, they experienced AVI-A surveillance and obligations as significant hurdles to their hoped-for reunification with their children. These obstacles compromised their mental and physical health. Cherise, for example, was only able to juggle criminal and family court demands by going without sleep. And yet it seems police did not view Suzie, who physically assaulted her partner, as a credible threat; she was able to walk away without formal repercussions.

The combination of probation, CPS, and AVI contact demonstrates that feminist practitioners' and researchers' early concerns have been realized: AVI can "inadvertently legitimize a miscarriage of justice" (Gardner, 2009, p. 70). But this miscarriage occurs not only because of concerns that practitioners may misuse a BIP-type, one-size-fits-all approach to intervention (Miller et al., 2005); it is because the AVI-A exacts monetary punishment while tying women to carceral surveillance, making them more visible, and therefore more vulnerable, to probation officers who can misuse their discretion, to CPS caseworkers who shame them and can remove their children seemingly at will, and to an AVI-A that is complicit in this harm. The extensive court-ordered referrals compromise women's right to self-determination and pose significant risk to their mental and physical well-being. The experiences of the women who attended without court orders, however, suggest that AVI can serve as a tool to promote personal agency. Without that personal agency AVI contact for low-income court-ordered women often felt, according to RyAnn, like "getting strangled to death."

# PART TWO

# Healing and Repairing the Breakage

CHAPTER 4

# Antiviolence Intervention Group

"CONNECTING A FEW DOTS . . ."
—QUISHANDRA

The women typically joined the antiviolence intervention group (AVI-G) a few days after their one-on-one antiviolence intervention (AVI) intake assessment and a week or more after they started probation or their CPS caseworker made their referral.[1] In contrast to the ways in which they viewed probation, CPS, and antiviolence intervention administration (AVI-A), the women described their AVI-G experiences positively, even as transformative. I begin this chapter with an overview of how the women attributed the group session format and group member composition to the AVI-G's positive impact. I then explain how members used the AVI-G to share their stories and break their isolation. Next, I explore the women's feelings of what Rosemary called "a common bond" or what QuiShandra described as the experiences of "connecting a few dots," and a gradual shift from feeling shame to hope. The chapter ends with two cases that highlight how the AVI-G facilitated the women's process of healing and repairing their breakage: QuiShandra's transformative experience and the difference Regina made in the lives of other AVI-G members.[2] For additional context regarding each woman's intersecting identities, refer to table 1, "Women's individual identities and pathways," in the introduction.

## GROUP FORMAT: "A CIRCLE OF FEELINGS"

The women who were court ordered to antiviolence intervention shared that their group membership provided them with support, connection, and opportunities for self-reflection (for similar findings, see Larance, 2006; Larance and Rousson, 2016; Miller, 2005; Scaia, 2017). The women in *Broken* credited the group format with facilitating group member interactions by centering their experiences, while offering support and information. Olivia referred to the format as "incidental teaching," and for her, "that's what made it so memorable and [made] such an impact." In each group session members shared a recent concern or celebration. The cofacilitators then used the women's contributions as teaching moments.[3] Olivia credited this process with "making . . . emotional kinds of connections . . . in the heat of the moment when we're going around and just sharing some of our most personal parts of our lives, but voluntarily, and doing it in a sense that we're looking for perspectives. You know, somebody please tell me what I did wrong. How? What? . . . I remember feeling . . . that emotional connection with women."

Similarly, Sheniqua described this form of interaction as "teaching our stories." It was a process that brought clarity and self-fulfillment. "Someone will say like a story," Sheniqua explained, "and she will say, 'Hey, this is a lesson in this story,' you know . . . and say it to somebody and they get like an 'ah ha' moment, I feel good. I feel like I'm doing my part."

This format cultivated rich discussion that, according to Tyra, "created a circle of feelings." Unlike her parenting classes and other CPS referrals, the AVI-G was powerful for Tyra because it "didn't have the feeling like a class." The AVI-G was, Tyra explained, "a neutral place for us to come and express ourselves, and our concerns, our heartbreaks and heartaches, and our strengths, and motivations, and downfalls, and just encouraging and lifting each other up, and giving each other advice and a place to come where we don't have to feel like we're being judged by everything that comes out of our mouth."

The circle and shared conversation generated feelings of safety. As Manuela explained, "I knew . . . nobody would hurt me. Nobody would judge me . . . I felt safe, protected, and understood . . . You're not afraid anymore [in the AVI-G] because you're in the womb."

### Group as Counter Cultural

"The willingness to be open about personal stuff," according to bell hooks (1989), is a "real race and class issue." Hooks explains that this is the case because "so many black folks have been raised to believe that there is just so much that you should not talk about, not in private and not in public . . . One point of blackness then became—like how you keep your stuff to yourself, how private you could be about your business" (p. 2). Indeed, in *Broken*, women from different racial and class backgrounds reflected on how personal disclosure among strangers, both sharing their experiences and listening to other people relate theirs, was counter to their family cultures or cultural backgrounds. Emersyn pointed out that engaging with a group of strangers and talking about her feelings was not something her family supported. "It was frowned upon," Emersyn said, "you didn't talk about your feelings." But for Emersyn the AVI-G was different. In group, she explained, "I quickly found [the AVI-G] a support system which surprised me because I more expected to be judged, maybe, by the ladies. You kind of get this women power thing . . . I made a couple of friendships . . . we chatted. Feeling like you're not alone."

Similarly, the process of sharing with strangers was counter to Jatara's culture. As she put it, "In our culture, meaning the African American culture, we look at things like that as you're weak [if you talk about personal stuff]. You never talk about stuff. You mainly just argue. You didn't get to know you. You just say what pissed you off and don't do it again."

Because the AVI-G offered a countercultural framework for interaction, Jatara found that the group process "made me in touch with me and to be able to communicate . . . I was looking forward to it . . . going to communicate with other women, and just talking about different struggles of life."

Although disclosing her thoughts and feelings to others was not part of Phoebe's background either, the AVI-G provided a welcome space for her to vent. She explained, "I come from a background where I don't really have people that I can vent to or talk to without feeling like you're wrong, you're stupid, why would you do that . . . without feeling judged and down. Coming to [the AVI-G], you're coming to this place where you're not going to get that . . . you could be yourself, and you could talk about what you need to talk about." The countercultural group format promoted connections among women with similar experiences, helping them mitigate the breakage of their other systems interactions.

## Almost Strangers

Although the women who were new to the AVI-G were initially hesitant to participate in a group process with people they did not know, many of them later claimed that their group interactions were possible *because* they were strangers. QuiShandra found that sharing with "almost strangers" who became "new friends" allowed her to avoid "super messy" family ties. Her point demonstrates what sociologist Mark Granovetter (1973) refers to as "the strength of weak ties." New acquaintances can strengthen each other's social networks and information sharing in ways that existing relationships with friends and family cannot. People who have never met, as sociologist Mario Small's (2009) work shows, typically have separate "clustered" friendship networks, and by meeting, can then form "bridges" between those networks. People with the same "intimate ties," like QuiShandra and her family members, however, are more likely to share information within their clustered networks. For QuiShandra, disclosing personal information to her family gave her a "headache" and induced "stress" because they "spread rumors," "misconstrue your story," and "go tell the wrong person" in ways that only complicated her situation. But with "new friends" made in group, she recalled, "You just kind of create . . . a bond . . . In some way everyone can relate to one another and has been through something traumatic, you know."

With a quiet yet assertive tone, Devore agreed. She had stopped asking her family members for relationship support because they did not have an "in-between" in how they responded. Her family members were too "straightforward" in telling her, "'Fuck that bitch!' . . . 'Leave her alone!'" These kinds of responses from her family members left her feeling more alone; she concluded she "might as well just be by myself." Devore yearned for connection with people who understood her situation and domestic violence. The AVI-G provided that possibility. There, Devore explained, it was "very helpful" to talk to women she did not know, as she was "trying to move on through the pain of her, [and] of what I did [to her]." Likewise, Phoebe found it comforting to share among strangers. "I did need to be around people I didn't know," she explained, "and . . . just release anything that I was going through at the time." Anonymity facilitated a healing process among people who "got it."

*Sharing Stories and Breaking Isolation*

Before the AVI-G, the women's stories were narrated for them in police reports, muted in court proceedings, overlooked in probation check-ins, and misrepresented in CPS caseworker interactions. The ability to have one's voice heard and believed, however, is critical to who we are and to our well-being. The human voice communicates presence, power, participation, protest, and identity (Reinharz, 1994). Ethnographer Elaine Lawless (2001) observes how "telling our stories is a positive, therapeutic act that aids the storyteller in trying to make sense of a life that otherwise might appear too fragmented, purposeless, or chaotic" (p. 16). Sharing stories in the midst of those who understand may be, according to psychiatrist Bessel van der Kolk (2014), "the most powerful protection against becoming overwhelmed by stress and trauma" (p. 81).[4] Telling their stories and listening to each other provided the various group members I interviewed for *Broken* opportunities to identify and name their own experiences. The group in turn also provided an embodied experience where the women exchanged visual and auditory subtleties, such as a knowing glance through tears, a shifted body position showing interest or concern, the curve of a smile signaling understanding, a similar tone of voice expressing shared outrage or sympathy, and synchronized breathing patterns—all integral to feeling physically and emotionally safe with others who understood their situation.

Regardless of how many AVI-G sessions they had attended, the women mentioned the positive experience of collectively sitting in the circle and sharing their stories. Essence had recently finished her third group. Although she knew the women were "not in a position" to change anything about her legal system contact or outcome, "it helps mentally" to discuss the pain and frustration among others who could identify with her situation. After five groups, Valerie described listening to others' stories and sharing her story as, "something that made me feel acceptance and okay, and . . . never judged . . . I would ask something and they . . . would just be okay with it and explain things to me." For Benita, who attended six groups, listening to the shared stories helped her consider that maybe she was not alone. Benita spoke reflectively as she recalled, "[group] helps a lot . . . talking to [the cofacilitators] and all the girls in there hearing their stories, so I just be like, okay, maybe . . . I'm not the only one!" With just a few sessions to go, Devore pointed out that the AVI-G was helpful not simply because of "a particular day or session" topic. Instead, she explained, "It was just every day I go. Every time I go, everybody had an opportunity to talk about what's bothering them at that point, at that time, and then we worked on it." Having finished the previous year, Ikeeylah remembered that telling her story "out loud . . . helps to get it out . . . you can just be healed." Olivia, who finished years ago, explained, "The nice thing about [the AVI-G] was knowing that I wasn't the only one . . . that had

been in this type of situation . . . I was able to relate to other women."
Years after Lola's AVI-G participation she furrowed her brow and
reflected, "I wasn't the only one that had a story to tell . . . there are
other people that are out there that went through the same thing that I
went through . . . I wasn't alone."

Lily credited the group with changing her life. When she started the
AVI-G more than ten years ago she "had nobody." Lily explained,

> I didn't have any friends because I got high . . . At that point I was at home
> alone. [My baby's father] was in the house. [He was] the drug dealer. I
> couldn't talk to anybody because he'd beat me . . . I was on eggshells. There
> was nothing I could do right, so I was really at home scared for my life . . .
> So, it was just me. So, when I went in that group, I had nobody but me. I
> didn't even like myself.

Lily cried as she explained that the [AVI-G] "was the foundation of me
starting over . . . I got best friends out of the group." The AVI-G provided the infrastructure for Lily to build a new life by ending her isolation: "Because of the stories you like connected with the women. You
got to grow and knew them, and then because once you felt like you
knew them, you had that bond with them, and so it was like this positive atmosphere. Everyone would help. They would get through their
situations together."

Lily connected her increased capacity to maintain her sobriety to the
opportunity to share her story and break her isolation in a supportive
group atmosphere.. When Lily first began probation, she continued to
"drop dirty" for the next 11 months—despite the cost and continued
monitoring. Joining the AVI-G was a turning point. It was the "first
time" Lily felt supported by others. For her, she explained, the difference was "having that positive support . . . and then making a few
friends, and seeing people going along the same journey and not judging
you." The process of sharing stories in a judgment-free environment,
while also ending their isolation, was a kind of salve the women used to
ease the pain of their personal breakage and begin to heal, making way
for the journey forward.

AVI-G INTERACTIONS

While listening to and sharing their stories in the circle, the women
benefitted from the therapeutic factors of group dynamics (Yalom,
2005). Social scientists have identified such factors in BIPs for men
(Holtrop et al., 2017; Lindsay et al., 2008) as well as survivor support

and intervention for women (Larance, 2006; Larance and Porter, 2004; Larance and Rousson, 2016; Miller, 2005; Scaia, 2017). In the AVI-G, these factors included, but were not limited to, forming "a common bond," as Rosemary put it, or "connecting a few dots," as QuiShandra described the matter, and moving from shame to hope.

## A Common Bond

Sociologist Erving Goffman's (1963) labeling theory suggests the experience of coming to systems attention for a range of relationship experiences may mean that, regardless of how these women viewed themselves before these events, they now felt alone and stigmatized. That stigma catalyzed feelings of shame and embarrassment that caused further breakage in a very public way. Becky was upset when extended family told her grandparents about her arrest. Devore hid her CLS involvement from family. Emersyn did not tell her mother about her court-ordered obligations until she had no other options. Lola felt "it's embarrassing" to only have a warehouse job because of her convictions. Tyra was "embarrassed all over again" after she was evicted from transitional housing and she was "embarrassed" to enter the AVI-G because "my kids were gone." To manage their vulnerability, some women made the choice *not* to tell friends and family about their systems involvement—again, unless they absolutely had to. This self-isolation exacerbated their feelings of loneliness.[5] If the women did disclose their AVI-G involvement, they would often, like Moneesha, refer to it as "my therapy," or, like Tyra, as "my class," or, like Christine, as "my women's group"—in other words, they chose language that belied any connection to the carceral system. Nonetheless, for many, the AVI-G was the only formal space where they could share what others had done to them, what they had done to others, and the strain of legal systems contact among those who understood. Their shared vulnerability created what Rosemary, a slight woman who spoke quickly, described as a "common bond" between group members. After 11 sessions, she recognized this collective identity as the following: "We've all been to jail. We've all been through something . . . rather tragic with our relationships . . . There is that commonality that we're all one mind, and we're all struggling." Abby, after her 12th AVI-G, echoed Rosemary's sentiment by expressing her shock that among the 12 women in her group, *all* of them—including her—had survived men's sexual violence at some point in their lives. This common bond was one of feeling "reassured" for Cherise. Having completed her last group, she was in touch with another member whose former partner "still wants sort of control and [was] kind of using the children as pawns."

Likewise, Christine, who had attended 12 groups, learned early on that the severity of her unjust arrest story and abusive relationship were not unique. She found validation in connection with a woman whose experiences reflected her own:

> There is a lady [in group] . . . our situations almost mirror [each other] . . . It's been pretty helpful to have her [in group] . . . She went to jail also because she slapped her husband. Kind of the ways that her husband would treat her and talk to her are pretty similar [to how my husband treated me] . . . It was relieving just knowing we kind of had that in common. She and I will text back and forth [between groups], and I can tell her what's going on . . . She understands.

Having finished group years before, RyAnn described this common bond as being "believed" and having "credibility" with "other women who could empathize." It was other women knowing "that smell" or "that look" an ex-partner had before being abusive, "so you didn't have to explain yourself." Olivia observed this commonality as follows: "A lot of the women, in the same situation . . . reached their breaking point . . . [and] finally stood up, finally said something, finally took a stand, and the tables were turned."

The common bond between the women was comforting, regardless of the circumstances that brought them to group. But for those wrongfully arrested, it also provided an avenue to explore their anger at the injustice of it all. Although Essence felt comforted by "listening to the other women's stories" that were so similar to hers, she was "very angry that this is even happening . . . these women are really defending themselves." With the clarity gained from the shared stories of other wrongfully arrested women, Essence thought, "I should have just never called the police. I should have just let him beat me up, choke me, whatever, and went to the doctor and took care of my injuries."

Bonding through a new awareness of the harms they endured and that some had caused, as well as systems injustice, made it possible for these women of diverse identities to communicate and form connections across class, race, age, income, and sexual orientation. For Darla, a low-income Black woman in her early 20s, learning that she was in the "same boat" as middle-class white women who had also been arrested for harming a partner was a "surprise." Once she got to know these women as fellow group members, Darla reasoned that despite their different identities, "We all get tired [of the abuse] at some point. We have our breaking points."

Tyra, who described herself as a low-income Black single mother, explained that meeting middle-class white women whose partners also abused them "was surprising." Being similarly situated made their emotional connection possible. Tyra put it this way: "Their lives were so different, and they were experiencing the same type of heartache and disappointment in relationship problems despite the fact that they were from different walks of life. We had something in common. That's what made [the group] easy . . . because we could relate to each other . . . We felt safe and not judged because we all had something that was in common."

A new awareness that women from very different backgrounds had also survived family and intimate harm brought clarity and comfort. Tyra felt that "just because I'm low-income doesn't mean that someone who has a better income or lives a more stable life hasn't experienced something similar to myself. It's just good to know that I'm not alone. I'm not by myself."

For Phoebe the common bond made race and age differences irrelevant. "When you get in that room and you're around all those women," she said, "you don't even see [their race] . . . You don't see the color; you don't see the age. You just hear the pain; you just hear the story; you just hear what they've been through."

Christine described the connection across identities as being "like a melting pot. There's just all walks and ages . . . I think there's a unity that is built in there, and just knowing that you have that support and friendships. You can go, and you can talk about things in a safe place."

Feeling connection across identities was also shared by women otherwise minoritized by their gender expression and sexual orientation. Sheniqua and Devore were concerned about joining the AVI-G because they assumed their sexual identities differed from the majority of the group members. Sheniqua described her caution in interactions with Probation Officer Rigor because she looked like a "big boy dyke"—50 pounds heavier than she "should be" and wearing big black sweatpants (see chapter 1). Similarly, she assumed her appearance and her sexual orientation would be a problem for other AVI-G members because "it kind of was" for her family, who made it clear "they would love it if I was with a guy." She was surprised, however, that as a masculine-presenting

Black bisexual cisgender woman, group members did not react negatively to her appearance or disclosures about male and female partners. Quite the opposite—Sheniqua smiled as she explained that she "got a lot of love from all the heterosexual women."

Devore was also "a little scared" to start group because she assumed she would be the only masculine-presenting Black lesbian. She grew up in a loving family who did not outwardly talk about her gender presentation or sexuality but did let her know her choice of partners would mean that she would "have to deal with God." As a self-protective measure, Devore initially disguised her sexuality in group by using the gender neutral pronoun "they" when speaking about her girlfriend. She was "shocked" to learn that she did not need this form of self-protection. Devore explained,

> When I went in there . . . I never said whether she was a girl or a man. I just left it. I just said "they" until other women started telling their stories . . . and I was shocked that some of them were girls and some of them were men. The women that's straight, they didn't treat lesbian women no different. We all in there for the same reason . . . It's not like it's one set race. I kind of like that too, as a mixture because it lets you know, hey, this is not just happening in the Black community. There was a lady in there that was Mexican. I was shocked she was going through it. A Caucasian person was going through it. It was me and another lesbian, and I was shocked . . . I thought I was going to be the only one with a girlfriend.

Devore's comfort with the other women made it possible for her to disclose her story. In the process she learned that domestic violence affected people across a range of different identities.

Sheniqua and Devore felt accepted by the other group members despite differences in gender presentation, racial identity, and sexual orientation. For Devore, that connection was lifesaving. She was mourning the loss of her relationship and her job of six years because of her domestic violence conviction. "I was really pissed off and hurt," she said. "Like everything I built just went down . . . I had to start all over . . . It's like I hit rock bottom." Interactions with other group members helped Devore "cope with other problems" as well as begin to heal from the "broken" relationship with the woman she had given her "heart to." Without the group members' support Devore believed she "would have just shut down, probably commit[ted] suicide." Common bonds brought validation of diverse life experience, connections across identities, and promoted mutual support. Feeling supported through connection, in Devore's case, literally saved her life.

## *"Connecting a Few Dots"*

Common bonds created feelings of safety, which made information-sharing possible. QuiShandra described the group process of exchanging information and discussing how to apply that information as "connecting a few dots." She explained that it involved getting "feedback . . . from my facilitator and women who may be experiencing some of the same issues or things that I'm going through." According to QuiShandra, it "really helps . . . [because] you can be a little bit confused about a few things." Valerie explained that she "loved this process," which she described in the following way: "[there are] other women there, and somebody to listen to me, and help me . . . [I] get advice from women that's been through it." Connecting a few dots was not only about relationship issues. The women shared multiple challenges, including unemployment or underemployment. They supported each other in finding and securing a first or second job. During Darla's first group she learned that Cherise, Phoebe, and QuiShandra needed to make more money to afford probation and antiviolence intervention. She shared that a family member had a security business and might be hiring. When the women expressed interest, Darla said, "Well, if you're serious, I'll tell my auntie to push you in . . . I'll put in a word for you." Darla's auntie employed Cherise and QuiShandra by the end of the week. Phoebe, however, decided the job was not for her.

For many women the process of "connecting a few dots"—shared information and strategies for how to apply that information to their daily lives—provided new ideas for what might be possible, and the courage to implement those changes. Benita explained that by listening to the other women she not only learned different ways "to deal with stuff" but also considered, "maybe I could try that." Tyra felt that because of this process she moved from "not having a voice" to learning how to "speak up . . . how to be true to myself so that I can be truthful to other people." Listening to how others dealt with their challenges and how they connected the dots for themselves gave Nikki "the guts" to do the same in her relationships. Nikki attributed her newfound courage and "strength to enforce" her new ideas to "hearing other people's stories about situations that they had found themselves in . . . especially getting in trouble with the law."

Social scientists refer to this reciprocally supportive process as mutual aid. Rooted in social work group practice, mutual aid refers to "people helping one another as they think things through" (Steinberg, 2014,

p. 2). Group members cultivate mutual aid through the exchange of thoughts, ideas, and feelings, and the process flourishes when members—rather than the social work practitioners or group facilitators—regard each other as the principal helpers (Steinberg, 2014). To cultivate mutual aid, the "whole person," rather than only the "needy" part of that person, must be part of the group process and all group members have the right to be heard (Steinberg, 2014). Moneesha was thoughtful and deliberate in her word choice as she recalled liking this member-focused approach because "everyone had a chance to participate." This approach to sharing and then applying information "changed" Imani's "way of looking at a lot of things." "Connecting a few dots," or mutual aid, is embedded in the social work ethic of the right to self-determination, which regards people as the experts in their relationships.[6] The knowledge gained during the AVI-G included, but was not limited to, a more complex understanding of "domestic violence" that centered coercive control; identifying the signs of abusive relationships, or red flags; and how to apply this increased awareness to their daily lives.

*Domestic Violence and Coercive Control*

Women described themselves as beginning the AVI-G with "narrow" or "limited" ideas of what domestic violence involved, focusing only on physical abuse that left visible injuries. In the AVI-G they gained a deeper understanding of intimate harm focused on how coercively controlling partners tailor their abusive actions to the vulnerabilities of the person they are harming. Olivia credited her early understanding of domestic violence with what she knew from "Lifetime movies . . . [where] the woman is just black and blue from head to toe." During AVI-G sessions Olivia learned that coercive control "can be worse than that—the mental of it . . . . You didn't have to be beat to a bloody pulp and dead on the side of the road to have went through a similar situation." This deeper understanding was validating for Olivia, who explained, "It's okay to feel the way you're feeling." Like Olivia, Tyra learned about coercive control and how it was the scaffolding of her husband's physical abuse. Without that information, Tyra recalled, "I think that I would not understand the ways that power and control worked and the different aspects of it . . . I know now it is not just physical abuse. I know that there are different lines of abuse underneath a bruise." Of all the referrals CPS made for Tyra, the AVI-G was the only place she learned about coercive control.

After three group sessions, Essence's growing understanding of coercive control gave her the opportunity to consider how it was specific to her arrest and CPS contact, both of which had been initiated by her former partner. Essence explained that because of the AVI-G she was "seeing more" complexity in the abuse she had endured throughout her life. Part of that complexity was a growing understanding "that men in this situation usually pick a child" to manipulate the child's mother. This made Essence "feel so much better," she explained, "because I thought I was going crazy like I didn't understand why [this happened to me]." For Christine, a more complex understanding of coercive control helped her "gain respect for [herself], and keep boundaries," which became a catalyst for changing her relationships with friends, family, and her husband.[7]

Sissy claimed that AVI-G conversations regarding coercive control, "change[d] my point of view." She came to the group hoping to understand more about how her child's father could coerce her into illegal behavior, such as stealing work boots for him. But she also learned that his constant phone calls and voicemails were forms of stalking that, if documented, she could use to support her court case. Initially, Sissy avoided the calls and deleted the voicemails, not wanting to take her already limited time to manage his behavior. But, Sissy explained, "those voicemails keep coming . . . over 100. I'd erase them all, and then another 100 the next day . . . Calling and calling and calling. I clear my phone, and the next two days it's full. I clear my phone, and then I don't even know how to save all that. Many of them went to voicemail."

AVI-G members encouraged Sissy to email the voicemails to herself and use them as proof of his abuse for the judge. Although she was reluctant to do this, Sissy said, "I started emailing [them] to myself. I was like, oh my gosh, I'm wasting more time emailing than [working]!" Group members also encouraged Sissy to "call the police" and "get him out of the house." They did so by asking her, "Why do you feel sorry for him?" and reminding her that when she went to court for a crime he coerced her into committing, "he didn't even pay a dime" defending her against the charges. With the case ongoing, Sissy expressed gratitude for the women's support, noting, "I learn[ed] to document everything . . . take pictures of everything."

Nikki credited her conversations with the women in the AVI-G with a deeper understanding of how her husband gaslit her during court appearances. Nikki realized that by withholding information and lying, her husband had effectively convinced the judge he was not only the victim of *her* abuse, but also a good father. She decided to challenge this false narrative with documentation and focus on herself rather than on him. Nikki explained the matter as follows:

> He took me to court and told all these lies about me . . . made me seem like just the biggest piece of crap on the planet. I went in there with all my support letters from [Alcoholics Anonymous], and [AVI] . . . and [probation] . . . I didn't go in there and say a bad word about him . . . I just stayed focused . . . I knew after being in [the AVI-G] and being in AA that if I didn't focus on myself and started focusing on him, I was going to lose ground.

For Sissy, Nikki, and others, group member suggestions and support were forms of mutual aid. They not only facilitated the healing process; they provided the guidance and support necessary to begin repairing the breakage.

*Red Flags*

Learning about the signs, or red flags, of coercive control in their relationships armed these women with the knowledge of how to avoid abusive partners and, for some, stop being abusive themselves. By understanding the signs of abuse, Lily could "see" the early abusive behaviors; moreover, she felt that those red flags "helped" avoid future abusive partners. For women who had both endured and caused harm, learning the signs, explained Joy, "was really helpful in discern[ing] what domestic abuse was and my role and my behavior versus someone else's." There were what Jatara called multiple "ah ha" moments when learning about red flags and then applying that information to their lives. For Jatara this was a "very powerful" process. As she put it, "Listening to the different stories of how these men manipulate women . . . you see these patterns of these men and how they try to control [women], so I'm able to spot it more and see that pattern in them." Shifting the focus to herself, Jatara continued, "You're only accountable for you. So it was life changing. It was everything I needed. It helped me get back to me." Getting "back to me" meant focusing on the changes she would make in future relationships.

In the AVI-G, Marcella also learned about herself, her history of surviving sexual violence, and depression. She used that new understanding to tease out how she "shut down" her "empathy" when she was "romantically involved." Through this process she identified not only how she was hurt but also what she called "power things" that she did to new partners that "were really manipulative." Nikki explained that she "didn't know how to leave [an abusive] situation before [the AVI-G]." She credited her increased understanding of coercive control and red flags with her insight that she would have to "just walk away" and "leave the situation immediately before it got to the point where it got physical." Nikki also attributed her increased awareness and feelings of personal responsibility with her success in achieving and maintaining sobriety to the AVI-G. She recalled, "I don't think I could have done AA without [the AVI-G] . . . [The AVI-G] was what I called my accountability group. I could have never stayed sober for those five years. There's no way . . . I don't know like where the awakening happened . . . There wasn't like this certain 'ah ha' moment. It was like a continual, like gradual progression."

Although Phoebe struggled with having been wrongfully arrested on a bogus warrant her partner had initiated, she credited the AVI-G with providing her help she did not initially think she needed—help in recognizing red flags when her ex-partner would "control" her through the way in which she responded to his abuse. "I actually really did need help, you know," Phoebe explained, "regardless if it was just moving forward, period, dealing with people or dealing with the situation. I need to learn how to not let [him] have that much control and power of my emotions." Phoebe now embraced the opportunity to understand the signs of abusive relationships and then use that information to empower herself despite his coercive control.

Devore also welcomed the opportunity to gain a new understanding of red flags. But she wished she had had the knowledge much earlier. If she had, Devore believed she would not have harmed her partner. Devore explained,

> I never saw those signs . . . that led me to this point. If I would have known about those signs in relationship[s] or if my mom, or dad, or somebody talked to me about relationships and what to look out for, at least I would have the chance whether or not just to . . . stay or to keep going . . . but I didn't have that opportunity. I was just going off of what I was feeling, but the signs was all there at the beginning, and I could have avoided going to jail or hurting her because I never knew.

Devore felt she now knew "what to look for in a relationship." She also explained that by "understanding more about relationships" she was able to "think before I make any decision involving physically hitting anybody." This increased awareness meant that, similarly to Nikki, she could now decide to "just leave the whole thing . . . and end it right here."

Sheniqua described the process of learning about red flags and implementing that knowledge as follows: "recognize it for what it is, and decide what you're going to do." Sheniqua felt this process would keep her safe from another abusive partner and also prevent her from "beating somebody's butt . . . down the line." Group content had the potential to promote safety across relationships.

*From Shame to Hope*

The women expressed feeling ashamed of the violence in their lives. This shame evolved from cultural and gendered socialization that often prioritizes women's responsibility for maintaining peaceful relationships, and it was complicated by their CLS or CPS contact or both. The shame initially felt immobilizing. But the shared connection of the AVI-G catalyzed the journey out of shame and toward hope. Emersyn tearfully stressed that being in the group was powerful because it allowed her to address these feelings: "You know, I was ashamed of myself . . . the support was nice." The group, Emersyn explained, enabled her to start moving from feeling ashamed to feeling supported and then to begin to move ahead with her life.

Interactions with other AVI-G members also helped Suzie move beyond the shame and feeling like a "monster" by helping her to see "the light at the end of the tunnel":

> The good thing about [group] was . . . I saw other people that had been through what I've been through, and to realize that we're just ordinary people . . . and to listen to what they've gone through and their relationships with the people that they had their fight with, so it was good . . . I did see the light at the end of the tunnel . . . and I got to feel like an everyday person which was awesome instead of the monster like I felt like I was.

By listening to and learning from others and sharing her story, Rosemary felt less ashamed for being a "bad" or "evil" person. "It's been a positive experience," Rosemary said, "to listen to other people and find out that you're really not that bad of a person, and that these things don't necessarily happen to bad people, or that people that go through this aren't weak-minded or evil. They're just people."

A more complex understanding of domestic violence, awareness of red flags, and the opportunity to move beyond shame brought connection, as well as a shift in focus. For *the heartbroken,* who had endured wrongful arrest and were often still in relationships with coercively controlling partners, the connection was tempered by a deeper clarity about the system's unfairness. For women who found themselves *at their breaking point,* the connection and information sharing were validating and even lifesaving. Their focus shifted from hating themselves for what they had done to disliking their actions and feeling supported in exploring alternatives.

## PERSONAL HEALING AND TRANSFORMATION THROUGH CONNECTION

A closer look at how QuiShandra and Regina experienced the AVI-G provides further context regarding the ripple effect of the AVI-G's personal and collective benefits. This ripple effect was evident in the women's descriptions of healing and transformation.

### QuiShandra: "You're a beautiful butterfly"

Soon after QuiShandra's first meeting with her probation officer, she learned that she was being evicted from her apartment owing to the domestic violence conviction. The local domestic violence shelter then denied her and her two children admission for the same reason. A week later, a family shelter finally admitted them. After only a few weeks, though, QuiShandra was "exited" from the shelter against her wishes. She explained what happened in this way:

> They told me I had to exit because I missed a meeting with a lady that was there, so I was just like what the heck? I was working two jobs at the time . . . My son was doing [school and sports]. I was going to church faithfully. I had a lot going on with my days . . . I never came back for meal time because I was already out throughout the day ripping and running.

"Ripping and running" included her obligations to remain probation compliant. Shelter administrators dismissed her pleas to reconsider the eviction. As a last resort she and her children moved in with her mother, with whom she had a "difficult" relationship. Now QuiShandra could not find a well-paying job in the formal economy that would help her meet the demands of court, probation, and AVI-A compliance. She explained,

> I can never find a good, steady, solid-paying job. Right now this job . . . it's with the cleaning and whatnot, but it's like an under-the-table job . . . Other than that, I have really been like in and out, in and out, in and out of jobs

left and right, and . . . it's really not paying the bills for real. It's because I've got like all these charges.

In addition to the probation and AVI-A financial obligations, there was the "mental thing" (see chapter 3), which made it difficult for QuiShandra to get through the day and posed barriers to participating in family rituals.

Then there was the AVI-G. At first, she did not want to go, but after the first session, there was something about meeting with "strangers" that were "almost friends" and "connecting a few dots" that felt transformative. After 20 sessions, QuiShandra referred to the AVI-G as

> another home for me . . . It's comforting because you like see women that you're growing with, that you're healing with, that you're able to connect with, that you're able to relate with, and that's been on this journey, and is pivotal . . . that can help give you feedback or laugh with you a little bit . . . [they] cry with you or . . . give you a hug when you need [one] . . . that's there every session.

She went on to explain the process of building connections with other women based on their shared challenges: "You just kind of create . . . a bond with this group of women. In some way everyone can relate to one another and has been through something traumatic, you know. Over the times . . . just going there . . . you kind of are able to connect with or you enjoy going to meet with these people."

QuiShandra reflected on what she had observed about other women in the AVI-G over those sessions:

> You're able to really like see how women can go into something and come out as something and be ten times better at whatever it is that they're doing. We'll walk in there on the first day, and you're looking like you're just super tired. You've been beat up, beat in, and out, down, drained out, and you'll walk out with a smile. You'll just start coming to group with like a whole new look. You'll come to group with a glow, and all the ladies will like know like, "Oh my God, girl, look at you! Oh my God!" It will be like that type of thing that [the AVI-G] kind of brings out of you. You can just really go on and seek better ways of living with a group of women, so it's pretty cool to grow.

In addition to what she observed in other women, QuiShandra noticed personal changes as well. "At the end of it all," she said, "it's like you're a beautiful butterfly . . . You know, you're able to like tell your story in a different way now." For QuiShandra that "different way" was feeling transformed by her AVI-G participation, in marked contrast to her probation officer and AVI-A interactions. In hindsight,

QuiShandra explains, "You do probation for probation . . . but you're doing the [AVI-G] for yourself."

### Regina: "Getting shit done"

While QuiShandra attributed the transformation she felt to connections she made with other women during the AVI-G, Regina (see chapter 1) intentionally leveraged her social and financial privilege to help other AVI-G members. Although Regina held a very different access to resources from the rest of the group members, she remembered sharing in and listening to conversations during group. From those conversations she observed that "life had really crushed" the majority of the other women. Regina decided early on to leverage her social networks to make "good stuff" happen for women outside of group. She not only helped women one-on-one; she engaged in what Mario Small (2009, p. 19) refers to as "actor driven brokerage"—actively connecting women to each other as well as to community resources. As a "broker," Regina could circumvent the shame many women felt in reaching out for institutional help on their own, leverage her capital, and effectively enable connections. This was possible both because of her desire to make a difference in the other women's lives and her social and financial resources.

Regina began by facilitating fellow group member Bea's "transition" from living with her abusive partner to living in a temporary domestic violence shelter.[8] Regina described her first impression of Bea as "very closed off and . . . hostile, angry, pissed off. Probably had lost faith [in the system]." During group, Bea mentioned the relentless abuse she suffered from her partner, and eventually asked Regina if she could help. Regina first called a friend who was a police officer to get an idea of her legal options in helping Bea. Armed with this information, Regina and Bea executed a plan. Regina drove to Bea's apartment and loaded Bea, her dog, and her belongings into Regina's luxury sedan. When Bea's abusive partner appeared out of "nowhere" and started shouting and verbally abusing her as she was trying to rapidly gather her things and leave, Regina stopped, stood in front of him, looked up at him, and shouted back, "Look, YOU ain't all THAT and a bag of chips, so let's just keep this moving!" According to Regina, he did "not dare" to challenge her. She and Bea quickly moved Bea's things out of the apartment, into the sedan, and onto the shelter.

Just before Bea's time in the domestic violence shelter came to an end, Regina convinced a local friend who was also a landlord to rent

Bea a room in his boarding house. Although the landlord did not like the idea of renting to women "in trouble," Regina smiled as she explained, "He owed me a favor." This initiated an informal process over the years that when an apartment in the house became vacant, the landlord gave women who had contact with either the local domestic violence shelter or the AVI-G (or both) first choice. Contrary to what he initially assumed, the women were desirable tenants who kept their rooms clean, the noise to a minimum, and their rent paid. Gradually, the entire boarding house was occupied by women from the county domestic violence shelter and the AVI-G. Regina also provided some of the women small loans, trips to a local clothing and furniture donation center, her hand-me-down business clothes, and short-term stays at her home. Regina smiled, remembering when Bea asked her why she was so nice to her and the other women. "I'm not," Regina laughed warmly, "I'm just for getting shit done!"

Regina was proud of the community resources and connections she mobilized for the women, all because their lives became intertwined when she too was court ordered to the AVI. But she "drew the line" when women started privately disclosing their sexual assault histories to her and asking for emotional support. "It just felt like it was so out of my wheelhouse that I didn't want to speak about it," she said. In hindsight, though, Regina reflected,

> If I would have been able to do it over, I probably should have done more to address when [they] brought up to me about the sexual abuse issues, but I was already doing so much that I felt like now I've got to take this on? . . . that I didn't want to speak about it. Probably should have contacted somebody to address that a little bit more.

Regina expressed her frustration with a system that seemed to especially punish low-income, systems-involved women. She encouraged a contextual approach that takes "things on a case-by-case basis." She insisted that "the system should be more sophisticated."

Regina observed the breadth of the challenges many of these women experienced but also the need for formal systems responses. As she put it, "The government is saying how many problems can we deal with? You're homeless. You just got out of jail. You've got a criminal record. You don't have any money. I get it. The government can't take care of everything, but I think that there's certain things that they can work harder on and better at . . . Anybody that's disenfranchised now? . . . you're fucked!" Regina went out of her way to make a difference in the women's lives. Although she recognized the systems-inflicted harm, she still blamed herself for not being able to do more for the other women.

## SUMMARY AND REFLECTIONS

As a seasoned AVI practitioner, I initially came to this research project especially curious about how AVI-G curricula content affected the women. As I asked them curriculum-focused questions it was evident that they were exposed to the session content, but also that this was not at all their primary takeaway from their AVI-G contact. Instead, they wanted to talk about how the AVI-G gave them opportunities to share and listen to each other's stories. I then learned that the AVI-G format facilitated human connection in ways that were unlike anything many of the women had experienced. For those who felt broken and alone, human connection eased the pain, promoted healing, and made way for change. In sharing with other women, whom QuiShandra at first called "almost strangers," they ended their isolation, found a common bond, connected the dots of information they shared and then applied to their own lives, and began to move from feeling shameful to hopeful. The women shared these experiences regardless of how they came to systems attention or if they attended on their own accord.

By centering their agenda rather than my own during our conversations, I learned how their AVI-G experiences were profoundly different from what they encountered when reporting to their probation officers, interacting with their CPS caseworkers, and navigating AVI-A. Certainly AVI-G session content was effective, but that was not their main takeaway. Instead, like QuiShandra, they wanted to talk about how transformative this process had been for them. The connection developed during this process was similarly powerful for the women who experienced the group as reaching across class, race, age, income, and sexual orientation. I cofacilitated a group in which Tyra mentioned how surprised she was that middle-class white women had "these problems." I was there when women disclosed in group what Regina had done for them and when Regina quietly smiled as women acknowledged their gratitude to her. It was only in confidence with me that she was animated in explaining what she had done and in wishing she could have done more.

Throughout this process I was reminded of Susan Miller's (2005) prescient warning. She cautioned that one of the multiple risks of developing AVI for women was that, in becoming "institutionalized and bureaucratized," staff would focus on operations, legitimacy, and expertise. What would be lost, Miller argued, is the larger mission of understanding the complexity of domestic violence and the appropriate ways for the legal system to respond to participants' circumstances. As a practitioner-researcher I am very familiar with the relentless tension between AVI legitimacy in terms of seeking funding and broad community support and the larger movement's social justice efforts in finding and securing housing, employment, childcare, and more. When centering the women's voices, however, it becomes clear that this desire for connection is also a social justice issue. This connection can happen through AVI-Gs, but if done without care, the AVI-Gs risk compromising the participants' right to self-determination. Although the women in this project experienced the AVI-G as a supportive space, that experience may have been amplified by the contrast with how unsupportive and isolating probation, CPS, and AVI-A contact were. It is important to note that staff who were bound by mandatory reporting obligations monitored the AVI-G. Furthermore, the mere existence of such interventions—which have relationships with the CLS and CPS, where the lines between the systems of power and support are blurred if not entirely absent—demonstrate how services staffed by social workers and a range of antiviolence practitioners have largely, if not entirely, been coopted by carceral systems.[9] The hope for holistically supporting systems-involved women lies in opportunities for them to informally and voluntarily assemble in ways that promote healing, autonomy, and moving forward with lives free from violence.

# CHAPTER 5

# After Antiviolence Intervention Group

*Connections, Going It Alone,*
*and Convictions*

"WE KIND OF JUST KICK IT AFTERWARDS."
—BECKY

In this chapter, I bring attention to the ripple effect of the women's voluntary connections made within, between, and after the AVI-Gs. As figure 6 shows, what began in the group sessions with sharing stories and forming common bonds grew into practical connections and years-long friendships that helped ease the burden of ongoing systems contact. The women used these informal connections to emotionally heal from intimate and systems-inflicted harms, and to begin to repair their breakage. This chapter also attends to the experiences of the women who chose to have limited or no contact with other group members beyond the AVI. The chapter finishes with a glimpse of the women's lives after their court-ordered obligations ended. By including the benefits some of the women found in informal connections, choices not to have contact, and how the legal system affected their lives years later, I encourage a more complex analysis of how carceral systems affect people over years.

## BETWEEN AVI-G SESSIONS: "FREE SPACE"

After finishing their weekly AVI-G session, the women moved out of the formal group room, through the agency lobby, and into the agency parking lot. In this space—between group and their daily lives—they "sat," as Rosalee put it, "[on the curb] with a cigarette and talked together," or, as Becky said, would "just kick it" until the bus arrived,

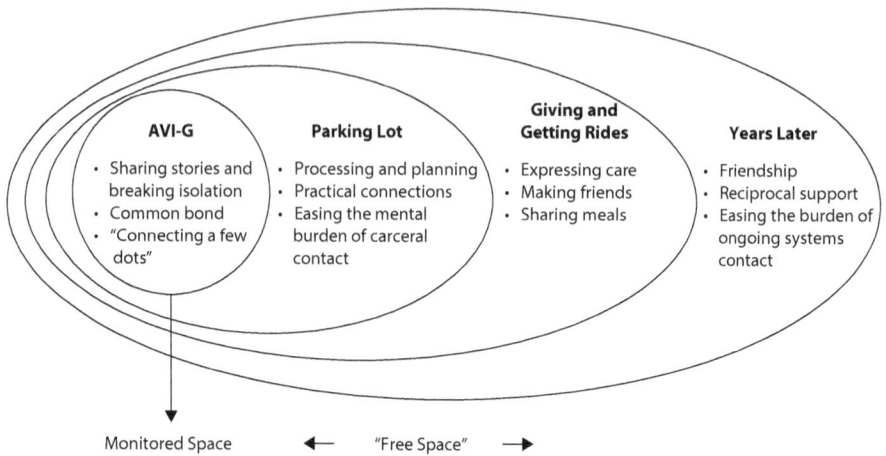

FIGURE 6. The Antiviolence Intervention Group ripple effect.

and then, according to Tyra, would slowly "walk . . . back to [their] cars." Here, the women created their own "free space" between their private lives and formal institutions where they could, in the words of social scientists Sara Evans and Harry Boyte (1992), "act with dignity, independence and vision" (p. 17). This shared space was visually evident to passersby, who could see clusters of the women long after the AVI-G ended.[1] In Emersyn's experience, groups of three or four women routinely congregated when "certain people would click with certain people or have a similarity or whatnot—a common bond." Here they did not feel compelled to expend emotional labor, obligated to pay fees, or monitored by systems actors. Here they could talk as long as they wanted about what they wanted. The act of creating this in-between space was not only an avenue toward restoring feelings of physical and emotional safety, but also a means of subtly resisting oppressive power.[2] This resistance was evident in how the women used this space to heal and move forward on their own terms, fortifying themselves for the continuing challenges ahead.

THE PARKING LOT

*Processing and Planning for AVI-G Interactions*

Some of the women used conversations in the parking lot to process what happened in the AVI-G, discuss group member interactions, to manage the cofacilitator-group member power dynamic, or, as Tyra put it, to engage in "brainstorming" for the next AVI-G. Nikki characterized these gatherings as an opportunity to discuss interactions from the group that had just finished. She recalled that these conversations "centered on what happened at group that day . . . sometimes elaborating on things [because] . . . there were so many of us [in the AVI-G] but . . . everybody would need a chance to share, so we wouldn't be able to like delve into certain topics for very long. In the parking lot we would try to touch back onto those topics with certain people who were really struggling."

Emersyn and other group members would "continue the conversation about . . . what was happening in the group. 'You know, so what are you going to do about your guy?' 'What's going to happen with the baby?'" In addition to conveying the transfer of information, these interactions involved subtle exchanges of care. Emersyn explained, "We'd stand in the parking lot and chat . . . you would send [women] a little wink or you'd see them getting teary . . . You might say something like, 'Hey, been through that,' or 'This is what I did.' . . . It was just kind of a friendship with somebody that maybe kind of understood your path."

While they smoked, talked, and listened, group members processed their recent AVI-G interactions. Rosalee remembered discussing a new group member sharing with others: "It was really good that she's finally coming out a little bit and talking to us, you know."

Conversations in the parking lot were also an opportunity to informally manage the cofacilitator-group member power dynamic, free from systems-generated repercussions; this was evident in the women's critiques of AVI-G cofacilitators. "Sometimes we'd talk about how [the cofacilitators] irritated us," Nikki explained, or "how we wished [a different cofacilitator] were there that day." It is possible that an unmonitored space to informally talk through group member interactions and critique cofacilitators made the sort of emotional labor expended during probation and CPS less necessary during the AVI-G.

The women used the space to plan for the content they would share in the next week's AVI-G. Tyra referred to this process as "brainstorming in the parking lot." Sometimes this brainstorming took place to "get reinforcements." For example, if a woman was considering disclosing a particular relationship scenario that might elicit mixed responses, she would secure other group members' support during these informal conversations. When she shared the information during the next AVI-G, she could then count on certain other women's responses. At other times, "brainstorming" meant deciding how much, if any, information to share in the next AVI-G: "Should I bring this up in group, or is this too much, or is it too little, or should I not say anything at all?" asked Tyra. The women's conversations in the parking lot served the strategic function of collectively preparing themselves for the next AVI-G.

### Practical Connections

Navigating written and unwritten legal system rules stirred feelings of loneliness and confusion; doing so was also exhausting. And expensive. An important function of the women's informal conversations was the practical assistance they generated. These connections enabled a kind of information-sharing that eased the women's financial burdens and provided critical knowledge of how to maneuver within the carceral system. RyAnn referred to this time as "the hookup hour":

> The women would get together in the parking lot . . . Say there was a woman who needed clothes for her kids, right. So, another woman may know like, "Hey, you know if you go to like the Salvation Army in this place, there is a woman by this name, and she'll help you." Or like, "Hey, this agency pays your [electric] bill." Or like, oh man, you know that if your car is broken down you [go here]. Or just times where it was just like talking about even like how to navigate court, like, "Oh man, I've got to go to court." "Oh, who's the judge you're seeing? Okay, say this." You know, or like don't do this or before you go make sure you've definitely paid this . . . or come to court with some money, you know.

Through the exchange of community and systems-specific information the women were collectively repairing their breakage. As QuiShandra put it, "Some people even, like I do . . . give a little bit of information. 'Oh, I've got a job that you can have' . . . so it's really, really good. You know, everybody can kind of connect with one another in different ways." Jatara explained that she and other members would "talk about, 'Girl, I don't know how I'm going to pay these probation fees. I don't know what I'm going to do. Should I do community service?'" Although practical information-sharing took place in the AVI-G, the venue limited time and content. The women voluntarily seeking each other out after the AVI-G created a space to exchange resources while controlling the process.

### Easing the Mental Burden

Time in the parking lot was also spent, as Moneesha described it, disclosing "personal things . . . going on in our lives," too private to share in the AVI-G. Tyra characterized these conversations as "something somebody said [in the parking lot] that . . . you didn't want to say in [the AVI-G]." The women made these disclosures and engaged in supportive discussions in ways that alleviated the mental burden of intimate and systems harms. Jatara described this mental burden as being collectively "in shock" about their current circumstances. The women therefore sought a place to vent, knowing that those listening could identify with their struggle, but would not necessarily try to "fix" anything. These conversations, Jatara explained, were all about "everybody rubbing each other's sores"—metaphorically alleviating the emotional and mental pain of their circumstances by holding space and creating connections. The space and conversations brought Sheniqua "peace. . . . [In the parking lot] I don't have to be like stressed out." In Imani's experience, those who were most likely to make these private disclosures were "whoever had the worst day and ended up in tears." Imani explained that, in response, "we would be like, 'We here for you.'"

This unmonitored space also allowed the women the opportunity to discuss and process the most private systems-related disclosures, while avoiding the risk that AVI-G cofacilitators would report them to probation or CPS. Jatara explained that, in the monitored AVI-G circle, "I didn't share that I was still messing around and still sleeping with [my child's] dad because that was a stipulation [of probation] and I wasn't supposed to. I wasn't supposed to have contact, but I mean [other group members] knew." Other group members knew, because Jatara discussed it in the parking lot, where she could talk among other women who understood and responded in a way that she found supportive. If she had disclosed these details in the AVI-G, she believed, the cofacilitators or other group members might have discouraged her contact with him or reported her to probation or both. Jatara pointed out that her situation was not unusual. Most of the women in her group were having sex with or somehow "messing around" with the former partner with whom they had had the incident and often, even, a legal no-contact order. For Jatara, the ongoing contact was strategic. Continuing to have sex with her son's father meant he would allow Jatara to see their child. Jatara acknowledged that her actions had legal risks, but she had to manage those risks her way—not having contact with her child was unthinkable. Jatara knew her son's father would most likely report her to probation, but it was a chance she had to take. It was also a risk that other women from group understood and would be open to listening about without involving further systems contact.

## GIVING AND GETTING RIDES

Mutual aid was evident across the women's interactions. Imani and others paid for another woman's AVI-A fee (see chapter 3) and Regina connected the women with a range of opportunities (see chapter 4). Indeed, the women throughout this project described ways they supported each other. Participating in this reciprocity was life-giving for many. Sometimes the women helped another group member out because they saw their former selves in that specific woman's struggle. At other times they wanted to ease the burden for those who were similarly systems-involved. Exchanging rides was a concrete way for the women to express care for each other. Taking car rides made getting to AVI and back home or to work much easier and took less time and effort than public transportation would have done. It also facilitated court compliance. Sheniqua explained that although she could not "give back monetarily," she gave car rides to other group members. Similarly, Joy "felt the need to express care" to other group members she saw in the parking lot. She did so "with a smile or positive word" and "gave . . . rides home." These exchanges led to Joy supporting Lily with rides to and from group, giving gently used hand-me-downs to her children, and helping her with her sobriety.

In addition to gestures of kindness, giving and getting rides provided another in-between space for the women to make and strengthen friendships through conversation. Imani, for example, made a close friend in the AVI-G, a friend who had a car and often gave her rides home; conversation and connection flowed during those trips: "We would kick it on the ride . . . talk over the phone [between groups] . . . and had lunch and stuff."

Similarly, Nikki remembered that although another group member lived 20 miles in the opposite direction from her home, she went out of her way to pick Nikki up to go to group and then drop her off afterward. This meant she did not have to rely on her mother for a ride, which was a tremendous relief, since she and her mother had never gotten along. It also alleviated her shame for having lost her driver's license from a conviction for driving under the influence of alcohol. "That's how her and I became so close," Nikki recalled. "She would drive the opposite direction to come and pick me up and take me to group because she knew me getting a ride from my mom caused so many problems." Those rides facilitated friendship through conversation in the car and over "appetizers or whatnot" on the way home.

Getting and giving rides also ignited what may very well be lifelong friendships whereby the women felt emotionally supported and at ease sharing limited resources. Tyra's, Lily's, and Jatara's time in the AVI-G overlapped. The women did not remember who joined the AVI-G first or who left first. When Tyra started the AVI-G she was pregnant. In the beginning she walked to group from her apartment and then back after group because her van was not working. But that soon changed. "Sometimes I took the bus. Sometimes one of the other girls gave me a ride that lived in the area or was going past," she recalled. Gradually, the women exchanged telephone numbers. "One of the beauties of exchanging numbers," Tyra said, was that "we were always able to call each other in the morning like, 'Hey, are you going to [the AVI-G]? Do you need a ride?'" Early on, Jatara saw Tyra walking and offered her a ride home. Soon afterward, Jatara started picking Tyra up to go to group. Tyra remembered, "Jatara was bringing me back and forth, and then [another group member] started bringing me back and forth." And then the other group member picked up Tyra, Jatara, and Lily, the latter of whom was living at the local domestic violence shelter. Tyra smiled as she explained that one day,

> I wasn't walking anymore. Then, I had friends. I had never had friends before, so that was new for me . . . Me and Jatara became really, really good friends. We've done so much together over the last couple years . . . and Lily. Lily is a pretty awesome girl . . . I appreciate her so much. There is plenty of times I've called her on a rampage, distraught or angry.

Lily explained, "Tyra was pregnant, I was pregnant . . . we've been through all of it from the moment that [CPS] ended up taking Tyra's baby from her. . . . We're . . . best friends." Although Lily's and Tyra's friendship started during their AVI-G participation, it flourished during the shared rides. "When the [AVI-G] was over, I was over," explained Lily, "but if I got a ride home, then I was talking to Tyra." Through the trust cultivated over the course of these conversations, Lily and Tyra did "normal best friend stuff." Lily would "borrow Tyra's van if I needed to go somewhere or she would take me places . . . I used to babysit the boys for her . . . [Our friendship] was just everything."

The women's friendship provided significant reciprocal support after their AVI-G contact ended but their involvement with family court did not: "If we had a breakdown because the court system or the court went wrong we would vent [to each other]," explained Lily. Similarly, Jatara and Tyra's close bond became stronger after the AVI-G finished. Years later, Jatara reflected, "I don't know how me and her became so close because we really didn't deal with each other much when we was a part of the [AVI-G]. We really formed a friendship [after]." More than 10 years later, and multiple states apart from each other, she and Tyra start each day with a phone call or text. "It's good to know that I'm not alone. I'm not by myself," Tyra explained. "There's someone that I can talk to." Tyra, Lily, and Jatara travel across a number of state boundaries to share time together during their children's school breaks and religious holidays.

## NOT CONNECTING

Not everyone formed connections in the parking lot or during shared rides. For some women, forming relationships was not an option owing to the limited time and the multiple obligations they had. Other women simply were not ready or chose not to connect as a form of self-protection. Sissy did not take time in the parking lot because she needed to get home and cook dinner for her small children. Now and then Devore "spent a short five minutes" to "get information about a job or a book that . . . helped somebody," but she was too tired to linger. She was focused on heading home to get some sleep after having worked the night shift and then going straight to the morning AVI-G. Although QuiShandra enjoyed interacting with other women during group and "on the way out" of the room, she typically did not have much time after the group session ended because her ride was waiting.

Olivia quickly headed for the highway after group to get to her university classes. She acknowledged that although she was busy with school, she "just wasn't ready to let people in" emotionally, feeling "broken down, brokenhearted." Similarly, Ikeeylah left to "go on with my day . . . [not] really looking to make connections." Christine did not have time to stop and talk in the parking lot either. She had a 60-minute drive home before she could breastfeed her baby. She also did not want to keep the babysitter any longer than necessary. Christine would, however, "text back and forth" during the week with another group member with whom she had grown close (see chapter 4). Although Tiffany was eager to make friends, the age difference between her and the other group members discouraged her from reaching out to them. "I know age doesn't really matter," she said, "but . . . I want friends that are my age . . . but they're all older." Phoebe would chat "now and then" but usually "made sure that I just came to that class, and when I left, I just left."

Manuela's choice not to connect with anyone in the parking lot was a matter of protecting herself and other group members. Her husband monitored her every move. Although staff denied his demands to participate in her AVI intake assessment, Manuela's husband brought her into the building for each session, waited in the agency lobby during the group, and escorted her out of the building afterward. Manuela explained that she did not interact with the women outside of group because she anticipated a "Who's that person?" questioning scenario from her husband. She acknowledged that her lack of connection with the women outside of group "gave him the power." Manuela also knew she did not have a choice. In the short term, he made sure she did not have a life outside his control. Limited time, personal boundaries, and protection for themselves and others were all factors in the women's decisions to not make connections after the AVI-G.

## AFTER CPS, PROBATION, AND AVI: YEARS LATER

The following section provides a glimpse of the women's lives a year or more after their CPS, probation, and AVI contact ended.[3] It demonstrates how the women's AVI-facilitated experiences and connections followed them years later. This section also shows the long-term consequences of their criminal convictions. I begin by highlighting the experiences of the women who were family court ordered to the AVI, followed by those ordered by criminal and family courts, and finally the women ordered to the AVI only by the criminal court.

### After CPS and AVI: Tyra

Tyra eventually freed herself from CPS involvement, achieving her goal of living with and raising her children, whom she described as "my fresh air." Who made this possible? It was Gloria, explained Tyra, her last CPS caseworker (see chapter 2). Gloria was different because she listened to Tyra, made meaningful referrals, and provided Tyra with "the whole layout"—describing the problem, how to correct the problem, and the time frame within which to make changes. When Tyra reflected on her journey, she pointed out that the "biggest issue with the [CPS] system in general is that there are people putting rules in place, and they haven't lived the life that they're trying to regulate. It's not fair." Years after her CPS involvement Tyra addressed this unfairness by securing a job advising CPS caseworkers on how to best intervene in the lives of families affected by domestic violence. Many of those Tyra advised had overseen her case in previous years.

*After CPS, Probation, and AVI: Valerie and Lily*

Months after Valerie assaulted her partner, he beat her until she was unconscious. When she recovered, she reported the incident to the police, fearing he would kill her. Although Valerie told him she did not want to press charges, she expressed ambivalence about the fact that the state had charged him with assault—"I'm kind of okay with it, but I'm kind of not." He was convicted and imprisoned. For now, she was safer, but she was also back in the familiar position of having to raise her children "by myself." When it came time for her ex-partner's release from prison, Officer Phoenix recommended to the court that it release Valerie from probation and allow her to move out of state to an undisclosed location with her children. The combination of Valerie being a young white woman who initially came to systems attention as a *real* victim, and being assigned to Officer Phoenix, who had a holistically responsive supervision approach, meant Valerie received support that allowed her to eventually move beyond punishment.

Lily's former partner also went to prison for felony domestic violence. When she was notified that he was up for early release she contacted her probation officer for permission to move out of state and, once that permission was granted, she left with her children. Although this had been her long-term plan anyway, it became a short-term plan when Lily learned of her partner's early release. The move was "horrible." Long before Lily and her children got to their destination hundreds of miles away their car broke down and had to be "scrapped." She left all their possessions behind with the hope that she could eventually go back and retrieve them. When Lily and her children arrived in their new state, she secured Section 8 housing and started a home-based business. But she quickly found herself at odds with her neighbors. There was "this guy and this girl" living next door who were fighting. Lily explained, "I knew his facial expressions, and so when he grabbed her to pull her back to the house, I yelled at him because they were in front of my house . . . I told him to get his hands off of her, and then he yelled back." Although the neighbor told her to "stay out of other people's business," Lily refused. She remembered her relationship when she was in the AVI-G: "I can't do that because [neighbors] ignored it when it was happening to me. If someone would have called [for help] . . . I know they heard . . . but no one ever called. I never want to be that person."

Lily shared this story to emphasize that her time in the AVI-G mattered long after her probation and CPS contact ended. She also wanted me to know that, although it took a while, she now worked in the financial sector. Lily "aced" her state licensing exam, earning "the first 100 percent I ever made on a test!" Although her criminal record initially delayed the final stage of her state licensure, an old friend known in the state's financial sector wrote a letter of support on her behalf. Lily and her children moved out of Section 8 housing and into their own home. She was maintaining her sobriety, and providing financially and emotionally for her children. All of this, Lily pointed out, meant that the psychiatrist who evaluated her when CPS opened her case was wrong— she was "*not* a failure!"

## After Probation and AVI: Lasting Systems Harm

For court-ordered women, discussions about their lives after AVI largely focused on criminal records and expungement.[4] The women typically had to finish probation and then wait a period of time (e.g., three to five years) before applying for expungement. They understood that the application required a filing fee and a weeks- or months-long waiting period for a criminal background check. Hiring a lawyer could help but, if their application was denied, the state required a several-year waiting period before reapplying. For low-income women who lacked resource-rich social networks, the opportunity to have a criminal record sealed or erased could be the deciding factor between long-term freedom of choice about where to live and work or a life sentence of limited options. For women who no longer had a criminal record, there were still reminders of their legal system's contact.

## Confusion and Shock: Phoebe and Ikeeylah

Phoebe was ecstatic when she finished both probation and the AVI. She contacted me the day after her last AVI-G, hoping a second interview would capture the changes she had made over the last year. "I definitely feel like all the work that I've done has reflected me doing well," Phoebe explained, "I haven't had any incidents with the police or anything since all this happened, and I never did . . . I've never been to jail, nothing, so I just don't see why [my conviction won't be dropped]." Phoebe hoped that all her work in the AVI would somehow mean her conviction would be wiped from her criminal record.

A few weeks later, Phoebe called to ask me for a third interview. She was crying. She had recently been offered a receptionist job paying $13.50 an hour. Although this was not as much as she had made before her conviction, "it's more than what I've been paid through me working this whole time" and there were "great benefits" for her and her children. Getting the job would mean having her own place again and her children moving back in with her. Phoebe was crying because she had just learned that, because of her domestic violence conviction, she did not pass the criminal background check. The $13.50 per hour receptionist job was out of reach. The prospective employer told her, "I really have a good feeling that if you were to go and explain this to the judge that this is really interfering with your ability to be able to work and your livelihood, the judge has a lot of power. [The judge] could consider that and something to happen for you to where you can go back to work."

Phoebe explained that the employer knew "nothing about everything" she had been through and "nothing about the legal system." Phoebe was also frustrated with her own confusion: "I thought I had time to successfully complete probation and *then* I would have an option to not have it on my record and be okay." She explained,

> I do feel like it's extremely unfair for this to be a first offense, a misdemeanor at that! I'm not a felon . . . I've done absolutely every single thing that they have wanted me to do at court. I've paid what I've needed to pay . . . I've suffered enough. I should at least be able to have my job and work . . . It's not much, but for me it's much . . . because I've been working my butt off to get a better job.

Phoebe could not bear the thought of waiting to apply for expungement. She explained, "Every time I hear [expungement], I just get into this state where I'm like, no, there has to be something else because . . . years?! . . . I have to suffer . . . years for a misdemeanor?! . . . I'm just like 'it's not even that type of case or conviction at all' . . . I think I've done enough . . . and I should at least be able to go to work!"

Phoebe was realizing that no matter how "well" she had done in the AVI, it was only the *beginning* of her punishment. From a legal systems perspective, she had *not* "done enough." Although no longer on probation and no longer obligated to pay AVI-A fees or attend the AVI-G, Phoebe had begun the post-probation portion of her "carceral citizenship" (Miller and Stuart, 2017). She would not be able to move out of her grandparents' place, afford an apartment, and have her children move back in with her.

Ikeeylah agreed to a plea deal only because her public defender told her that the misdemeanor domestic violence conviction would "drop off" her criminal record after she completed two years of probation and 30 AVI-Gs. It did "show up," however, when she applied for jobs. She explained, "I thought that it was off my record, but when the job I applied for came back and said that it was on there . . . I was confused." She contacted her former probation officer and learned that it would be "either two and a half years or another four years" before the record of the conviction was removed. Ikeeylah still did not have specific information. Although it was "not hard" finding a factory or grocery store job, the conviction prevented Ikeeylah from getting a job in the social work profession for which she had trained. Her only hope was to rely on the goodwill of strangers: "I've got to try to maintain a living and do what I went to school for with this on my record, hoping that someone somewhere gives me a chance . . . It's very hard and frustrating because I'm still paying the price for something that happened two years ago." Although off probation and finished with the AVI, she was not free. Her frustration was exacerbated by memories of people in the legal system telling her that the domestic violence misdemeanor conviction was "no big deal." As she put it, "Going through courts, and then talking to the judge, and the probation officer and everyone was making it seem like it's not a big deal . . . You know, you really shouldn't have been charged. You know, people just saying that it's not a big deal, but now it's becoming . . . a big deal because it's keeping me from what I set out to do."

Ikeeylah was confused and angry. Now she had no choice. All she could do was wait two to four years to *apply* to have the conviction removed from her record and hope that she would eventually be able to find work in her chosen field.

### Some Relief: Olivia and Jatara

Olivia's AVI fees and compulsory participation meant that she had to leave university, default on her student loans, and return to serving tables at a local restaurant. She reflected,

> For one, justice is not always served. That is for sure. That people are wrong-fully accused every day, and that the conditions for the people that might otherwise need help is not available . . . There's just not resources for those people that need them. I also learned a lot about myself, too. Just how strong

I actually am to be able to go through all that and come out on top is just unbelievable because that would break somebody it seems. Meeting a lot of the women in the program, it just did seem like looking back on it now, that a lot of the women were in there for the wrong reasons or they shouldn't have been.

Unlike most of the women, Olivia did not have a criminal record. Her parents had financially supported her in finding and securing a private defense attorney. That attorney negotiated a plea agreement according to which if she paid for the AVI and completed the AVI-G, her domestic violence conviction would be dropped, leaving her criminal record "clean."

Years later, Olivia's life was much different. She returned to school, changed majors, completed her degree, married a new partner, and had a job she loved. But there was one thing that remained from the time of her wrongful arrest and plea agreement. She had signed a child custody agreement written by her former partner's attorney, stating that she would have their child four days during the work week and the child would spend all weekends and holidays with his father. Olivia knew it was meant to be unfair. She was giving up all the "fun time" of weekends and holidays. But Olivia went along with the arrangement, hoping it would satisfy her former partner so he would leave her alone. She intended to make changes after she finished probation, but the agreement was still in place. "I just haven't been really prepared to fight that battle," she explained. Olivia knew her former partner had partly fulfilled the threat to keep their son from her when she had held that knife up years ago to protect herself.

Jatara did not have the time, money, or family support to challenge her conviction, nor did she have a plea agreement. As a single, low-income mother of two children she needed a well-paying job. She also needed physical distance from her son's father, who continued to harass and threaten her. When Jatara would not have sex with him when he wanted, he made false allegations to her probation officer that she had violated the no-contact order or he reported her to CPS for allegedly harming their child. She solved both problems by asking for and receiving her probation officer's permission to move out of state. An interstate move allowed her to avoid the grinding disappointment of being denied intrastate jobs. Although her domestic violence conviction would "sit on" her criminal background for at least seven years in her home state where she was convicted, prospective employers typically only do criminal background checks within the state of the advertised job.[5] Jatara was now employed out of state and a safe distance from her child's father. It was a welcome relief, she explained, to feel "almost free."

At the time of Jatara's second interview the required seven years to apply for expungement had passed. When I asked her if she would apply, she explained she would "have to go through the process all over again of going before the judge, and proving my life, and because of [the situation] with my youngest son's father, I'm not ready to do that right now." Child custody was still an issue. Although Jatara had sole custody on paper, if she challenged that at all or did anything to change her status, she feared her son's father would take him, which he had already done for months at a time. It was not worth the risk, especially given the uncertainty of what an expungement application process might entail. Despite all these challenges, Jatara thrived. A year after her last interview she texted me pictures of her and her two children smiling. Nearly grown, they were standing on either side of her with their arms around her. Jatara was wearing a university graduation gown, radiant, and holding up her degree. She had finished school at night, worked all day, and cared for her children, all while navigating the system.

### Day-to-Day Challenges: Imani and Nikki

Not long after completing the AVI Imani was fired from her full-time nursing job. Her employer had done a random background check and found the charges that "really looked bad"—charges that were later dropped in court. Imani pointed out that it seemed, at least from the employer's perspective, that the outcome of her trial was irrelevant. Her loss of employment meant Imani could no longer support herself or work toward becoming a probation officer. Now she could not afford to pay for the classes.

Imani cycled between three or four different part-time jobs to make enough money to pay the rent. With a new baby to care for, Imani considered other options, like the new podcast she and friends were creating. But honestly, all of this had to wait. Imani knew she did not have the time or money to focus on expungement. Right now she was more focused on a phone call she had just received from the county coroner. They asked her to identify the body of her deceased father. He had been missing for over a year. For now, Imani's day-to-day life, not the expungement, was her focus.

Nikki completed the AVI and probation more than six years ago. When I asked her whether or not she would apply for expungement, it was clearly not something she was considering. She hoped that it would eventually "drop off from a background search," but she imagined it would probably take "20 years" or more. Nikki shifted the focus of our conversation to her mother's recent death. For years she had taken care of her mother. When her mother passed, Nikki inherited an apartment building where she now lived and managed the other units, which meant her housing and living expenses were no longer a problem. A more pressing concern, however, were the day-to-day barriers posed by what Nikki called the "stinking domestic violence charge." "Because of the domestic violence on my life," she explained, "I've been cut off from so many things . . . I mean I can't even do stuff at my daughter's school. I mean I've been cut off left and right." Because of her criminal record she was not allowed to chaperone her daughter's elementary school field trips or become a leader for her daughter's community group. She was very happy to share, however, that after multiple attempts and letters of support, the community group's executive leadership made an exception, informing her "it sounds like you've been through an awful lot, but you've done a lot to change your life, so we're willing to give you a chance." Now, a year after their decision, Nikki explained, "That was a big thing for me when I was approved to become a . . . leader . . . I'm the only one that's kept [the group] together." For now, her focus was the joy of overcoming at least one barrier.

## Betrayal: Emersyn and Lola

Emersyn lost multiple jobs owing to probation's excessive demands. Over the course of her five-year probation term she was financially devastated (see chapter 1). Although Emersyn accepted a plea deal, none of this felt like a "deal."[6] When I asked about whether or not she would pursue expungement, she sounded exhausted with the mere thought of doing so. Emersyn remembered that when she asked her public defender about it, she gave "kind of a chuckle" in response, letting Emersyn know that expungement was not possible. Because Emersyn had more than one misdemeanor, her lawyer said it was unlikely that it would be approved. "I never pursued it," she said, "I just wanted to close the door." She continued, pointing out that applying for expungement

> would be a ton of time. I worry about the cost involved. I suspect there would be legal fees. The emotional stirring up is something. The exhaustion is certainly a concern . . . I feel like it could be a waste of time. I feel like I would hit roadblocks. I think it would be a fight. And ultimately, I guess I

question, because that system has, I feel, done me so wrong, I just don't feel like it's a fight I can win. And why put the effort into something that I'm not confident that I can have a decent outcome in?

Once again between jobs, Emersyn expressed frustration and trepidation about finding another job with a criminal record. She also reflected on the whole process. A year or so into her legal system journey she felt betrayed by her abusive partner. She also felt she had betrayed herself by retaliating. But now? Five years after probation was over, Emersyn explained that all the ways her partner had betrayed her were "healable wounds." The legal system-inflicted "wounds were much deeper . . . because it was financial, emotional, it affected my family, my job, my housing, everything." She doubted those wounds would ever heal.

More than 10 years had passed since Lola's last conviction. But she had two felonies. The first was a shoplifting charge the day after she turned 18. She had stolen shirts from a department store worth about $125. She explained that at that time "anything [stolen] over a hundred dollars was a felony. Me being so young, I was stupid. I was scared, and I didn't go to court . . . so by me not going to court, they charged me." The second conviction was after she used her car when responding to threats from her partner's "side chick." Lola explained that the woman he was cheating with was

> talking about she's going to blow up my house with my kids in it! She needs to know you're not going to tell nobody no stuff like that! . . . The next thing I know . . . I was sideswiping [their car with my car] . . . Then people were . . . literally telling their kids, "Get up on the sidewalk! Get on the sidewalk!" because I was just going crazy in this little court . . . I was just so angry . . . he was with someone else that . . . said she was going to blow up my house with my kids in there. Like that's all I have is my kids . . . I went crazy. I just went crazy!

The way she felt about herself in relation to those she loved was a large part of the collateral damage of her systems involvement. Now Lola's elderly mother needed in-home care and Lola assumed she would be the person to do it; however, the in-home care agency initially refused Lola's request to care for her mother because of her criminal record. Lola cried as she explained the shame involved in maneuvering through the official process:

> The only way I got [the in-home care designation] was because [my mother's] worker said, "Look, this is her daughter. She's not going to hurt her."

So, they said, "Okay, we've got a paper sheet to fill out, and we need her mother to fill it out too, so that we know that she knows she has a felony and that she agrees to work with her." You know, this is embarrassing. Your own mom? You've got to get a paper for your mom to fill out to take care of her?!

Lola's mother assured her that she would leave her home to Lola after she passed away, hoping that would ease her shame and embarrassment. Lola cried as she shared how much she would miss her mother. She also knew she would not be able to keep the home. The homeowners' association had a rule against people with felony convictions owning homes in the subdivision. Then there was the daily reminder that Lola could not earn an income that would make her an equal financial partner with her husband:

> I would love to meet him halfway. I just can't get a good job . . . It's so embarrassing. Like, "Oh, you have a record. We can't hire you." You know, even like I was trying to be a Lyft driver or an Uber driver just to make some extra money. You can't . . . He makes 30 dollars an hour, and I'm over here making 12-something an hour, and I have to work [another job] to make 16 dollars to make them both feel like something.

She felt ashamed and powerless. "It's just every day you wake up and you have that tarnished name," she explained. She would do anything to change that: "If there's any way I can work through this and I've got to spend money, I'm willing to do whatever. If I have to work four jobs, three jobs, whatever. If it's money . . . then I'll work as hard as I can to get this off. If I have to pay an attorney to help me get some of this stuff off, that's what I have to do because that's the only thing that's holding me back."

But there was nothing she could do. In the state where she was convicted, expungement was not an option for people who had more than one felony. That policy affected the way she felt about herself:

> My life would be so much better if I didn't have that black cloud over me, that background. My life would be so much different. I think I would love myself more if I didn't have that. I know I would. I'm just so hard on myself because I know this is something that I created. No one else . . . It was my choice, and I made some horrible choices. I chose to fight back when I should have just left the situation, so now I'm paying for it.

Lola felt she had betrayed herself. Her indelible criminal record made sure she remained in a state of self-blame, shame, and embarrassment. In any other case, the inability to get a job and own a home in a particular neighborhood would constitute illegal forms of discrimination

(Miller and Stuart, 2017). But for these women, it was state-sanctioned and seemingly encouraged. Their criminal records cancelled out their complicated human experience, leaving them reliant on the goodwill of others.

### Financial and Social Capital: Regina

The impact criminal convictions had on the lives of low-income women of diverse identities, as well as how they described the inaccessibility of expungement, sharply contrasted with Regina's experiences. When I asked Regina if she had applied to have her conviction expunged she paused and looked at me as if she had never thought about it before. Then she slowly explained, "I could have gone back and gone through the process of having it expunged. I never have because I really have not really felt like it was ever going to affect my life because it was so ridiculous. There was no substance. . . . It was a joke. . . . I've moved on with my life." Regina had moved on with her life because she could. She had resources that gave her options the other women did not have (see chapter 1). Aside from temporary embarrassment and a criminal record, her privilege and access to resources meant the conviction did not affect Regina's income, reputation, or life.

### "Ladies be careful": Sheniqua

When considering the effect that convictions can have on women's lives after probation, it is important to also consider that day in and day out these women navigated intimate harm. Sheniqua's story is a painful reminder of this. Sheniqua skillfully remained off Officer Rigor's radar (see chapter 1). She told her story in the AVI-G among the women she felt loved her (see chapter 4), finished probation, and managed to pay the AVI-A fees (see chapter 3). At our last contact Sheniqua was moving forward with her intention "to get myself together." But I was devastated to learn months later that early one morning she was killed by her partner. Abby, who was still in the AVI-G at the time of Sheniqua's death, was one of her fellow group members. Abby explained that Sheniqua "had just graduated from [the AVI-G], and her girlfriend had shot and killed her while they were sitting in the car. It wasn't the girl for the reason she had to take [AVI]. It was a new girlfriend." The week following Sheniqua's death the AVI-G cofacilitator initiated a discussion to both process Sheniqua's passing and point out the danger inherent in

Sheniqua's story. According to Abby, the cofacilitator explained the matter as follows: "That's why I keep telling you ladies be careful. Yes, you're here for using violence in a relationship, but that doesn't mean it's ever not been done to you or doesn't mean that it can't not be done to you."

Court records show that Sheniqua's partner went to prison for murdering her. Of course, we will never know her motivation or their relationship dynamic. Sheniqua worried about being misread and then mistreated by those in the legal system because of what she described as her "Black big boy dyke" appearance and identity. Her outward presentation belied her history of having endured harm from parents and partners. May her memory live on in efforts to intervene in people's lives beyond the "victim-offender binary"—toward the more complicated human experience of, for some, having both harmed and been harmed by others, and always being deserving of supportive systems responses rather than relentless CLS-sanctioned punishment. Perhaps such a view will provide the hope of living another day free from violence.

## SUMMARY AND REFLECTIONS

This chapter demonstrates how some women found comfort in connection with each other after their time in AVI-G was over. They cultivated these connections for weeks or even years by creating and strategically using the "free space" (Evans and Boyte, 1992) in the parking lot and during shared rides. Their experiences encourage closer consideration of the power of informal, voluntary relationships among systems-involved people to promote healing, repair their breakage, and find ways forward. Their stories also illuminate how important the right to self-determination is in choosing *not* to be in contact with others outside of group. These women also seemed to be less likely to participate in this research, a limitation of the findings.

A view of the women's lives years later brings the systems-inflicted breakage of community-based carceral consequences into sharper focus. For low-income women lacking diverse social networks, the very idea of applying for, let alone obtaining, expungement was out of reach. To balance this inaccessibility with the need to earn an income, some women moved away, many hoped for the goodwill of strangers, and others resigned themselves to focusing on daily challenges that felt more within their control. For low-income women with criminal convictions there was no life free from carceral citizenship (see National Inventory of Collateral Consequences of Conviction, n.d.). Their experiences remind me of how Sissy described the routine abuse and coercive control from her child's father—it was "like furniture." In other words, it was always there; they had to maneuver around it, but they couldn't waste their time thinking too much about it because, as RyAnn so aptly put it, "life went on life-ing." There was neither the time nor the energy for this to be their primary focus. For diverse low-income women who lacked extensive social networks, their criminal records became part of this "furniture," which was ultimately the risk, or, in Sheniqua's case, the reality, of killing a partner or dying at the hands of the one they loved.

# CHAPTER 6

# A Call to Action

"THEY HAVEN'T LIVED THE LIFE THAT THEY'RE
TRYING TO REGULATE."
—TYRA

Although the women came to systems feeling *heartbroken* or *at their breaking point,* they felt further broken by what Sage, for example, referred to as the "thing on top of thing"—namely, the CLS, CPS, and AVI-A contact, which was excessively punitive, retraumatizing, and financially devastating. Their detailed accounts demonstrate that formal systems meant to address harm became complicit in causing harm, often replicating the abuse they experienced in their intimate relationships. But the women also found and created avenues toward healing and repair: a probation officer with a holistically responsive supervision style, a CPS caseworker who provided what Tyra called "the whole layout," and AVI-G facilitated connections. This chapter is a general call to action for practitioners, policymakers, and researchers involved in the lives of women who have survived and caused harm. However, in this call I specifically speak to practitioners.[1] This call to action builds on women's accounts—urging practitioners to work beyond the victim-offender binary—by (1) expanding the early battered women's movement's vision for continued social change, and (2) guiding systems actors in promoting healing and repair. Answering this call by bridging macro and micro approaches is fundamental to meeting the needs of those in the community whose voices are otherwise muted or ignored.

## 1. EXPANDING THE EARLY BATTERED WOMEN'S MOVEMENT'S VISION

First-generation battered women's movement activists put the issue of men's violence against women on the US political agenda and shaped life-saving interventions. They challenged the lack of a legal system response to domestic violence in ways that saved lives, but also had unintended consequences. Activists from diverse backgrounds continue to expand on this early work by meeting the needs of Black women, Indigenous women, women of color, people who are disabled, those without US citizenship documentation, new immigrants, and LGBTQIA+ people, as well as by creating interventions for those who have harmed their partners.[2] Thus, the movement continues to self-correct, learn from its mistakes, and reinvent itself (Arnold and Ake, 2013). It is time for practitioners to simultaneously work toward macro and micro change that will intentionally untether AVI services from the harm meted out by the CLS and CPS.[3] Macro change will involve practitioners engaging a view beyond the victim-offender binary, reflexivity, playing an active role in social change, using language that accurately reflects systems-involved people's experiences, and challenging current federal funding priorities.

### A View Beyond the Victim-Offender Binary

The early battered women's movement supported women made vulnerable by men's violence against them, with the core principles of promoting women's safety and right to self-determination and holding men accountable for the harm. *Broken* demonstrates that although this victim-offender binary helped many, it is fraught with limitations that cause further harm. This call to action urges practitioners to intentionally support women of diverse identities who are affected by probation, CPS, and AVI through innovative interventions and broad social change efforts.[4] This intentional focus recognizes that carceral interventions in communities exist on what law professor Fiona Doherty (2016) refers to as a "continuum of excessive penal control", similar to the prison-industrial complex (Richie, 2012). These macro and micro interventions will involve the following:

- Partnering with social justice movements to focus on tangible social change outcomes including healthcare, community safety, living-wage employment, low- and no-cost childcare, and affordable housing.

- Advocating for "Ban the Box" efforts to promote fair hiring practices, in tandem with expungement-focused advocacy and critical examination of how charges, as well as misdemeanor convictions, can also mean loss of employment.[5]
- Linking eradication of interpersonal domestic and sexual violence to ending violence globally.[6]
- Working to end domestic and sexual violence through broad, coordinated community responses that center the voices of those affected in collaboration with community-based advocates and activists.[7]
- Foregrounding research, analysis, and interventions informed by queer theory, intersectional feminism, and critical race theory.[8]
- Recognizing that people's intersecting identities, such as those having to do with disability, class, race, income, gender, sex, age, and national origin, are inextricably linked to how they experience intimate and institutional power.
- Challenging wrongful arrest of the *heartbroken* and advocating for those misidentified as "offenders."[9]
- Addressing the harm experienced and caused by women *at their breaking point* by incorporating a human rights framework focused on just processes and positive outcomes.[10]
- Implementing trauma-informed and holistically responsive practices across systems.
- Proactively discussing and addressing women's use of nonfatal, non-self-defensive force in traditional survivor-centered settings. This will provide opportunities to address any force the women are currently using and preemptively raise awareness of the systems involvement and injury that can result.
- Developing interventions outside the CLS through grassroots collaborations that promote positive public health outcomes.[11]
- Defining accountability as centering healing, hope, and broad transformation for people who have caused harm and clearly differentiating that focus from their CLS and CPS punishment.[12]
- Holding institutions that intervene in systems-involved people's lives responsible for embracing cultures, practices, and policies that promote, rather than undermine, efforts toward individual and community healing and repair.

- Addressing co-occurring mental health diagnoses and substance use challenges in ways that consider both as matters of health and well-being rather than reasons for criminalization.

### Engaging Reflexivity

Reflexivity is the process of examining one's own belief system and how it influences one's work. Working beyond the victim-offender binary requires practitioners to regularly reflect on our personal feelings, judgements, experiences, and motives. This self-reflection requires us to humbly recognize that, as human beings, we all exist on the same spectrum of being harmed and causing harm. Therefore, all of us must regularly and deeply examine our belief systems, relationships, and actions in a collective effort to then address harm, and ultimately, contribute to freedom from harm. By engaging in reflexivity we challenge our judgments and perceptions through deep listening that facilitates empathy, potentially mitigating harm we may cause others. Reflexivity also facilitates curiosity about ourselves and others. As the Bail Project's founder Robin Steinberg (2023) points out, "curiosity is the precondition for compassion" (p. 198); thus, empathy, curiosity, *and* compassion are fundamental to evolving our notion of justice.[13]

### Asserting Our Role

Expanding the early battered women's movement's vision will require practitioners who receive women court-ordered to AVI to proactively assert their role as working alongside—rather than within—these systems. Too often AVIs, for example, are bound to the carceral system without question or consideration. For example, AVI policies often require participants to provide a police report to prove or disprove their account. Rather than developing AVIs based on systems' requests, I encourage practitioners to proactively develop services based on the experiences and needs of systems-involved people (see United Nations, 2022). In addition, there must be a concerted effort to "call in" rather than "call out" (Ross, 2016) systems partners in ways that center the larger goal of holistically meeting peoples' needs. Through these efforts practitioners will, for example, recognize when participants are overburdened with multiple systems referrals, and make necessary adjustments. These efforts will be reminiscent of voluntarily assembled consciousness-raising groups, which shaped early transformative social justice movements that spur vicarious healing.[14]

### Practitioner Language

The language practitioners use when speaking to or about systems-involved people should simultaneously reflect the experiences of those served and promote the practitioners' role beyond the carceral system. Too often practitioners who work outside the legal system use CLS language—for example, referring to someone as a "victim," "offender," "probationer," or "primary aggressor"—which places people in carceral-focused categories and likely misrepresents the complexity of their experiences (see Burk, 2004). Not only does CLS language lack the necessary complexity to capture the human experience; it risks alienating systems-involved people. Furthermore, using CLS language undermines practitioner efforts to assert their role beyond the carceral system. Practitioner language will instead strive to represent the experiences of women who are systems-involved. A first step is to ask people what language feels most accurate and helpful, and listen to and implement their feedback. Building a vocabulary grounded in the experiences of those whose lives practitioners enter—separate from that dictated by the carceral system—is a necessary, ongoing process.[15]

### Funding

The Violence Against Women Act (VAWA) codified the victim-offender binary in federal funding priorities for law enforcement and systems-identified survivors.[16] While activists and practitioners often critique VAWA funding priorities for preferencing the CLS (Goodmark, 2012, 2022; Messing et al. 2015), few consider the lack of financial support for community-based agencies serving systems-identified "offenders." Meeting the needs of people who have both survived *and* caused harm will require the redistribution of funds from the CLS to local agencies that provide a range of services. This would build financial capacity across families and communities. The +SHIFT Program (Larance et al., 2019a) in Victoria, Australia, for example, receives state government funding for a wide range of community-based services for women with survivorship histories brought to systems attention for causing harm (Family Safety Victoria, 2021). In addition, some US AVIs have secured Victims of Crime Act funds by documenting group members' domestic violence survivorship. Others have received foundation grants and funding from their community's United Way, a local fundraising affiliate. Furthermore, funding should be available for "promising practices" rather than a primary focus on "evidence-based" interventions to encourage innovation and creativity through building alliances between practitioners and people made vulnerable by their marginalized identities.[17]

## 2. GUIDING SYSTEMS ACTORS IN HEALING AND REPAIRING THE BREAKAGE

Practitioners are situated in people's lives in ways that can exacerbate systems-inflicted breakage or mitigate the harm. Micro change efforts to work beyond the victim-offender binary will require practitioners to actively support systems-involved women.[18] All attempts to be aware of the potential for causing further breakage, and intervening in that process, are fundamental to facilitating positive change.

In light of the breakage the women in this book experienced early in their lives and through systems contact, I suggest the powerful metaphor of Kintsugi pottery. In Kintsugi, when a piece of pottery breaks, rather than discarding it, the potter mends it with precious metal. The result is a pot that is beautiful *because* of the breakage and visible repair. Practitioners have the opportunity to facilitate Kintsugi-style healing and repair by advising probation officers, CPS caseworkers, and AVI providers in their ongoing efforts to improve social justice-focused, client-centered services. An essential aspect of micro practice is context. As Regina points out, "You've . . . got to look at things on a case-by-case basis." I encourage practitioners to consider the suggestions below within the context of the communities they serve.

### Probation

Probation officers using a punitive, rigorous approach to supervision anticipate and, in some cases, promote failure for women already marginalized by ableism, racism, classism, sexism, homophobia, and poverty. Probation can further compromise people's safety and well-being. When probation officers interact with people under their supervision they are, by association, interacting with their extended networks. Thus, probation officers who harm people on probation are harming the community, implicitly giving permission for those on probation to do the same. Probation has the potential to be supportive, with the aim of ending all CLS involvement. This will require dramatic culture change and a range of practices.

*Supervisory style and discretionary toolkits.* Practitioners must proactively educate women about probation, a probation officer's role in their lives, and the inherent power imbalance that places them at risk of institutional harm. This information will empower women to tailor their expectations, as well as their body language, words, and tone during probation interactions. Understanding the reporting relationship dynamics can contribute to women's positive mental health and well-being.

A holistically responsive probation supervisory style encourages accessibility, kindness, and flexibility, provides explicit support and sharing of resources tailored to each person's diverse needs, and attends to people's mental and physical well-being as well as the social factors that may undermine both. Probation can be an avenue toward success for women across a range of different identities and needs; it includes increased access to community resources. In contrast, probation officers using strict monitoring methods may be inadvertently colluding with abusive partners and undermining women's capacity to heal and move forward. To facilitate success, probation officers need a contextual understanding of women's challenges. Open-ended initial and year-end interview questions, for example, could help officers tailor probation to their needs (see Morash, 2010 for suggested questions).

Probation departments should inform officers that how they communicate with those on their caseloads matters. For example, research has linked recidivism to more punitive supervisory styles (Morash et al., 2016; Morash et al., 2019), while women's belief that they will find employment, and success in doing so, are linked to officers using communication styles that promote openness and participation in decision-making (Roddy and Morash, 2020).

Technology and groupwork may reduce the emotion work involved in in-person probation reporting. For example, during the global COVID-19 pandemic, many probation departments used virtual reporting. An in-person option is probation group reporting (Henderson and Avalon, 2018), which may simultaneously improve the reporting experience and facilitate meaningful connections between diverse systems-involved women. Probation group reporting—in tandem with vouchers for childcare, transportation, and food—could help low-income women across a range of different identities end their probation contact. It could also facilitate the positive social interactions known to promote positive mental health among women on probation (Malcome et al., 2019). Women searching for employment could also use the transportation vouchers to bridge a "spatial mismatch" (Roddy et al., 2022) between where the jobs are and where they live, which often poses a barrier to employment for low-income women.

*Drug and alcohol testing.* The women joked that simply calling in to learn whether or not they had to arrive within the next eight hours to test made them want to use substances. The process was confusing, time intensive, costly, traumatizing, and made the women feel set up to fail. A positive test result could mean further sanctions, including additional fees and jail time, and disproportionately affected low-income women. A probation-wide culture shift will demand that drug and alcohol testing *not* be routine. Drug and alcohol testing should only be considered if it is reasonably related to the offense *and* the probation department is committed to a therapeutic approach in coordination with skilled treatment counselors for those with addiction issues. This change will be significant. For example, available guidelines on probation drug testing were last updated more than three decades ago (see American Probation and Parole Association, 1991). Experts in addiction medicine (Jarvis et al., 2017; Rastegar and Fingerhood, 2020; Reichert, 2020; Reichert, Weisner, and Otto, 2020) recommend that drug testing for people with addiction histories, or those at risk of addiction, be used in recovery settings rather than as punishment. Furthermore, referrals to Alcoholics Anonymous should not be an instrument of punishment (Rastegar and Fingerhood, 2020).

*Fines, fees, and costs.* Low-income women had difficulty complying with their court-ordered financial obligations. Evidence suggests that low-income people's inability to pay these fines, rather than a new offense, may result in further legal systems involvement and possibly referrals to a collection agency (Pager et al., 2022). Practitioners should make efforts to eliminate them.

*Turnover and recordkeeping changes.* The women bore the burden of probation's bureaucratic failures in ways that drained them of money and time and undermined their mental and physical health. The system must make improvements in documentation and streamline staff changes. The women recognized the irony involved in the fact that although probation was meant to hold them accountable, no one was holding probation accountable. Judges should expect probation officers and departments to consider women's histories as well as their current challenges. Probation-involved people must have accessible, safe avenues to notify judges if their probation officers are being unreasonable or abusive or both. Without transparency, low-income women have no hope of managing these deficits. Indeed, the harm caused in these instances begs the question: "What is probation an alternative to—and for whom" (Phelps, 2020, p. 274)?

## CPS Caseworkers

Although each woman's CPS contact was situation-specific, CPS caseworkers employed a failure to protect ideology across interactions. This ideology cast the women as "failed" mothers because of their domestic violence survivorship, substance use, and mental illness histories. Furthermore, police presence during CPS interactions emboldened caseworkers, leaving the women feeling "tricked and betrayed," as Tyra put it. Unraveling this ideology and these practices will involve significant CPS culture change that centers an awareness of relationship-specific coercive control and how CPS workers' responses to it may be entrenched in racism, classism, sexism, and homophobia. Furthermore, CPS caseworkers and family court judges could often benefit from training about how "lying" or "resistance" may be protective strategies of mothers struggling to parent in the midst of their own challenges and cultural expectations regarding mothering and motherhood. Thus, rather than being "liars" or "resistant," CPS-involved women are utilizing their limited discretion in the midst of carceral power. Therefore, this ideological unraveling for CPS caseworkers will entail collaboration with AVI practitioners that centers the understanding that protecting children also means supporting their mothers. Steps forward require practitioners to proactively educate CPS-involved women about caseworkers' roles in their lives and the inherent power imbalance that places them at risk of institutional harm. This information will empower them to tailor their behavior and expectations during interactions, contributing to their positive mental and physical health. The points that follow include Tyra's suggestions for CPS caseworkers as well as empirically based policy recommendations.

*Having faith and listening.* Providing caseworkers implicit racial bias training can assist them in recognizing their own challenges while meeting people where they are (see, e.g., Center for the Study on Social Policy, 2019). Likewise, motivational interviewing skills are necessary tools for caseworkers dedicated to guiding CPS-involved families toward community resources as well as reunification (Children's Bureau, 2017). Furthermore, the Safe and Together Model (Humphreys et al., 2018; Safe and Together Institute, n.d.) provides a framework for CPS caseworkers to more effectively respond to people affected by domestic violence. It also promotes a deeper understanding of mothers who are the "nonoffending" parent by encouraging caseworkers to partner with them and intervene with abusive fathers.

*Meaningful referrals.* The women in *Broken* experienced referrals as random, unhelpful, punitive, and a waste of time. To change this dynamic, CPS caseworkers must be transparent about their reasons for making each referral, expected benefits, completion timeline, and support for achieving completion. Providing resources like transportation and childcare are integral to the women's success. Tyra and Lily, for example, emphasized the importance of their Parent Partner (Parenting Matters, n.d.), a strengths-based program that employs parents who have successfully navigated CPS to mentor CPS-involved families.

*"The whole layout."* Caseworkers should provide CPS-involved families with clear expectations and a time frame for anticipated reunification. This includes upfront explanations about why caseworkers may change roles in women's lives, what their new roles are, and how long they anticipate being in that role. From Tyra's perspective, "the whole layout" includes communicating (1) CPS's definition of the problem, (2) the way she needs to correct it, (3) the timeframe for correction, and (4) the consequences she will encounter if she does not correct it within the established timeframe. With this information Tyra felt better equipped to meet CPS caseworker expectations and work toward reunification, reducing her feelings of being "set up to fail."

*Documentation.* All CPS caseworker case notes, emails, and informal written communications shape how those monitoring CPS-involved caregivers view their case, often for years. Caseworkers who are less familiar with domestic violence may not recognize coercively controlling behaviors when reading documentation they receive about ongoing cases. Moreover, caseworkers may not recognize the protective strategies of mothers who are navigating abusive partners' tactics. To address documentation challenges, the Safe and Together Model's (Humphreys et al., 2018) case reading practice and training intervention may be helpful. These tools can be used to train CPS caseworkers in becoming more effective in their case note production and analysis. They can become more familiar with coercive control as a protective strategy and learn how to effectively document it.

*Policy recommendations.* Policy reform will offer structural protections against the failure to protect ideology in CPS practices. Such protections are evident in policy configurations used in Iowa and Oregon, which offer examples of unconditional prohibitions on CPS identifying survivors of domestic violence based on the harm they have endured in their intimate relationships (Victor et al., 2021).

### Antiviolence Intervention

As *Broken* has shown, AVI can cause harm to low-income court-ordered women of diverse identities. Most women in this project could not afford the group session fees, had limited access to transportation, lacked the necessary childcare to attend group, and experienced negative mental and physical health implications. Because of their court orders, they also risked jail time and further financial and social penalties for noncompliance. Family court–ordered women who struggled to attend the groups risked additional sanctions that affected their ability to reunite with their children. Thus, court ordering already marginalized women to AVI risks weaponizing their circumstances against them.

Women who are *heartbroken* as well as those *at their breaking point* need a viable way forward that enables them to exist beyond the carceral system, while simultaneously working alongside the system. For the former it means practitioners intervening and advocating for them and for systems change in ways that ensure they will not become systems-identified offenders. For the latter, it involves supportive services, beyond the carceral system, that promote their healing and well-being while also addressing the harm caused. The way forward is fraught with contradictions. For example, the legal system requires court-ordered women to provide proof of AVI contact. Without that proof, the women risk extensive jail time, and perhaps extended time on probation and additional fines. CPS-involved women risk not being reunited with their children. But by deciding to provide proof of AVI contact, AVI practitioners risk being complicit in systems-inflicted harm. Ways to mitigate the harm within an AVI setting include considerations for (1) support and intervention and (2) battering intervention standards.

## Support and Intervention

Practitioners can facilitate Kintsugi-style healing and repair in multiple ways that include attention to intersectionality and coercive control, assessment, contact with referring entities, AVI-Gs, access to services, curricula, and promising practices:

*(A) Intersectionality and coercive control.* Because gender-responsive and culturally specific interventions can be misused in ways that are ableist, sexist, racist, classist, and homophobic—inadvertently legitimizing stereotypes (McCorkel, 2013)—working beyond the victim-offender binary requires an intersectional understanding of individual lived experiences. This understanding must engage humility that centers learning from people about how their race, gender, sexuality, class, income, abilities, and other identities and social locations shape who they are and how they experience the carceral system. Unfortunately, stereotypes of cisgender heterosexual white femininity too often decentralize the experiences of socially marginalized people. For example, criminologist Hillary Potter (2008) points out that Black women fight back against their abusive partners at greater rates than white women, some seeing themselves as "dynamic resisters." Furthermore, Black women are often pathologized or misdiagnosed with personality disorders (DeGenna and Feske, 2013) rather than understood through the lens of structural oppression. Likewise, identity and entitlement abuse (see Donovan and Barnes, 2020) of or by LGBTQIA+ people is often misunderstood, overlooked, or unassessed. Suzie, for example, seemed to be a risk to her partner but she successfully evaded the police and prosecution by the law. In contrast, Sheniqua worried how her physical appearance would shape punitive system responses, but she was murdered by her partner. Disabled women, like Abby, may feel powerless in making changes to services ill-suited to their needs. A person's intersectional identities influence their power in relationships, as well as the systems-inflicted harm that may follow from their interactions with systems' actors.

Too often practitioners have narrow ideas of what domestic violence entails. They may focus entirely on the physical harm without recognizing who holds the coercive power in the relationship and the broad social consequences of that power. Identifying relationship-specific coercive control is a challenging process that may rely more on situational and organizational contexts and temporality than practitioner skill (Barlow et al., 2019; Brennan et al., 2019; Robinson et al., 2018). In this way, engaging an intersectional lens and expanding our understanding of intimate harm have the capacity to promote positive mental and physical health outcomes across settings.

*(B) Assessment.* The initial AVI intake assessment is an opportunity to provide relevant support and community resources for *the heartbroken* and those *at their breaking point.* An intake assessment provides AVI practitioners with the necessary information to reroute women wrongfully arrested (*the heartbroken*) to the relevant entities on a voluntary basis. For example, the harm caused to women like Essence who survived strangulation during the incident that resulted in their wrongful arrest and then AVI referral may remain invisible to police. Often, they have children with the person who strangled them; their abusive partner likely avoided arrest and, in addition, has a history of sexually abusing them (Messing et al., 2018). Black women are at a higher risk of attempted strangulation, being strangled more frequently, and being killed by strangulation more often than white women (Messing et al., 2018). A woman who has been strangled can suffer long-term fear, post-traumatic stress disorder, neurological damage, or miscarriage, and is seven times more likely than a woman who has not been strangled to be killed by her partner (Campbell et al., 2007; Monahan et al., 2022). Therefore, among a range of issues, it is essential that practitioners screen for a history of strangulation (e.g., in the cases of Olivia and Valerie), make necessary referrals, and provide resources (see Beverly, 2020).

A thorough initial intake assessment also provides practitioners with the necessary information to best serve the personal, relationship, and systemic needs of women who have caused harm and often have domestic and sexual violence survivorship histories (those *at their breaking point*). An assessment should holistically explore a woman's relationship experiences rather than solely focus on whether or not she is a victim or an offender. If a woman's legal case has not yet been adjudicated, however, it is important that AVI practitioners especially take care in how they speak about her, document her case, and support her *lack* of disclosure as institutional responses to her disclosures may impede efforts to seek justice (National Clearinghouse for the Defense of Battered Women, 2001; Pence et al., 2011). A framework for holistic assessment will engage critical context (Larance, 2021; Larance et al., 2022) at the time of initial assessment and throughout services by: (1) grounding the intake and intervention process in listening to what women have to say, and responding empathically with resources; (2) learning from women how their multiple identities shape their interpersonal interactions and institutional experiences; (3) considering their motivation and intent if they describe using harmful actions, as well as the impact of those actions, particularly incidents that may have taken place after the referring incident; and (4) gathering and documenting longitudinal relationship histories that illuminate how the women may have also experienced harm.

Focusing on context, as well as engaging in an assessment of fear, will guide necessary safety and support planning and provide women with supportive resources. When assessing whether or not women fear their current or former partner, one should also ask about whether or not they dread their partner's presence or what they could find out about them (Larance, 2017).[19] Although questions about fear are important, they are subjective (see House, 2001). For example, often women who have survived and caused harm will not identify themselves as fearful, minimizing their risk as an adaptive coping mechanism (see Campbell et al., 2007). Therefore, disclosure of fear does not necessarily indicate their level of risk. However, also discussing dread, or a culturally appropriate term that captures this concept, is a way to understand the relationship-specific coercive control women may have endured, are still enduring, or may be using. Practitioners must realize that women with domestic and sexual violence survivorship histories often over disclose what they perceive themselves to have done wrong in their relationship. Furthermore, they often do not initially disclose the harm they have endured.

Following the initial intake assessment, AVI practitioners must engage in an ongoing assessment that identifies the spectrum of harm in women's lives (Kertesz et al., 2021; Larance, 2006). Practitioners need to also pay close attention to the language used in documentation (e.g., assessment forms and case notes) and how confidential information is stored (Larance and Kertesz, 2023). These are pressing issues for consistent skilled supervision.

*(C) Referrer contact.* Practitioners should communicate with those who refer women (e.g., probation officers, CPS caseworkers, therapists)

to AVIs in ways that educate the referrers and promote women's autonomy and family safety. The first contact with a referral source may be an ideal time to point out that the AVI provider's larger goal is likely the same as the referrer's goal (e.g., ending domestic violence), but their roles in that process may be very different (e.g., the practitioner provides healing and awareness of nonforceful behaviors; probation officers and CPS caseworkers monitor compliance).

Each engagement with referrers is also an opportunity for AVI practitioners to consider how the practitioner-referrer relationship reflects the integrity of the services provided without causing further harm to those referred. For example, when referrers request information about women's disclosures during the AVI-G, inform them that the group space is where the practitioners facilitate healing and repair and promote an awareness of viable options to using force. The group space is also a place where women can confidentially explore their ideas and experiences.[20] Typically, probation officers' and CPS caseworkers' inquiries stem from their role in reporting on the women's change process. Therefore, sharing Larance and Rousson's (2016) Conceptual Model of the Change Process, which details how women experience an AVI-G, can be used in lieu of disclosing group member interactions.

A tangible way to promote court-ordered women's autonomy and family safety is only communicating whether or not referred women have had AVI contact—not disclosing payment or in-group conversations.[21] AVI staff may relay this information in a range of ways. The method used in the research community involved entering attendance information into a password-protected online system available to probation officers and CPS caseworkers 24 hours a day, seven days a week. When an AVI staff member entered a woman's absence, the system default was to flag her as noncompliant. Although this process is used for its convenience and efficiency, problems arose when staff entered this information without, first, contacting the woman to ask about the circumstances surrounding her absence, what assistance she needed to be systems compliant, and then making informed decisions about how to support her, proceed with documentation, and communicate with the referrer. A common justification for not contacting her before entering her absence is that doing so would be collusion with an offender; therefore, to do this would be to not hold her accountable. However, there are a range of reasons why a woman may miss group—for example, her childcare provider may cancel at the last minute, or her partner may intentionally sabotage her attendance (see Larance and Rousson, 2016;

Scaia, 2017). Therefore, practitioners must consider how automated agency practices may be colluding with the CLS and CPS—and, by extension, abusive partners. Practitioners working beyond the binary will consistently aim to interrupt and avoid that collusion.

At any given time, AVI practitioners working with court-ordered clients are in the difficult position of acting as agents of social control or social change. Working toward social change—with women currently under social control—demands that practitioners engage a trauma-informed approach to their perception of and reporting about court-ordered women's AVI-G participation. Supporting systems-involved women means recognizing that they may be justifiably concerned about disclosing relationship details in a monitored space. Too often practitioners refer to women who are less verbal in group as resistant or unmotivated. Rather than being resistant, women court ordered to AVIs are utilizing their limited personal discretion to navigate institutional power. While practitioners across settings often have broad discretion in how they wield power, women court ordered to services are at their mercy with no way of knowing how their disclosures may be used against them. Women who do not verbally share during the group process may be engaging silence to protect themselves and their families. Rather than demonstrating a lack of motivation, group member silence often signals they are differently motivated, enduring an unfamiliar system of punishment. Considering what counts as participation also demands a deeper understanding of and respect for how people from different cultures and family backgrounds—particularly those with survivorship histories—experience group dynamics. Thus, AVI practitioners requiring specific verbal disclosures for documented CLS or CPS compliance may be privileging a (re)traumatizing dominant framework for participation that risks further marginalizing people.

*(D) AVI-Gs.* Battering Intervention Programs (BIP) were created to address the gendered socialization of cisgender heterosexual men and their abuse against cisgender heterosexual women. Women who have survived and caused harm should not be included in BIPs, described as being in BIPs, or be considered BIP group members (Dasgupta, 2002; Harasim-Pieper, 2011; Kertesz, Humphreys and Larance, 2021). Effective AVI for women is distinctly different from traditional BIPs. Instead, interventions must be grounded in an understanding of contextual, historical, social, and political factors that shape socialization across identities and life experiences. Program staff must continually assess for

women's use of self-defense in the referring incident, as well as historically, and advocate for them accordingly.

Likewise, practitioners must support women from minoritized communities in ways that attend to their specific needs. For example, there is always the risk that women in same-sex relationships who are court ordered to groups with women in heterosexual relationships may feel alienated by a dominant heteronormative discourse that often shapes group content (Ristock, 2001). Referred individuals should therefore be consulted about whether or not they feel comfortable in groups with heterosexual women and then be offered the option of individual sessions. Implementing approaches informed by minority stress theory (Alessi, 2014) can also contribute to the focus on healing and repair. One should also consider how women being similarly situated in their lives, regardless of their identities, may promote what Rosemary called "a common bond," one that could even, Devore suggested, prevent suicide—that is, when women from a range of different identities "felt" what Sheniqua called "the love." Nonetheless, people from LGBTQIA+ communities may not only prefer but be better served by community-specific groups and resources.

In addition, trauma-informed AVI-G cofacilitation is not about urging group participants to focus on the past. Instead, it is about supporting people as they focus on the present and gradually work toward violence-free futures. If group members do decide to disclose how they have been hurt, how they have hurt others, or both, it is both possible and necessary to supportively acknowledge the spectrum of their experiences. This approach engages practitioner empathy, compassion, and reflexivity. Central to this process is an understanding of accountability that centers a woman's personal journey of integrity, rather than responsibility to referring entities. Accountability cannot be imposed; rather, it must focus on personal, interpersonal, and community healing and restoration (Asar, 2021; McLeod, 1998; Sered, 2019). Equally important, but rarely considered, is that the AVI must be accountable to group participants through transparency.

(E) Increasing access. No-cost intervention,[22] childcare, and virtual assessment and group options directly support women's court-ordered AVI access; unfortunately, however, only some programs in the United States provide no-cost AVIs.[23] Regarding childcare, allowing young children to accompany their mothers into the AVI-G should be an option. Providing childcare vouchers for those attending in-person groups and access to virtual assessment and groups are also alternatives. The global COVID-19 pandemic demonstrated that virtual groups promote accessibility. Although there are safety considerations (Larance and Scaia, 2020), virtual assessment and group options can reduce the expenditure of time, money, and energy for women juggling multiple court-ordered obligations while also increasing accessibility.

AVI's harmful aspects for low-income court-ordered women should be considered alongside the experiences of women who voluntarily participate to meet their own goals. Joy and Marcella used interactions in the AVI-G to explore their behavior; Sissy used it to navigate the CLS while also receiving support and practical guidance; and Suzie used her AVI contact as an avenue toward self-discovery and as proof for her wife that she was committed to changing her behavior. The women's strategic AVI use provides a glimpse of how antiviolence intervention can effectively and autonomously operate outside court orders.

Providing women access to information and community contacts during group sessions can be a powerful experience. If group members agree and confidentiality is maintained, practitioners can invite community members with specific expertise to share information during the first or last few minutes of an AVI-G—for example, a trusted defense attorney answering women's general legal questions, a banker sharing budgeting and financial tips, and a yoga practitioner guiding a brief relaxation technique. All can be avenues toward healing and repair.

*(F) Curricula and promising practices.* There are a range of published curricula and guiding frameworks informed by the lived experiences of women who have survived and caused harm that hold promise in contextually addressing women's use of force in community-based settings (see Battered Women's Justice Project, 2020; Center for Court Innovation, 2021; Harasim-Piper, 2011; House, 2001; Kertesz et al., 2021; Larance et al., 2009; Larance et al., 2019a; Mulvaney, 2022; Pence et al., 2011; Van Dieten et al., 2014). Practitioners can learn from these resources and use them to create agency-specific curricula informed by and tailored to the needs of group participants in the agency's specific geographic and social location. Effective and supportive AVIs will engage people through content that promotes healing and, for women resorting to non-self-defensive nonfatal force, alternatives to those actions. They will also engage the larger community in broad social change work.

Critically, *Broken* reveals that systems-involved women's opportunities to share their stories, be heard, listen to others' stories, and be believed were the most beneficial aspects of their AVI contact and, for many, their carceral involvement. Therefore, although the curriculum is important, it is an application of philosophy and tools. Group cofacilitators from a range of different identities who are well-versed in the intersectional dynamics of coercive control and anti-oppressive practices, as well as group cofacilitation skills, and reflexive about their own journeys can support women in ending their isolation, forming connections, and increasing their awareness of viable alternatives. For some women, those AVI-G connections made interactions outside the group possible. Their bonds beyond a monitored space can sustain them in ways that agency contact alone may not.

### Battering Intervention Standards

Over the past 30 years, there has been an effort to standardize practice interventions for men court ordered to BIPs for abusing women, with a range of outcomes (Boal and Mankowski, 2014). As of 2020, 45 states had some form of battering intervention standards (www.biscmi.org; BISC-MI, n.d.). Over the last 15 years there has been a push to include services for all people who have caused harm in these standards. This approach is problematic, as cisgender heterosexual women of diverse identities and people from LGBTQIA+ communities often use force in different contexts and for different reasons, with very different outcomes. Standardizing interventions based on those originally designed for heterosexual cisgender men is misguided. State standards striving to incorporate parameters for work with people from diverse populations must do so in ways that attend to different lived experiences across multiple identities and evolve with current research and anti-oppressive grassroots practices (Kernsmith and Kernsmith, 2009; Larance, 2006; Larance and Rousson, 2016; Mulvaney, 2022). What may seem necessary as a general intervention standard in one time and place and for one population may have wide-ranging unintended collateral consequences that cause harm rather than promote healing and repair.

## LOOKING AHEAD

Reflecting on the lessons in *Broken* and implications for practice, policy, and research moving forward, it is important to return to the women's words. When Tyra reflected on her journey, having finally received the support and friendship she desired, she shared,

> Now I feel like I could write a whole book, and I promise I would sing every word. I would. I'd write a book, and I'd sing every word of it. It would be a whole book of songs. That's what I tell people, too. When people be like, "Oh, you gonna tell your story?" No, I'm going to sing you my song because this is a song, my life is a song. The beginning of it is fast beat. It's higher-pitched, and it's angry, but the end of my song is slow-tempo and beautiful.

Practitioners are well-positioned to holistically support women's songs of transformation rather than stories of breakage. By centering the voices of women who, in the words of Tyra, have "lived the life," may we all work beyond binary conceptualizations of those who have caused and often survived harm and facilitate their healing and repair.

APPENDIX

# Research Methods

In 2015, after nearly two decades as a social work practitioner, I enrolled in the University of Michigan's joint doctoral program in social work and sociology. As a practitioner, I learned from hundreds of systems-involved women but I yearned to understand their lives more deeply through the lens of a practitioner-researcher. In the fall of 2016, I received University of Michigan Institutional Review Board approval (IRB) [HUM00111067] to begin my dissertation research project, "Through Her Eyes."

## RECRUITMENT

Between January 2017 and August 2019, respondents were recruited from a community-based AVI in the eastern standard time zone of the United States, where I had previously worked. An agency staff member provided past and current group members general information about the project, along with my contact information.

Thirty-eight women contacted me and scheduled interviews. Five of the thirty-eight women did not complete their scheduled interview. Four of those five women did not come to or cancel the interview. I contacted them, inquiring about their safety, but I did not receive responses. From my practice experience, I understood that their lives were chaotic, and that research might only add to that chaos (see Phoenix, 1994). One of those five women explained that the 30 dollar gift card was inadequate financial reimbursement for revisiting the trauma of her abusive relationship.[1] She was also concerned that her abusive husband would compromise the confidentiality of the interview data. The women who participated did so with the intention of being able to tell their stories. Although many of these women experienced income or housing insecurity, making the 30 dollar gift card desirable, they said that participating in the project was not

185

about the money. They wanted to tell their story and have it make a difference for others. All of them explained that throughout their interactions with police, court, probation, and CPS, they felt silenced or disbelieved or both. In contrast to those experiences, participating in this research provided the possibility of being fully heard and believed.

## LIMITATIONS

In addition to being involved with the agency-based recruitment, one respondent shared that she contacted two former group members and encouraged them to participate. Both declined. The first woman did so because she was embarrassed: she was addicted to heroin and her husband had died by suicide. The second woman did not want to revisit a relationship and a CLS experience that marked a dark period in her life. Their situations point to the need for research on the experiences of women for whom healing and repair were inaccessible. Additionally, no transgender women or nonbinary people responded to recruitment, which means their voices were left unheard in *Broken* (but please see Goodmark, 2013; Kattari et al., 2022).

## MIXED QUALITATIVE METHODS

It was my goal to gather data that would best bring attention to the complexities of systems-involved women's lives, meeting them where they were rather than how they are often portrayed (see National Association of Social Workers, 2020). I therefore utilized a range of mixed qualitative methods including the following: demographic questionnaires; in-depth trauma-informed life-history interviews (Richie, 1996), some of which were semi-ethnographic; go-along interviews (Kusenbach, 2003); middle-position interviews; and detailed field notes. In addition to providing the formal contact, I had many informal conversations with women over the course of the project and in the years after. During this extensive, embodied process, I engaged in the emotional labor of a feminist social work researcher (Hochschild, 1983; Mehrotra, 2017).

### Building Rapport and the Demographic Questionnaire

I began each interview by explaining that the purpose of the project was to understand the women's journeys from their perspectives and through their words. This explanation elicited connections that were evident in the women's words and body language. For example, Becky exhaled and said, "I love it . . . If only [the CLS] could see it through my eyes!" Before each of the interviews, I engaged in what I view as trauma-informed interview practices, such as providing interviewees with an overview of what they could generally expect at the beginning, the middle, and the end of our time together. I then reminded them that they were the experts in their situations, that their stories mattered, that they could shape the interview process as they desired, and that they could end the interview at any time, for any reason, and still receive the gift card. During the interviews, I checked in with the women to make sure they still wanted to proceed, and asked them if they needed to take a break. I actively listened through my body language, tone of voice, silence, and expressions of emotion.

I then used a demographic questionnaire to guide the initial portion of the inquiry. It included information about how they self-identified, when they had AVI contact, whether they were court ordered, the status of the relationship with the other person involved in the referring incident(s), if they had had contact with domestic violence survivor support services, and their community and network support systems. Beginning the interviews in this way allowed me to simultaneously gain an overview of their circumstances and begin to build rapport.

### In-Depth Trauma-Informed Life History Interviews

Like other researchers (Miller, 2005; McCorkel, 2013; Richie, 1996; Watkins-Hayes, 2019), I created an interview guide to frame the life history interview discussions. Inquiry prompts included issues around the women's families of origin, their experiences growing up, their early relationships, the interactions that led to their systems involvement, their systems experiences, and, when applicable, what their lives after systems contact were like. I encouraged the women to tell their stories in a manner that made sense to them and I followed their lead. Rather than searching for a singular truth, I sought to understand how the women viewed and made sense of their journeys.

Interviews often included the women's tearful disclosures of how they had endured domestic and sexual violence, as well as the shame they felt for having resorted to actions in which they never imagined they would engage. Some of the women disclosed having survived sexual violence for the first time in their lives. As a result of my practice experience, I could anticipate when the women were going to disclose sexual trauma: they often paused and looked down before detailing the experience. The topic we were discussing just before their disclosure was not necessarily related to their disclosure in a way that I could always follow, but it made sense to them. Although 22 of the 33 women disclosed some form of sexual abuse, I suspect that the number of women experiencing abuse was actually higher, given the stigma associated with these disclosures.

### Semi-ethnographic Life History Interviews

I refer to 32 of the 51 trauma-informed life-history (Richie,1996) interviews as semi-ethnographic because they took place in the women's own space—that is, their home or neighborhood—rather than a university office or a reserved room in a library. My data gathering for these interviews began on my drive to their homes. This gave me firsthand knowledge of how far they likely had to travel to fulfill court obligations, often on a daily basis. Meeting where they lived also meant that I met family members and became familiar with their neighborhoods and community surroundings.

Our interactions during these interviews enabled a rich range of information-sharing and embodied observation that was rarely possible in more formal settings. The women commonly showed me visible proof of their systems-inflicted harms. For example, they retrieved piles of informal notes jotted down on legal pads or bits of paper they had taken while on probation to "cover all of the bases." They flipped through their notes, detailing how their shorthand clarified for them when and where they needed to show up and how to remember which systems actors they had to answer to, why, and when. In some cases, these notes were more than a decade old, kept under their bed, in a dresser drawer, or in a kitchen cabinet as protection against the system "coming back" for them. The women also shared hundreds of pages of official court and probation documents, correspondence with probation officers, and AVI-A receipts they kept as proof of payment and session completion. They also shared text messages between them and their abusive partners, providing examples of what they had been through and for how long. In some instances, the women's abusive partners showed up unannounced. Navigating the dynamic of abusive partners boldly inserting themselves in the women's interviews gave me an idea of what the women dealt with on a daily basis. It was one thing to have a woman describe the abuse to me but quite another to unexpectedly encounter her confrontational abusive partner firsthand, despite the fact that I had years of experience cofacilitating groups for men who harmed their partners.

### Go-Along Interviews

After the trauma-informed life history interviews, some women invited me to go with them to legal and health-focused institutions. They wanted emotional support offered through my physical presence. They also wanted me to see first-hand what it was like for them to interact with people representing these institutions. During these go-along (Kusenbach, 2003) interviews I asked questions and documented my observations in ways that overcame many of the limitations of more traditional participant observation. I not only observed how women navigated these spaces but how systems actors treated them.

### Middle-Position Interviews

Throughout the project, the women also asked me for advocacy and instrumental support that, at times, I was well positioned to offer. Their requests placed me in a practitioner-researcher version of Elizabeth A. Armstrong's and Laura Hamilton's (2013) "middle position." In this position I met requests by providing social work case management and in ways I believe sociologists uniquely situated in the field should (see National Association of Social Workers, 2020). I embraced a basic tenet of feminist social work research—praxis—the inseparability of theory and action (Gringeri, Wahab, and Anderson-Nathe, 2010).[2] For example, after Tyra's first interview, she called me to tell me "just one more thing." She could not accept the job she was offered because her driver's license was suspended—more collateral damage from her husband's coercive control. Tyra could not afford the driver's license reinstatement fee. The job would require proof of a driver's license. Tyra not only needed the job to get out of Section 8 housing and support herself and her children; she *wanted* the job.

I was well positioned to provide the necessary advocacy and support for her driver's license reinstatement process. These efforts resulted in her driver's license being reinstated and her getting the job. There were other situations where the women's requests were beyond what I could manage and the outcome was not what they had hoped it would be. In all cases, however, I connected the women with necessary referrals.

*Field Notes*

I took detailed ethnographic field notes (Emerson, Fretz, and Shaw, 2011; Richie, 1996) before and after every interview. Before the interview, I documented my memories of the women I already knew and my perceptions of all the women from our initial telephone conversations. This included their tone of voice, the stated reasons for or concerns about participation, the conversations with children they were having in the background, and any side comments they may have made during our initial phone calls.

When interviewing the women in their homes, neighborhoods, or family members' homes, I drove myself, arrived early, and parked outside. I texted them to let them know I was outside preparing for the interview. I then took notes on my laptop computer describing the neighborhood or interview setting including visual and auditory observations. I also used the time as a personal check-in, allowing me space to reflect and prepare while documenting my thoughts and what I hoped for from our time together. This portion of my field notes included the respondent's unique personal identification number, the interview date, the interview time, the interview length, and descriptive and commentary sections.

Shortly after the interview I documented my recollections in a "writing mode" (Emerson et al., 2011) that allowed me to get as much information down as possible while it was still fresh in my mind. I wrote the descriptive impressions in a way that allowed for the possibility that others might perceive them differently, yet I situated my impressions in the time and place of the interview. In a separate section I noted how my memories of the respondent (for those with whom I had already had contact years prior) compared or contrasted with what I had learned or perceived during the interview. I also detailed as much as I could recall regarding what the interview space looked like, what sounds I heard, where we sat, the woman's physical appearance, and her personal affect.

In a final commentary section I documented my feelings and thoughts about the interview's content, my impressions of the interaction, and any emerging themes. I took care to avoid making assumptions or drawing conclusions too early from the interview interactions or narrative. Each time a woman contacted me outside the interview, I noted the nature and content of that contact in a postscript section similar to Robert Emerson and others' (2011) "episodic" field notes. While analyzing my data, I returned to the field notes multiple times in a "reading mode," where I reflected and read them for ways to "create rather than . . . record reality" (Emerson et al., 2011, p. 86). Immediately after the go-along and middle-position interviews, I made quick shorthand notes to myself in a notebook and then typed more detailed notes on my laptop when I returned to my computer. This enabled me to capture an idea or a quotation verbatim.

As an AVI-G cofacilitator, I had prior contact with 15 of the respondents (see table 1 in the introduction) during intake assessments or in the group space or both. I was also responsible for communicating the women's group attendance and payment status to their supervising probation officer or group attendance to their CPS caseworker or both. All of the 15 women greeted me in a way that suggested they were happy to see me,[3] but they also indicated the difference in our roles as many still referred to me as "Miss Lisa," a title of respect I never asked for but often received. Like sociologist Julie Bettie (2014), I was "not really an insider but not a complete outsider either" (p. 17). Once the interview started, these 15 women implicitly gave me "outsider within status" (Collins, 1986). They did so by freely discussing other women who had been in their group by name, sharing unprompted updated personal information about themselves and others, and openly detailing their feelings about probation officers and CPS caseworkers who had monitored their AVI attendance. They also commonly emphasized their points with "you know" or "you remember." Each time I responded to their assumption of mutual recall by asking for further clarification, and often by asking them to imagine I knew nothing about their journey and to expand on their statement with as much detail as possible.

Interviewing women with whom I had had previous contact was especially emotionally labor-intensive (Campbell, 2002; Hochschild, 1983; Mehrotra, 2017). For example, years before this I had cofacilitated Emersyn's and Tyra's AVI-Gs, and I anticipated that they had responded to recruitment to talk about their group experiences. It quickly became apparent that they came for their own reasons (see Venkatesh, 2002), relating what had previously gone untold in their surveilled AVI environment where they could not anticipate the repercussions of their disclosures. Both women were generously detailed in recounting their systems experiences. As a researcher, I was honored that they trusted me with their stories. As a practitioner, I was devastated to learn my unintended role in their systems-inflicted harm. Why did I not know the extent of what they were going through when they were in the group I cofacilitated? If I had known these things, what could I have done differently? I realized that it is especially difficult to recognize the breadth of systems harms while enmeshed in the system (see figure 5 in chapter 3). I worked through much of the rawness of these feelings with my dissertation committee cochairs, in extensive field notes, and research memos. That said, I do not think these feelings will ever be resolved, and that lack of resolution, I have come to believe, inspires my ongoing work.

*No Prior Contact*

Building rapport with the 18 women with whom I did not have prior contact was more gradual. These women were typically more guarded about revealing systems and group-related information, generally maintaining the AVI-G confidentiality rule of not discussing group member identities or disclosures with anyone outside the group. This made it more difficult to elicit detailed responses when I inquired about their relationships with other group members beyond the AVI-G. Once I established a rapport, however, many of these women generously detailed their own experiences. Although my personal identities were quite different from those of the majority of the women, I found that I was often able to build connections based on being a mother and a nontraditional student. This shared understanding appeared in discussions about finding childcare or attending to very young children who accompanied them to their interviews, or in other women's frustrations that their teenagers called multiple times throughout the interview after being told to wait and not disturb them. My being a nontraditional student, despite apparent racial and class status differences, was a particular curiosity for the women who had not yet attained their desired educational or career goals. Some women expressed admiration for my "going back to school" and a belief that now, by meeting me and seeing what I was trying to do with this research, they felt they were helping me get through school and make a difference in the lives of others. Perhaps they were not "so old" themselves and "could go back one day," they reasoned.

DATA ANALYSIS

I removed all names and identifying information from the transcribed interviews. Owing to strict IRB guidelines, as well as women's ongoing abusive relationships and legal proceedings, I also omitted some demographic information (e.g., their country of origin, children's names). I analyzed and re-analyzed transcripts and fieldnotes in their entirety over the course of the project using Dedoose 8.0.42, a browser-based collaborative qualitative data analysis program. This software enabled an additional layer of analysis through open coding of shared themes. I engaged in open thematic coding by compiling a master list of the general deductive and inductive codes and a list of themes for further consideration. The initial open codes were as follows: charges; court/jail; CPS (child protective services); education; her family; housing; immigration; intervention; mobility/transportation; money; parking lot; partner's family; personal development; police; pregnancy; presenting incident; probation; religion; sexual abuse; sexual identity; shelter (DV/homeless/other); stigma; substance use; and survivor. I also read each interview transcript several times in its entirety and made memos of my impressions as well as the individual women's familial, relational, and system's experiences. The combination of using qualitative software to identify common themes and reading full transcripts multiple times allowed for rigorous iterative analysis.

As an experienced practitioner, it was especially important that I challenge myself as a researcher "to see the familiar in new light" (Charmaz, 2014, p. 133) throughout the process. Analyzing extensive narrative sections using word-by-word constructivist-grounded theory (Charmaz, 2014) enabled me to do so. This approach guided my focus, capturing the meaning of the women's words and experiences—situated within their intersectional identities—as they intended, rather than from my own perspective.

ENGAGING CRITICAL CONTEXT

In summary, I integrated my practice and research knowledge throughout data collection and analysis in a four-part iterative process I refer to as "engaging critical context" (Larance, 2021). It includes

1) incorporating Black feminist epistemology's (Collins, 2009) central tenets of focusing on marginalized women's lived experience with a belief that knowledge about their circumstances is produced through conversation with them;

2) applying an intersectional (Crenshaw, 1991) analysis by learning from them how their multiple identities shape their daily lives and interactions with probation officers, child protection workers, and group cofacilitators;

3) employing a contextual feminist research perspective (Dobash, Dobash, Wilson and Daly, 1992; Miller, 2005) that considers a person's motivation and intent when using harmful actions and the impact of those actions; and

4) gathering a longitudinal relationship history that illuminates how a woman who has caused or allegedly caused harm may have also been harmed. Critical context enabled me to piece together the women's complex life experiences from their perspectives (p. 47).

This process centered the diverse women's individual voices, while mapping their collective systems-inflicted harms. This work has been fact checked with original sources since the dissertation's publication. Everything in this book supersedes the dissertation.

# Notes

1. All the women's names used in *Broken* are pseudonyms. In most cases they chose their pseudonym; in other cases they asked me to select one for them.

2. Women often use the terms *choking* and *strangulation* interchangeably (see Monahan et al., 2022). Essence's former partner strangled her by tightening his hands around her neck to stop her breathing.

3. Although I note throughout *Broken* when the women used the term *African American* to describe themselves and others, I use the term *Black* throughout this work. I do so because, as Washington (2001) points out, "discrimination against people of African descent has historically been based on skin color, not nationality" (p. 1280). I share Coleman's (2020) reasons for capitalizing the term *Black*, "to convey elements of shared history and identity."

4. Women with survivorship histories who have harmed their partners typically do not experience "justice" in what is commonly referred to as the "criminal justice system." Instead, they experience the decontextualized impact of the law. Therefore, what many refer to as the criminal justice system, I refer to as the criminal legal system.

5. While much of the literature on the carceral system focuses on women in prison, this work focuses on women in the community who are legal systems-involved.

6. In the research community, a criminal court order for a domestic violence and non-domestic violence offense (assault, drug possession) was issued by the presiding judge requiring a person on probation to do or abstain from specific actions. A person who does not comply with court-ordered conditions may incur additional fees and may face sanctions, including jail time, completion of additional assessments, program participation, and additional time on probation. Similarly, a family court order was issued by a family court judge as recommended by

each woman's CPS caseworker and monitored by CPS or another assigned child welfare worker. Reunification with their children depended upon their compliance.

7. From 1974 to 1980 there were a range of grassroots-activist-led urban and rural efforts across the United States focused on helping women who were harmed by their intimate male partners. By 1982, the "'battered women's movement' had come to symbolize the conglomeration of organizations serving abused women and their children. Embodied in over 300 shelters, 48 state coalitions of service providers, a national grassroots organization, and a multitude of social and legal reforms" (Schechter, 1982, p. 1). The early movement focused on cisgender women harmed by their intimate cisgender male partners. As the movement evolved it has become more inclusive and more recently has been referred to as the feminist antiviolence movement (Sweet, 2021). Throughout *Broken* I refer to it as "the movement."

8. The leadership of lesbians of color was central to the battered women's movement, but largely overlooked (Kanuha, 1990; Schechter, 1982).

9. The first mandatory arrest law was passed in Oregon in 1977; only a few other states followed this practice until 1983 (Goodmark, 2012).

10. Shepard and Pence (1999) point out that the battered women's movement was "marked by a reproduction of the race, class, and heterosexist oppression that dominates the social relations in this country," (p. 7) with middle-class white women holding many of the movement's structural leadership positions. In contrast, Black women, Indigenous women, and women of color held "reactive rather than proactive leadership roles, [and were] far more cautious about mapping out strategies for reform that would involve an expanded role for police and courts in women's lives" (Shepard and Pence, 1999, p. 7).

11. Although Crenshaw (1991) coined the term *intersectionality*, her scholarship contributed to a rich extant body of work (see Blackwell, 2011; Collins, 2009; Combahee River Collective, 1977; King, 1988; Ling, 1989).

12. See Elliott et al. (2005) and SAMHSA (2014) for descriptions of trauma-informed approaches and principles.

13. In practice settings it is important that the language used accurately describes the spectrum of harm caused and experienced. Doing so discourages a one-size-fits-all approach to intervention. See Pence and Dasgupta (2006) and Larance and Miller (2017).

14. Certainly, the ability to exploit this privileged access is not specific to men, as women can and do use personal information to hurt their partners. However, the ability to do so does not necessarily mean they hold the coercive control in their heterosexual relationships, given the difference in the kind of access they have to structural power.

15. Because the women in this project used the language of being in a "same-sex" or "lesbian" relationship interchangeably, I also do. Legal scholar Kimberlé Crenshaw's (1991) intersectional analysis is crucial to better understanding the significance and meaning of violence in those relationships (Renzetti, 1998).

16. For an example of gaslighting, see psychologist Jennifer Freyd's concept of DARVO, an acronym for "Deny, Attack, Reverse Victim and Offender," often used by those who have caused harm, particularly sexual assault, when

confronted with their actions. See Jennifer J. Freyd, "What is DARVO?" Freyd Dynamics Lab, accessed November 17, 2023, https://dynamic.uoregon.edu/jjf /defineDARVO.html.

17. These concerns were articulated externally during New Jersey Coalition to End Domestic Violence Subcommittee on Women's Use of Force meetings and internally during formal and informal conversations.

18. These were JBWS colleagues Jane Baldwin Shivas, Maryann Lane Porter, Allison Hoffman-Ruzicka, and Lisa MacGray. I also received guidance from Shamita Das Dasgupta (Manavi), Andrea Bible (National Clearinghouse for the Defense of Battered Women), Anne Marshall (Praxis), Sister Mary Nerney (STEPS to End Family Violence), Tina Olsen (Domestic Abuse Intervention Programs), and Nancy Worcester (Wisconsin Coalition Against Domestic Violence). Additionally, I consulted Erin House's (2001) Domestic Violence Project/SAFE House Center Advocacy Guide, and 2002 and 2003 special issues of *Violence Against Women*. All brought a gender-responsive, intersectional lens to Vista.

19. McCorkel (2013) illuminates the explicit purpose of a prison drug addiction treatment program for women focused on "'breaking down' a self" (p. 3). In contrast, the women in *Broken* used the language of being or feeling broken to describe their experiences.

20. While Duran (2006) used the term *soul wound* to describe Native Americans' intergenerational and historical trauma, Menakem (2017) uses the term more broadly to denote the pain of family and structural abuse, as well as the genetic transmission of trauma in the midst of white supremacy.

21. The outcome of institutional betrayal can be betrayal trauma (Freyd, 1997).

22. "Self-defense" is placed in quotation marks because it is CLS language that has become the implicit litmus test of justified versus unjustified force, signaling how the victim-offender binary shapes ideas of justice with little consideration of context.

23. This phenomenon has been well documented in other settings by sociologist and legal scholar Dorothy Roberts (2018, 2020).

## I. PROBATION

1. Here financial capital is the money necessary to pay for the following: court/probation fines, fees, and costs; AVI fees; a car; bus tokens; and any other expenditures necessary to meet court-ordered obligations. Social capital is defined here as access to and benefits that flow from social networks. Small (2009) defines social capital as "obligations that people who are connected may feel toward each other, the sense of solidarity they may call upon, the information they are willing to share, and the services they are willing to perform" (p. 6). Cultural capital is understood here as the women's awareness that engaging in emotion work during probation reporting was advantageous in possibly avoiding further sanctions. Cultural capital has been defined as "class-based knowledge, skills, linguistic, and cultural competencies, and a worldview that is passed on via family and is related more to educational attainment than to occupation" (Bettie, 2014, p. 208).

2. Community service may include completing a designated number of hours of volunteer work at a non-profit agency with documented proof provided to the court. The women who had community service as part of their consequences met at the jail on week days and completed assigned tasks such as raking leaves, shoveling snow, and cleaning up trash on the side of the highway for approximately eight hours at a time.

3. For example, if the person convicted of the crime broke the other person's glasses, they would be ordered to reimburse the person for the cost of new glasses.

4. According to Watkins-Hayes (2009) group solidarity is "composed of self-identification with the social group, a sense of closeness to one's group, and a belief that one's fate is linked to that of the group" (p. 128).

5. The probation officers' pseudonyms evolved from the women's descriptions of the probation officers' supervisory styles. The women supervised by "Officer Phoenix" (a middle-aged white man) described his supervisory style as supportive, respectful, flexible, and understanding. The women supervised by "Officer Rigor" (a middle-aged woman of color) described her supervisory style as rigorous and arbitrarily harsh, and that she recommended extensive sanctions for any perceived violation. Regina referred to her as a "Nurse Ratched type of person," referencing the main antagonist in Ken Kesey's 1962 novel *One Flew Over the Cuckoo's Nest* and the 1974 thriller by the same name, starring Jack Nicholson. Similarly, Emersyn referred to her as "a pit bull in power." Nikki referred to Officer Rigor as a "sneaky snake," with "the human element . . . very much missing from [Rigor's] personality." Nikki reasoned that Officer Rigor's style probably "had a lot to do with her being unhappy in her own life." Nikki's point, as well as Officer Rigor's identities as a woman of color, necessitates further consideration of the additional challenges Rigor may have faced in balancing her identities with her professional obligations. Whereas Phoenix's identities entitled him to a certain kind of power and respect, Rigor's did not. Watkins-Hayes's (2009) notion of "racialized professionalism" acknowledges this additional burden Rigor may have felt. Therefore, the way both Officers Phoenix and Rigor shaped and deployed their discretionary toolkits (Watkins-Hayes, 2009) was likely a mechanism for managing their professional identities.

6. Morash et al. (2019) also refer to the differences in probation supervision as shifting back and forth over time between rehabilitation-oriented and punitive responses to technical violations. Here Officer Phoenix's approach was rehabilitation-oriented, whereas Officer Rigor's approach was punitive.

7. Other women drove approximately the same distance, but it was not unusual for some women to drive 40 miles one way.

8. The "victim" was Regina's daughter's abusive ex-boyfriend. When Regina happened to see him in town, she walked up to him, put her hand on his shoulder, and told him she was watching him. He called the police and alleged that Regina assaulted him. Regina was approximately five foot three and slim. He was a young, muscled, six foot two, two hundred plus pound athlete. After Regina was convicted of assault, he continued to make false allegations against her.

9. Miller and Stuart (2017) define "carceral citizenship" as, "a distinct form of political membership experienced by and enacted upon people convicted of a crime . . . [it] begins at the moment of a criminal conviction and is distinguished from other forms of citizenship by the restrictions, duties and benefits uniquely accorded to carceral citizens, or to people with criminal records" (p. 533). Although their definition pertains to formerly imprisoned people, the women on probation had similar experiences, such as differential treatment by agencies and employers, owing to their convictions and probation supervision.

10. In the United States, felony and misdemeanor offenses are marked as different in federal, state, and municipal status. Felonies are considered to be more serious and more frequently result in prison for longer than a period of one year. Misdemeanors, if they result in incarceration, involve time in a city or county jail.

## 2. CHILD PROTECTIVE SERVICES

1. For example, in California the "*failure* or inability of the parent or guardian to adequately supervise or protect the child" may be interpreted as evidence to support neglect (Welf. and Inst. Code § 300; Pen. Code § 11165.2, cited in Children's Bureau, 2019, p. 15; emphasis added). Substantiated neglect is indicated by a caregiver's failure to perform socially expected and legally required caretaking obligations (Dubowitz et al., 1993). The goal of FTP statutes are "to encourage caretakers to report instances of childhood abuse and interpersonal violence, thereby reducing the violence to which a child is exposed" (Mahoney, 2019, pp. 435–436).

2. Charges include misdemeanors or felonies, with civil penalties, criminal penalties, or both.

3. BCS is defined as "judicial collusion with batterers through the criminalization of domestic violence survivors" (Bierra and Lenz, 2019, p. 107).

4. See Douglas (2018) regarding systems abuse.

5. A person appointed by the court to represent the best interests of a person unable to represent themselves.

## 3. ANTIVIOLENCE INTERVENTION ADMINISTRATION

1. For additional detail that supports each woman's narrative, readers should refer to table 1, "Women's individual identities and pathways," in the introduction.

2. Van der Kolk (2014) points out that "attempts to maintain control over unbearable physiological reactions can result in . . . physical symptoms, including fibromyalgia, chronic fatigue, and other autoimmune diseases" (p.53).

3. Phoebe was referring to Walker's (1979) "cycle of abuse" theory. The cycle consists of abusive partner's using a common pattern of "tension-violence-honeymoon" periods. The theory has fallen out of favor owing to survivors' detailing that there is no predictable common pattern and pointing out that the "honeymoon," if experienced, is another form of abuse. Furthermore, the cycle is problematic because of its reliance on stereotypes of white femininity that

decentralize the experiences of women of color, placing them at risk of being pathologized (Faigman and Wright, 1997; Jacobsen et al., 2007).

4. During her first interview, Marcella explained she voluntarily joined the AVI to learn more about her behavior in intimate relationships. A year later she had a pending court date for an assault charge. Although Marcella had stopped attending AVI on her own, she believed she would soon be court ordered. She hoped the judge would view her initial voluntary contact favorably.

## 4. ANTIVIOLENCE INTERVENTION GROUP

1. The women referred to the AVI-G as "group" or "the group." Those terms are used interchangeably in this chapter.

2. For additional context regarding each woman's intersecting identities, refer to table 1, "Women's individual identities and pathways," in the introduction.

3. The women had contact with five AVI-G cofacilitators. When asked about their group experiences, some women briefly focused on cofacilitator effectiveness. For example, an effective cofacilitator, according to Devore, was "a good listener." As Joy saw it, an effective cofacilitator was a person who did "not talk a lot." Sheniqua thought that a cofacilitator should understand the power of "teaching our stories," and Jatara believed that the hallmark of such a person was that she "stay[ed] calm . . . [and] didn't judge." Suzie, meanwhile, stressed that a successful cofacilitator used a "kind tone of voice." But all the women directed the conversations toward what was meaningful about being in the AVI-G.

4. Van der Kolk (2014) points out that "No doctor can write a prescription for friendship and love" (p. 81).

5. Holt-Lunstad et al. (2010) concluded that loneliness is as harmful to physical health as smoking 15 cigarettes a day.

6. See NASW Code of Ethics: 1.02 Self-Determination: "Social workers respect and promote the right of clients to self-determination and assist clients in their efforts to identify and clarify their goals. Social workers may limit clients' right to self-determination when, in the social workers' professional judgment, clients' actions or potential actions pose a serious, foreseeable, and imminent risk to themselves or others." See "Highlighted Revisions to the Code of Ethics," National Association of Social Workers, February 19, 2021, https://www.socialworkers.org/About/Ethics/Code-of-Ethics/Highlighted-Revisions-to-the-Code-of-Ethics.

7. Miller (2005) observed that group cofacilitators cautioned women in abusive relationships against changing their behaviors in ways that could put them at risk with abusive partners. This caution was also encouraged during the AVI-Gs.

8. Although Bea did not participate in this project, I assigned her a pseudonym to humanize the process of telling this story. I remember Bea from her time in group when I was an AVI-G cofacilitator.

9. The focus and philosophy of these interventions greatly varies across the United States (Larance et al., 2019).

## 5. AFTER ANTIVIOLENCE INTERVENTION GROUP

1. As a group cofacilitator I typically left the building an hour or more after the last evening group. When walking to my car I noticed women from the AVI-G talking to each other in small groups across the parking lot.

2. Van der Kolk (2014) points out that moving beyond trauma requires that traumatized people have "experiences that can restore the sense of physical safety" (p. 87). He also asserts that "severely traumatized people may get more out of simply helping to arrange chairs before a meeting ... than they would from sitting in those same chairs and discussing the failures in their life" (p. 87).

3. Although Abby's, Becky's, Benita's, Cherise's, Essence's, and QuiShandra's voices have been amplified throughout this work, they are not included in this section because they were on probation and participating in the AVI-G at our last contact.

4. The process of getting rid of a criminal record by the court ordering it to be set aside.

5. Lily did not have this experience.

6. Although the decision of whether to offer a plea deal to the defendant was up to the prosecutor, the offer was extended to all the women in this book. Goodmark (2019) points out that prosecutors have the option of considering the history of violence and victimization in determining what charges to bring. The details of an actual plea deal depended upon the charges, the prosecutor, and what precedent was established in similar cases. For resources see Asmus (2004, 2017).

## 6. A CALL TO ACTION

1. For social workers, this call to action should align with the larger goals of the Grand Challenges of Social Work (2021).

2. See Almeida and Lockard (2008); Avalon Healing Center, accessed November 27, 2023, https://avalonhealing.org/; "What is the Duluth Model?" Domestic Abuse Intervention Programs: Home of the Duluth Model, accessed November 27, 2023, https://www.theduluthmodel.org/; Emerge: Counseling and Education to Stop Domestic Violence, accessed November 27, 2023, https://www.emergedv.com/; INCITE!, accessed November 27, 2023, https://incite-national.org/; The Northwest Network, accessed November 27, 2023, https://www.nwnetwork.org/; "Our Mission: End All Forms of Gender-Based Violence in the South Asian Community," Manavi, accessed November 27, 2023, http://www.manavi.org/.

3. For social workers this will mean endeavoring to fulfill the fundamental goals of Social Work's Grand Challenges (January 2021), while recognizing the art of social work practice (Graybeal, 2007) in ways that embrace the profession's rich, yet complicated, social reform history (see Berringer, 2019; Kanuha, 1998; Specht and Courtney, 1994).

4. This call focuses on the experiences of women owing to the research population's composition. I encourage further research to determine promising ways forward across communities.

5. See Avery and Lu (2021). See also "Our Cause: Criminal History Reform," The Papillion Foundation: The Greatest Crime Is a Wasted Life," accessed November 27, 2023, https://www.papillonfoundation.org/cause/reform.

6. See Richie's (2012) "Violence Matrix," which identifies the spectrum of violence in Black women's lives situated within overlapping, multilevel state structures that reproduce intimate harm.

7. See Shepard and Pence (1999).

8. See Mehrotra (2010); Mulvaney (2022); Crenshaw (1991); Matsuda (1991); Richie et al. (2021); and Davis et al. (2022).

9. See Asmus (2004, 2017); Center for Court Innovation (June 2020). The Center for Court Innovation is now the Center for Justice Innovation. See Center for Justice Innovation, accessed November 27, 2023, www.innovatingjustice.org; Don't Call the Police: Community-Based Alternatives to Police in Your City, accessed November 27, 2023, dontcallthepolice.com; and the National Defense Center for Criminalized Survivors, accessed November 27, 2023, www.ncdbw.org. The latter is a program of the Battered Women's Justice Project (formerly The National Clearinghouse for the Defense of Battered Women).

10. A human rights approach to health incorporates considerations relevant to AVI. https://www.ohchr.org/sites/default/files/Documents/Issues/ESCR/Health/HRBA_HealthInformationSheet.pdf

11. Whitaker et al., (2007) highlight the advantages and challenges of a community-based collaboration between the state of Massachusetts and the Centers for Disease control. Public health focused collaborations are promising.

12. See Almeida and Lockard (2008), Center for Court Innovation (April 2022), Herman (2023), Sered (2019), and Simmons (2019) for accountability focused conversations.

13. Compassion is the desire to take action to help another person. Empathy is an awareness of another person's emotional experiences, and it includes attempts to feel emotion from another person's perspective. Both are important in working beyond the victim-offender binary.

14. Sarachild (1975) points out that during the second wave of the women's liberation movement consciousness-raising groups focused on "studying the whole gamut of women's lives, starting with the full reality of one's own . . . [seen as a] method for arriving at the truth and a means for action and organizing" (pp. 145–147).

15. For guidance with language development, see American Psychological Association (2021); the Berkeley Underground Scholars Language Guide (2019); Tu and Penti (2020).

16. See Department of Justice (2022). As Attorney General Garland put it, "The department of Justice welcomes the reauthorization of the Violence Against Women Act and will continue to use the resources at our disposal to prevent and respond to gender-based violence and provide critical services for survivors." See "Justice Department Applauds Reauthorization of the Violence Against Women Act," Office of Public Affairs, U.S. Department of Justice, March 16, 2022, https://www.justice.gov/opa/pr/justice-department-applauds-reauthorization-violence-against-women-act.

17. See Graybeal (2007), who problematizes social work's increasingly narrow focus on evidence-based practice by emphasizing the art of social work practice.

18. See "Publication Topics," NCDW, accessed November 27, 2023, https://www.ncdbw.org/publications-by-topic.

19. The VIGOR (cf. Hamby, 2014) provides a framework for women making decisions about their safety. See "The Vigor," Life Paths Research Center, accessed November 27, 2023, https://www.lifepathsresearch.org/the-vigor/.

20. The exceptions are women expressing an intent to harm themselves or someone else and reporting child abuse or neglect.

21. The limits to confidentiality are followed throughout the research community AVI-Gs.

22. Virani (2021) recommends eliminating all fines and fees associated with domestic violence convictions, including court-ordered BIPs.

23. For example, select programs in Maryland and New Mexico.


APPENDIX: RESEARCH METHODS

1. I decided on the $30 gift card amount by considering the average US minimum wage of $7.25/hour, doubling it, and estimating that most interviews would last approximately two hours. Although I wanted to offer more, the IRB expressed concern that a higher amount would be coercive.

2. Freire (2001) originally defined praxis as "reflection and action upon the world in order to transform it" (p. 5).

3. This suggests possible response bias in that those women who were unhappy with me or the work I did didn't contact me to be interviewed.

# References

Alessi, Edward J. (2014). A framework for incorporating minority stress theory into treatment with sexual minority clients. *Journal of Gay & Lesbian Mental Health*, *18*, 47–66.

Allen, Harry E., Latessa, Edward J., and Ponder, Bruce S. (2015). *Corrections in America: An introduction* (14th ed.). Prentice Hall.

Almeida, Rhea V., and Lockard, Judith. (2008). The cultural context model: A new paradigm for accountability, empowerment, and the development of critical consciousness against domestic violence. In N.J. Sokoloff (Ed.), *Domestic violence at the margins* (pp. 301–320). Rutgers University Press.

American Probation and Parole Association. (1991). *Drug testing guidelines and practices for adult probation and parole agencies.* U.S. Department of Justice Office of Justice Programs Bureau of Justice Assistance. https://www
.ojp.gov/ncjrs/virtual-library/abstracts/american-probation-and-parole
-associations-drug-testing-guidelines

American Probation and Parole Association. (1997). *Purpose.* https://appa-net.
org/eweb/Dynamicpage.aspx?webcode=IB_PositionStatementandwps_key=
dc223702-d690-4830-9295-335366a65d3e#:~:text=Purpose,by%20proba-
tioners%20in%20the%20community

American Probation and Parole Association. (2013). *Probation & parole directory.* American Probation and Parole Association. https://www.appa-net
.org/eweb/Dynamicpage.aspx?webcode=IB_PositionStatement&wps_
key=dc223702-d690-4830-9295-335366a65d3e

American Psychological Association. (2021). *Equity, Diversity, and Inclusion Toolkit.* APA.org. https://www.apa.org/pubs/authors/equity-diversity-inclusin-
toolkit-journal-editors.pdf

Anderson, Kristin L. (2009). Gendering coercive control. *Violence Against Women*, *15*(12), 1444–1457.

Annie E. Casey Foundation. (2023). *Black children continue to be dispropor-tionately represented in foster care.* https://www.aecf.org/blog/us-foster-care-population-by-race-and-ethnicity

Armstrong, Elizabeth A., Gleckman-Krut, Miriam, and Johnson, Lanora. (2018). Silence, power, and inequality: An intersectional approach to sexual violence. *Annual Review of Sociology, 44,* 99–122.

Armstrong, Elizabeth A., and Hamilton, Laura T. (2013). *Paying for the party: How college maintains inequality.* Harvard University Press.

Armstrong, Elizabeth M., and Bosk, Emily A. (2020). Contradictions and their consequences: How competing policy mandates facilitate use of a punitive framework in domestic violence-child maltreatment cases. *Child Maltreatment,* 1–11.

Arnold, Gretchen, and Ake, Jami. (2013). Reframing the narrative of the battered women's movement. *Violence Against Women, 19*(4), 557–578.

Asar, Janice Gassam. (2021). 2021 MacArthur fellow Ibram Kendi discusses racial healing and the power we all have to create change. *Forbes: Diversity, Equity, and Inclusion.* https://www.forbes.com/sites/janicegassam/2021/10/07/2021-macarthur-fellow-ibram-kendi-discusses-racial-healing-and-the-power-we-all-have-to-create-change/?sh=1db69759728d

Asmus, Mary. (2004). *At a crossroads: Developing Duluth's prosecution response to battered women who fight back.* Praxis International.

Asmus, Mary. (2017). *Got justice? Options for prosecutors when battered women fight back.* National Clearinghouse for the Defense of Battered Women.

Avery, Beth, and Lu, Han. (2021). *Ban the box: U.S. cities, counties, and states adopt fair hiring policies.* National Employment Law Project. https://www.nelp.org/publication/ban-the-box-fair-chance-hiring-state-and-local-guide/

Bagwell-Gray, Meredith E., Messing, Jill T., and Baldwin-White, Adrienne. (2015). Intimate partner sexual violence: A review of terms, definitions, and prevalence. *Trauma, Violence, & Abuse, 16*(3), 316–335.

Ballan, Michelle S. and Frye, Molly B. (2012). Self-defense among women with disabilities: An unexplored domain in domestic violence cases. *Violence Against Women, 18*(9), 1083–1107.

Barlow, Charlotte, Johnson, Kelly, Walklate, Sandra, and Humphreys, Les. (2019, July 22). Putting coercive control into practice: Problems and possibilities. *The British Journal of Criminology, 60,* 160–179.

Battered Women's Justice Project. (2020). Understanding and addressing women's use of force: A retrospective. [Webinar]. Vimeo. https://vimeopro.com/bwjp/bwjp-webinar-recordings/video/436164963

Battered Women's Justice Project. (2021). *Coercive control codification: A brief guide for advocates and coalitions.* https://www.bwjp.org/assets/documents/pdfs/cc-codificationbrief.pdf

Berk, Richard A., Campbell, Alec, Klap, Ruth, and Western, Bruce. (1992). A Bayesian analysis of the Colorado Springs spouse abuse experiment. *Journal of Criminal Law and Criminology, 83,* 170–200.

Berkeley Underground Scholars Language Guide. (2019). https://undergroundscholars.berkeley.edu/blog/2019/3/6/language-guide-for-communicating-about-those-involved-in-the-carceral-system

Bernstein, Elizabeth. (2010). Militarized humanitarianism meets carceral feminism: The politics of sex, rights, and freedom in contemporary antitrafficking campaigns. *Signs*, 36(1), 45–71.

Berringer, Kathryn R. (2019). Reexamining epistemological debates in social work through American pragmatism. *Social Service Review*, 608–639.

Bettie, Julie. (2014). *Women without class: Girls, race, and identity*. University of California Press.

Beverly, Nicole. (2020). *Finding Nicole: A true story of love, loss, betrayal, fear and hope*. Self-published.

Bierra, Alisa, and Lenz, Colby. (2019). Battering court syndrome: A structural critique of "failure to protect." In Jane K. Stoever (Ed.), *The politicization of safety: Critical perspectives on domestic violence responses* (pp. 91–118). New York University Press.

BISC-MI. (n.d.) https://www.biscmi.org/resources/other-states-standards/

Blackwell, Maylei. (2011). *¡Chicana power! Contested histories of feminism in the Chicana movement*. University of Texas Press.

Bloom, Barbara, Owen, Barbara, and Covington, Stephanie. (2004). Women offenders and the gendered effects of public policy. *Review of Policy Research*, 21, 31–48.

Boal, Ashley L., and Mankowski, Eric S. (2014). The impact of legislative standards on batterer intervention program practices and characteristics. *American Journal of Community Psychology*, 53, 218–230.

Brave Heart, Maria Y. H., Chase, Josephine, Elkins, Jennifer, and Altschul, Deborah B. (2011). Historical trauma among indigenous people of the Americas: Concepts, research, and clinical considerations. *Journal of Psychoactive Drugs*, 43(4), 282–290.

Brennan, Iain R., Burton, Victoria, Gormally, Sinead, and O'Leary, Nicola. (2019). Service provider difficulties operationalizing coercive control. *Violence Against Women*, 25(6), 635–653.

Burk, Connie. (2004). *Advocacy model language versus Criminal legal system language*. Northwest Network of Bisexual Trans, Lesbian & Gay Survivors. https://static1.squarespace.com/static/566c7f0c2399a3bdabb57553/t/566c9ccfc21b865cfe7826c3/1449958607207/DV-vs-Legal-language-handout-3.05.pdf

Campbell, Christopher M. (2016). It's not technically a crime: Investigating the relationship between technical violations and new crime. *Criminal Justice Policy Review*, 27(7), 643–667.

Campbell, Jacquelyn C. (1995). *Assessing dangerousness: Violence by sexual offenders, batterers and child abusers*. Sage.

Campbell, Jacquelyn C., Glass, Nancy, Sharps, Phyllis W., Laughon, Kathryn, and Bloom, Tina. (2007). Intimate partner homicide: Review and implications of research and policy. *Trauma, Violence, & Abuse*, 8(3), 246–269.

Campbell, Rebecca. (2002). *Emotionally involved: The impact of researching rape*. Routledge.

Center for Court Innovation [Center for Justice Innovation]. (2020). *Shrinking the footprint of police: Six ideas for enhancing safety* [Handout]. https://

www.courtinnovation.org/sites/default/files/media/document/2020/Handout
_CCI_ShrinkingtheFootprint_07092020.pdf

Center for Court Innovation. (2021). Women who use force: Intimate partner violence caused by women [Webinar]. https://www.courtinnovation.org /publications/Webinar-Women-Who-Use-Force

Center for Court Innovation. (2022). Guiding principles for engagement and intervention with people who cause harm through intimate partner violence [Fact sheet]. https://www.courtinnovation.org/publications/fact-sheet-guid-ing-principles-engagement-intervention-ipv

Center for the Study of Social Policy. (2019) inSIGHT: A workshop on implicit racial bias for child protection workers. https://cssp.org/resource/insight-a-workshop-on-implicit-racial-bias-for-child-protection-workers/

Charmaz, Kathy. (2014). Constructing grounded theory (2nd Ed.). Sage.

Child Abuse and Treatment Act (CAPTA). (1974). https://www.govinfo.gov /content/pkg/STATUTE-88/pdf/STATUTE-88-Pg4.pdf

Child Abuse and Treatment Act (CAPTA). (2010). 42 U.S.C. § 5101, U.S. G.P.O. https://www.govinfo.gov/content/pkg/USCODE-2010-title42/html /USCODE-2010-title42-chap67.htm

Child Maltreatment. (2020). U.S. Department of Health and Human Services, Administration for Children and Families, and Administration on Children, Youth and Families. Children's Bureau. https://www.acf.hhs.gov/sites/default /files/documents/cb/cm2020.pdf

Children's Bureau. (2017). Fact sheet. Motivational interviewing: A primer for child welfare professionals. Child Welfare Information Gateway. https:// www.childwelfare.gov/pubpdfs/motivational_interviewing.pdf

Children's Bureau. (2019). Definitions of child abuse and neglect. Child Welfare Information Gateway. https://www.csdepj.gouv.qc.ca/fileadmin/Fichiers_clients /Documents_deposes_a_la_Commission/P-124_Rapport_Childrens_bureau _ACYF_ACF_HHS.pdf

Clear, Todd R., and Latessa, Edward J. (1993). Probation officers' roles in intensive supervision: Surveillance versus treatment. Justice Quarterly, 10(3), 441–462.

Coleman, Nancy. (2020, July 5). Why we're capitalizing Black. The New York Times. https://www.nytimes.com/2020/07/05/insider/capitalized-black.html

Collins, Patricia H. (1986). Learning from the outsider within: The sociological significance of Black feminist thought. Social Problems, 33(6), 14–32.

Collins, Patricia H. (2004). Black sexual politics: African Americans, gender, and the new racism. Routledge.

Collins, Patricia H. (2009). Black feminist thought: Knowledge, consciousness and the politics of empowerment. Routledge.

Comack, Elizabeth (2018). Coming back to jail: Women, trauma, and crimi-nalization. Fernwood Publishing.

Combahee River Collective. (1977). A Black feminist statement. https://www .blackpast.org/african-american-history/combahee-river-collective-state-ment-1977/

Crenshaw, Kimberlé W. (1991). Mapping the margins: Intersectionality, iden-tity politics, and violence against women of color. Stanford Law Review, 43(6), 1241–1299.

Crenshaw, Kimberlé W. (2016). Keynote address: On intersectionality. Presented at Women of the World Festival, London. March 14.

Crowe, Ann H., Sydney, Linda, DeMichele, Matthew, Keilitz, Susan, Neal, Connie, Frohman, Sherry, Schaefer, William M., Jr., and Thomas, Mike. (2009). *Community corrections response to domestic violence: Guidelines for practice.* American Probation and Parole Association. https://www.appa-net.org/eweb/docs/appa/pubs/ccrdv.pdf

Dasgupta, Shamita D. (2002). A framework for understanding women's use of nonlethal violence in intimate heterosexual relationships. *Violence Against Women*, 8(11), 1364–1389.

Davis, Angela Y., Dent, Gina, Meiners, Erica R., and Richie, Beth E. (2022). *Abolition. Feminism. Now.* Haymarket Books.

DeGenna, Natacha M., and Feske, Ulrike. (2013). Phenomenology of borderline personality disorder: The role of race and socioeconomic status. *HHS Public Access*, 201(12), 1027–1034.

DeKeseredy, Walter S. (2021). Bringing feminist sociological analyses of patriarchy back to the forefront of the study of woman abuse. *Violence Against Women*, 27(5), 621–638.

DeKeseredy, Walter S., and Dragewicz, Molly. (2009). *Shifting public policy direction: Gender-focused versus bi-directional intimate partner violence. A report.* Queens Printer for Ontario.

Department of Justice. (2022). *Justice Department Applauds Reauthorization of the Violence Against Women Act.* https://www.justice.gov/opa/pr/justice-department-applauds-reauthorization-violence-against-women-act

DeVault, Marjorie L. (1990). Talking and listening from women's standpoint: Feminist strategies for interviewing and analysis. *Social Problems*, 37(1), 96–116.

Dichter, Melissa E. (2013). They arrested me—and I was the victim: Women's experiences with getting arrested in the context of domestic violence. *Women & Criminal Justice*, 23, 81–98.

Dobash, Russell P., Dobash, R. Emerson, Cavanagh, Kate and Lewis, Ruth. (1998). Separate and intersecting realities: A comparison of men's and women's accounts of violence against women. *Violence Against Women*, 4, 382–414.

Dobash, Russell P., Dobash, R. Emerson, Wilson, Margo, and Daly, Martin. (1992). The myth of sexual symmetry in marital violence. *Social Problems*, 39(1), 71–91.

Doherty, Fiona. (2016). Obey all laws and be good: probation and the meaning of recidivism. *Georgetown Law Journal*, 104, 291–354.

Donovan, Catherine, and Barnes, Rebecca. (2020). *Queering narratives of domestic violence and abuse.* Palgrave Macmillan.

Douglas, Heather. (2018). Legal systems abuse and coercive control. *Criminology & Criminal Justice*, 18(1), 84–99.

Dragiewicz, Molly. (2011). *Equality with a vengeance: Men's rights groups, battered women, and antifeminist backlash.* Northeastern University Press of New England.

Dragiewicz, Molly and DeKeseredy, Walter S. (2012). Claims about women's use of non-fatal force in intimate relationships: A contextual review of Canadian research. *Violence Against Women*, 18(9), 1008–1026.

Dubowitz, Howard, Black, Maureen, Starr Jr., Raymond H., and Zuravin, Susan. (1993). A conceptual definition of child neglect. *Criminal Justice and Behavior*, 20(1), 8–26.

Dunford, Franklyn W., Huizinga, David, and Elliott, Delbert S. (1990). The role of arrest in domestic assault: The Omaha police experiment. *Criminology*, 28, 183–206.

Duran, Eduardo. (2006). *Healing the soul wound: Counseling with American Indians and other native peoples*. Teachers College Press.

Durfee, Alesha. (2012). Situational ambiguity and gendered patterns of arrest for intimate partner violence. *Violence Against Women*, 18, 64–84.

Durfee, Alesha. (2015). "Usually it's something in the writing": Reconsidering the narrative requirement for protection order petitions. *University of Miami Race & Social Justice Law Review*, 5, 469–484.

Edelson, Jeffrey, and Tolman, Richard M. (1992). *Intervention for men who batter: An ecological approach*. Sage.

Eisenberg, Sue E., and Micklow, Patricia L. (1977). Assaulted wife—Catch 22 revisited. *Women's Rights Law Reporter*, 3–4, 138–177.

Elliott, Denise E., Bjelajac, Paula, Fallot, Roger D., Markoff, Laurie S., and Reed, Beth G. (2005). Trauma-informed or trauma-denied: Principles and implementation of trauma-informed services for women. *Journal of Community Psychology*, 33(4), 461–477.

Emerson, Robert M., Fretz., Rachel I., and Shaw, Linda L. (2011). *Writing ethnographic fieldnotes* (2nd ed.). University of Chicago Press.

Evans, Sara and Boyte, Harry. (1992). *Free space: The sources of democratic change in America*. The University of Chicago Press.

Faigman, David L., and Wright, Amy J. (1997). The battered woman syndrome in the age of science. *Arizona Law Review*, 39(67), 67–115.

Family Safety Victoria. (2021). *Provide dedicated funding for future perpetrator programs*. https://www.vic.gov.au/family-violence-recommendations /provide-dedicated-funding-future-perpetrator-programs

Felitti, Vincent J., Anda, Robert F., Nordenberg, Dale, Williamson, David F., Spitz, Alison M., Edwards, Valerie, Koss, Mary P., and Marks, James S. (1998). Relationship of childhood abuse and household dysfunction to many of the leading causes of death in adults: The adverse childhood experiences (ACE) study. *American Journal of Preventive Medicine*, 14(4), 245–258.

Ferraro, Kathleen. (2006). *Neither angels nor demons: Women, crime, and victimization*. Northwestern University Press.

Fong, Kelley. (2019). Concealment and constraint: Child protective services fears and poor mothers' institutional engagement. *Social Forces*, 97(4), 1785–1810.

Fong, Kelley. (2020, August 11). *"The tool we have": Why child protective services investigates so many families and how even good intentions backfire* [Briefing report]. Council on Contemporary Families. https://contemporary families.org/cps-brief-report/

Freire, Pablo. (2001). *Pedagogy of the oppressed* (30th ed.). Continuum.

Freyd, Jennifer J. (1997). Violations of power, adaptive blindness and betrayal trauma theory. *Feminism & Psychology*, 7(1), 22–32.

Gardner, Donna. (2009). Victim-defendants in mandated treatment: An ethical quandary. In Kathy A. McCloskey and Marilyn. H. Sitaker (Eds.), *Backs against the wall: Battered women's resistance strategies* (pp. 69–86). Routledge.

Garner, Joel, Fagan, Jeffrey, and Maxwell, Christopher. (1995). Published findings from the spouse assault replication program: A critical review. *Journal of Quantitative Criminology, 11*, 3–28.

Gilfus, Mary E. (1999). The price of a ticket: A survivor-centered appraisal of trauma theory. *Violence Against Women, 5*(11), 1238–1257.

Glenn, Evelyn N. (1994). Social constructions of mothering: A thematic overview. In Evelyn N. Glenn, Grace Chang, and Linda R. Forcey (Eds.), *Mothering: Ideology, experience, and agency* (pp. 1–32). Routledge.

Goffman, Erving. (1963). *Stigma notes on the management of spoiled identity.* Prentice-Hall.

Gomez, Jennifer M. (2023). *The cultural betrayal of black women and girls: A black feminist approach to healing from sexual abuse.* American Psychological Association.

Gondolf, Edward. (2012). *The future of batterer programs: Reassessing evidence-based practice.* Northeastern University Press.

Goodmark, Leigh. (2008). When is a battered woman no longer a battered woman? When she fights back. *Yale Journal of Law and Feminism, 20*(75), 75–129.

Goodmark, Leigh. (2012). *A troubled marriage: Domestic violence and the legal system.* New York University Press.

Goodmark, Leigh. (2013). Transgender people, intimate partner abuse, and the legal system. *Harvard Civil Rights-Civil Liberties Law Review, 48*, 51–104.

Goodmark, Leigh. (2019). The impact of prosecutorial misconduct, overreach, and misuse of discretion on gender violence victims. *Dickinson Law Review, 123*(3), 627–659

Goodmark, Leigh. (2022). 'Something on women': Carceral feminist clamored for the Violence Against Women Act. What the nation got in return was more violence. *Inquest: A Decarceral brainstorm.* https://inquest.org/something-on-women-vawa/

Grand Challenges of Social Work. (January 2021). *Progress and plans for the grand challenges: An impact report at year 5 of the 10-year initiative.* https://view.pagetiger.com/grand-challenges-impact-report-2021

Granovetter, Mark. (1973). The strength of weak ties. *American Journal of Sociology, 78*, 1360–1380.

Graybeal, Clay T. (2007). Evidence for the art of social work. *Families in Society, 88*(4), 513–523.

Gringeri, Christina E., Wahab, Stephanie, and Anderson-Nathe, Ben. (2010). What makes it feminist?: Mapping the landscape of feminist social work research. *Affilia: Journal of Women and Social Work, 25*(4), 390–405.

Hamby, Sherry. (2014). *Battered women's protective strategies: Stronger than you know.* Oxford University Press.

Hamby, Sherry, and Grych, John. (2013). *The web of violence: Exploring connections among different forms of interpersonal violence and abuse.* Springer.

Hamilton, Laura T., Armstrong, Elizabeth A., Seeley, J. Lotus, and Armstrong, Elizabeth M. (2019). Hegemonic femininities and intersectional domination. *Sociological Theory*, 37(4), 315–341.

Harasim-Pieper, Monika. (2011). Women who use force in their intimate partner relationships: Toward a common language and understanding. *Women Who Use Force Ad Hoc Committee of Ohio Domestic Violence Network.* http://www.ncdsv.org/images/ODVN_WomenWhoUseForceIntPartner RelTowardCommonLanguageAndUnderstanding_9-2011.pdf

Harding, Sandra. (1987). *Feminism and methodology: Social science issues.* Indiana University Press.

Harris, Alexes. (2016). *A pound of flesh: Monetary sanctions as punishment for the poor.* Russell Sage Foundation.

Hartsock, Nancy C.M. (1983). *Money, sex, and power: Toward a feminist historical materialism.* Northeastern University Press.

Henderson, James and Avalon, Stephanie. (2018). Implementing probation group reporting: Innovative and effective supervision in domestic violence cases. *The Battered Women's Justice Project.* https://www.bwjp.org/assets /implementing-probation-group-reporting-050718.pdf

Henry, Colleen, Victor, Bryan G., Ryan, Joseph P., and Perron, Brian E. (2020). Substantiated allegations of failure to protect in the child welfare system: Against whom, in what context, and with what justification? *Child and Youth Services Review*, 116, 1–9.

Herman, Judith L. (1992). *Trauma and recovery: The aftermath of violence—from domestic abuse to political terror.* Basic Books.

Herman, Judith L. (2023). *Truth and repair: How trauma survivors envision justice.* Basic Books.

Herman, Judith L., Perry, J. Christopher, and van der Kolk, Bessel A. (1989). Childhood trauma in borderline personality disorder. *American Journal of Psychiatry*, 46(4), 490–495.

Hirshel, David, Buzawa, Eve, Pattavina, April, and Faggiani, Don. (2007). Domestic violence and mandatory arrest laws: To what extent do they influence police arrest decisions. *Journal of Criminal Law and Criminology*, 98(1), 255–298.

Hochschild, Arlie. (1983). *The managed heart: Commercialization of human feeling.* University of California Press.

Holt-Lunstad, Julianne, Smith, Timothy B., and Layton, J. Bradley. (2010). Social relationships and mortality risk: A meta-analytic review. *PLoS Medicine*, 7(7), 1–20.

Holtrop, Kendal, Scott, Jenna C., Parra-Cardona, J. Ruben, Smith, Sharde M., Schmittel, Emily, and Larance, Lisa Young. (2017). Exploring factors that contribute to positive change in a diverse, group-based male batterer intervention program: Using qualitative data to inform implementation and adaptation efforts. *Journal of Interpersonal Violence*, 32(8), 1267–1290.

hooks, bell. (1989). *Talking back: Thinking feminist, thinking black.* South End Press.

House, Erin. (2001). *When women use force: An advocacy guide to understanding the issue and conducting an assessment with individuals who have used force to determine their eligibility for services from a domestic violence agency.* Domestic Violence Project/SAFE House.

Humphreys, Cathy, Healey, Lucy, and Mandel, David. (2018). Case reading as a practice and training intervention in domestic violence and child protection. *Australian Social Work, 71*(3), 277–291.

International Association of Chiefs of Police. (1967). *Training key 16: Handling disturbance calls.*

Jacobsen, Carol, Mizga, Kammy, and O'Orio, Lynn. (2007). Battered women, homicide convictions, and sentencing. *Hastings Women's Law Journal, 18*(1), 31–65.

Jarvis, Maregaret, Williams, Jessica, Hurford, Matthew, Lindsay, Dawn, Lincoln, Piper, Giles, Leila, Luongo, Peter, and Safarian, Taleen. (2017). Appropriate use of drug testing in clinical addiction medicine. *Journal of Addiction Medicine, 11*(3), 163–173.

Jones, Alexis. (2018). Correctional Control 2018: Incarceration and supervision by state. *Prison Policy Initiative.* https://www.prisonpolicy.org/reports/correctionalcontrol2018.html

Kaeble, Danielle, and Cowhig, Mary. (2018). *Correction populations in the United States, 2016.* Department of Justice, Bureau of Justice Statistics. https://bjs.ojp.gov/content/pub/pdf/cpus16.pdf

Kanuha, Valli K. (1990). Compounding the triple jeopardy: Battering in lesbian of color relationships. *Women & Therapy, 9,* 169–184.

Kanuha, Valli K. (1996). Domestic violence, racism, and the battered women's movement in the United States. In Jeffrey L. Edleson and Zvi C. Eisikovits (Eds.), *Future interventions with battered women and their families* (pp. 34–50). Sage.

Kanuha, Valli K. (1998). Professional social work and the battered women's movement: Contextualizing the challenges of domestic violence work. *Professional Development: The International Journal of Continuing Social Work Education, 1*(2), 4–18.

Kattari, Shanna K., Kattari, Leonard, Lacombe-Duncan, Ashley, Shelton, Jama, and Misiolek, Brayden A. (2022). Differential experiences of sexual, physical, and emotional intimate partner violence among transgender and gender diverse adults. *Journal of Interpersonal Violence, 0*(0), 1–25.

Kelley, Susan. (2017). People with disabilities are more likely to be arrested. *Cornell Chronicle.* https://news.cornell.edu/stories/2017/11/people-disabilities-more-likely-be-arrested.

Kernsmith, Poco, and Kernsmith, Roger. (2009). Treating female perpetrators: State standards for batterer intervention services. *Social Work, 54*(4), 341–349.

Kertesz, Margaret, Humphreys, Cathy, and Larance, Lisa Young. (2021). *Interventions for women who use force in a family context: An Australian practice framework.* Melbourne: University of Melbourne. https://vawc.com.au/kertesz-m-humphreys-c-larance-l-y-2021-interventions-for-women-who-use-force-in-a-family-context-an-australian-practice-framework-melbourne-university-of-melbourne/

Kim, Mimi. (2013). Challenging the pursuit of criminalization in an era of mass incarceration. The limitations of social work responses to domestic violence in the USA. *British Journal of Social Work, 43,* 1276–1293.

Kim, Mimi. (2015). *Dancing the carceral creep: The anti-domestic violence movement and the paradoxical pursuit of criminalization, 1973–1986* [Working paper]. Institute for the Study of Societal Issues, University of California–Berkeley.

King, Deborah K. (1988). Multiple jeopardy, multiple consciousness: The context of a black feminist ideology. *Signs, 14*(1), 42–72.

Knickmeyer, Nicole, Levitt, Heidi M., Horne, Sharon G., and Bayer, Gary. (2003). Religious oriented coping strategies of Christian battered women. *Journal of Religion & Abuse, 5*(2), 29–53.

Kusenbach, Margarethe. (2003). Street phenomenology: The go-along as ethnographic research tool. *Ethnography, 4*(3), 455–485.

Labrecque, Ryan M. (2017). Probation in the United State: A historical and modern perspective. In O. Hayden Griffin and Vanessa H. Woodward (Eds.) *Handbook of corrections in the United States* (pp. 155–164). Routledge.

Larance, Lisa Young. (2006). Serving women who use force in their intimate heterosexual relationships: An extended view. *Violence Against Women, 12*(7), 622–640.

Larance, Lisa Young. (2017). Response to "Addressing violence by female partners is vital to prevent or stop violence against women: Evidence from the Multisite Batterer Intervention Evaluation," by Murray Straus. *Violence Against Women, 23*(1) NP1.

Larance, Lisa Young. (2021). *Talking back to the web of power: Women's legal, child protection, and antiviolence intervention entanglement and resistance.* [Doctoral dissertation, University of Michigan]. ProQuest Dissertations and Theses Global.

Larance, Lisa Young, Andersen, Paula, and Vicary, Dave. (2019a). *+SHIFT: A draft curriculum framework for intervention with women in Victoria, Australia who have used force in their intimate relationships.* Baptcare and Berry Street, Melbourne, Australia.

Larance, Lisa Young, Goodmark, Leigh, Miller, Susan L., and Dasgupta, Shamita D. (2019b). Understanding and addressing women's use of force: A retrospective. *Violence Against Women, 25*(1), 56–80.

Larance, Lisa Young, Hoffman-Ruzicka, Allison, and Shivas, Jane B. (2009). *Vista: A program for women who use force.* Jersey Center for Nonviolence.

Larance, Lisa Young, and Kertesz, Margaret. (2023). Methodological and ethical considerations when working beyond the victim-offender binary: A Brief Report on the unintended consequences of the C-ABI. *Journal of Family Violence. Special Issue: Ethical governance and integrity in domestic violence and abuse research.* https://link.springer.com/article/10.1007/s10896-023-00584-w

Larance, Lisa Young, Kertesz, Margaret, Humphreys, Cathy, Goodmark, Leigh and Douglas, Heather. (2022). Beyond the victim-offender binary: Legal and anti-violence intervention considerations with women who have used force in the U.S. and Australia. *Affilia: Feminist Inquiry in Social Work, 37*(3), 466–486.

Larance, Lisa Young, and Miller, Susan L. (2017). In her own words: Women describe their use of force resulting in court-ordered intervention. *Violence Against Women, 23*(12), 1536–1559.

Larance, Lisa Young, and Porter, Maryann L. (2004). Observations from practice: Support group membership as a process of social capital formation among female survivors of domestic violence. *Journal of Interpersonal Violence, 19*(6), 676–690.

Larance, Lisa Young, and Rousson, Ashley N. (2016). Facilitating change: A process of renewal for women who have used force in their intimate heterosexual relationships. *Violence Against Women, 22*(7), 876–891.

Larance, Lisa Young, and Scaia, Melissa P. (2020). Mandated group intervention for women who have used force: Considerations during the COVID-19 Pandemic. In M. P. Scaia and J. Heath (Eds.), *Draft Adaptation of the European Network Guidelines of Working Responsibly with Perpetrators of Domestic Violence During COVID-19* (pp. 39–43). Global Rights for Women. www.globalrightsforwomen.org

Latessa, Edward J., and Smith, Paula. (2015). *Corrections in the community* (6th ed.). Routledge.

Lawless, Elaine. (2001). *Women escaping violence: Empowerment through narrative*. University of Missouri Press.

Lawson, Jennifer. (2019). Domestic violence as child maltreatment: Differential risks and outcomes among cases referred to child welfare agencies for domestic violence exposure. *Children and Youth Services Review, 98*, 32–41.

Lazarus-Black, Mindie. (2007). *Everyday harm: Domestic violence, court rites, and cultures of reconciliation*. University of Illinois Press.

Lindsay, Jocelyn, Roy, Valerie, Montminy, Lyse, Turcotte, Daniel, and Genest-Dufault, Sacha. (2008). The emergence and the effects of therapeutic factors in groups. *Social Work with Groups, 31*(3–4), 255–271.

Ling, Susie. (1989). The mountain movers: Asian American women's movement in Los Angeles. *Amerasia Journal, 15*(1), 51–67.

Magen, Randy H. (1999). In the best interest of battered women: Reconceptualizing allegations of failure to protect. *Child Maltreatment, 4*(2), 127–135.

Mahoney, Amanda. (2019). How failure to protect laws punish the vulnerable. *Health Matrix: The Journal of Law and Medicine, 29*(1), 429–461.

Malcome, Marion L.D., Fedock, Gina, Garthe, Rachel C., Golder, Seana, Higgins, George, and Logan, T.K. (2019). Weathering probation and parole: The protective role of social support on black women's recent stressful events and depressive symptoms. *Journal of Black Psychology, 45*(8), 661–688.

Mann, Susan A., and Kelley, Lori R. (1997). Standing at the crossroads of modernist thought: Collins, Smith, and the new feminist epistemologies. *Gender & Society, 11*, 391–408.

Martin, Margaret E. (1997). Double your trouble: Dual arrest in family violence. *Journal of Family Violence, 12*, 139–157.

Matsuda, Mari. (1991). Beside my sister, facing the enemy: Legal theory out of coalition. *Stanford Law Review, 43*(6), 1183–1189.

McCall, Leslie. (2005). The complexity of intersectionality. *Signs: Journal of Women in Culture and Society, 30*(3), 1771–1800.

McCorkel, Jill A. (2013). *Breaking women: Gender, race, and the new politics of imprisonment*. New York University Press.

McGuire, Danielle L. (2010). *At the dark end of the street: Black women, rape, and resistance—a new history of the civil rights movement from Rosa Parks to the rise of black power.* Vintage Books.

McLeod, Melvin. (1998). *"There's no place to go but up"—bell hooks and Maya Angelou in conversation.* Lion's Roar: Buddhist Wisdom for Our Time. https://www.lionsroar.com/theres-no-place-to-go-but-up/

Mehrotra, Gita. (2010). Toward a continuum of intersectionality theorizing for feminist social work. *Affilia: Journal of Women and Social Work, 25*(4), 417–430.

Mehrotra, Gita. (2017). Considering emotion and emotional labor in feminist social work research. In Stephanie Wahab, Ben Anderson-Nathe, and Christina Gringeri (Eds.), *Feminisms in social work research: Promise and possibilities for justice-based knowledge* (pp. 259–275). Routledge.

Menakem, Resmaa. (2017). *My grandmother's hands: Racialized trauma and the pathway to mending our hearts and bodies.* Central Recovery Press.

Messing, Jill Theresa, Patch, Michelle, Wilson, Janet Sullivan, Kellen, Gabor. D., and Campbell, Jacquelyn. (2018). Differentiating among attempted, completed, and multiple nonfatal strangulation in women experiencing intimate partner violence. *Women's Health Issues, 28*(1), 104–111.

Messing, Jill Theresa, Ward-Lasher, Allison, Thaller, Jonel, and Batwell-Gray, Meredith E. (2015). The state of intimate partner violence intervention: Progress and continuing challenges. *Social Work, 60*(4), 305–313

Miller, Rueben Jonathon and Stuart, Forest. (2017). Carceral citizenship: Race, rights and responsibility in the age of mass supervision. *Theoretical Criminology, 21*(4), 532–48.

Miller, Susan L. (1989). Unintended side effects of pro-arrest policies and their race and class implications for battered women: A cautionary note. *Criminal Justice Policy Review, 3*(3/89), 299–317.

Miller, Susan L. (2005). *Victims as offenders: The paradox of women's violence in relationships.* Rutgers University Press.

Miller, Susan L. (2018). *Journeys: Resilience and growth for survivors of intimate partner abuse.* University of California Press.

Miller, Susan L., Gregory, Carol, and Iovanni, LeeAnn. (2005). One size fits all? A gender-neutral approach to a gender-specific problem: Contrasting batterer treatment programs for male and female offenders. *Criminal Justice Policy Review, 16*(3), 336–359.

Miller, Susan L., and Manzur, Jamie L. (2021). Safeguarding children's wellbeing: Voices from abused mothers navigating their relationships and the civil courts. *Journal of Interpersonal Violence, 36*(9–10), 4545–4569.

Miller, Susan L., and Smolter, Nichole L. (2011). "Paper abuse": When all else fails, batterers use procedural stalking. *Violence Against Women, 17*(5), 637–650.

Mirchandi, Kiran. (2003). Challenging racial silences in studies of emotion work: Contributions from antiracist feminist theory. *Organizational Studies, 24*(5), 721–742.

Mohanty, Chandra. (1991). Under western eyes: Feminist scholarship and colonial discourses. In Chandra T. Mohanty, Ann Russo, and Lourdes Torres

(Eds.), *Third world women and the politics of feminism* (pp. 51–80). Indiana University Press

Monahan, Kathleen, Bannon, Sarah and Dams-O'Connor, Kristen. (2022). Nonfatal strangulation (NFS) and intimate partner violence: a Brief Overview. *Journal of Family Violence, 37,* 75–86.

Morash, Merry. (2010). *Women on probation and parole: A feminist critique of community programs and services.* Northeastern University Press

Morash, Merry, Kashy, Deborah A., Cobbina, Jennifer E., and Smith, Sandi W. (2019). Technical violations, treatment and punishment responses, and recidivism of women on probation and parole. *Criminal Justice Policy Review, 30*(5), 788–810.

Morash, Merry, Kashy, Deborah A., Smith, Sandi W., and Cobbina, Jennifer E. (2016). The connection of probation/parole officer actions to women offenders' recidivism. *Criminal Justice and Behavior, 43*(4), 506–524.

Morgaine, Karen. (2017). Positionality and privilege in qualitative research: Feminist critical praxis. In Stephanie Wahab, Ben Anderson-Nathe, and Christina Gringeri (Eds.), *Feminisms in social work research: Promise and possibilities for justice-based knowledge* (pp. 226–239). Routledge.

Mulvaney, Conor. (2022). *Invisible pain and overlooked violence: Abusive partner interventions in the LGBTQIA+ Community.* Center for Court Innovation.

National Association of Social Workers. (2020). *Code of ethics.* https://www.socialworkers.org/About/Ethics/Code-of-Ethics/Highlighted-Revisions-to-the-Code-of-Ethics

National Clearinghouse for the Defense of Battered Women [National Defense Center for Criminalized Survivors]. (2001). *DRAFT: An Important Note about Assessment Tools.* National Clearinghouse for the Defense of Battered Women.

National Inventory of Collateral Consequences of Conviction. (n.d.). https://niccc.nationalreentryresourcecenter.org/

Osthoff, Sue. (2002). But Gertrude, I beg to differ, a hit is not a hit: When battered women are arrested for assaulting their partners. *Violence Against Women, 8*(12), 1521–1544.

Pager, Devah, Goldstein, Rebecca, Ho, Helen, and Western, Bruce. (2022). Criminalizing poverty: The consequences of court fees in a randomized experiment. *American Sociological Review,* 1–25.

Parenting Matters. (n.d.). *Parent partner.* https://parentingmattersfl.org/programs/parent-partner/

Pate, Anthony M. and Hamilton, Edwin E. (1992). Formal and informal deterrents to domestic violence: The Dade County spouse assault experiment. *American Sociological Review, 57,* 691–697.

Pence, Ellen, Connelly, Laura, and Scaia, Melissa. (2011). *Turning points: A nonviolence curriculum for women.* Domestic Violence Turning Points.

Pence, Ellen and Dasgupta, Shamita D. (2006). Re-examining "battering": Are all acts of violence against intimate partners the same? Praxis International.

Phelps, Michelle S. (2017). Mass probation: Toward a more robust theory of state variation in punishment. *Punishment & Society, 19*(1), 53–73.

Phelps, Michelle S. (2018). Mass probation and inequality: Race, class, and gender disparities in supervision and revocation. In Jeffery T. Ulmer and

Mindy S. Bradley (Eds.), *Handbook on Punishment Decisions: Locations of Disparity* (pp. 44–63). Routledge. https://www.prisonpolicy.org/scans/phelps/mass_probation_and_inequality.pdf

Phelps, Michelle S. (2020). Mass probation from macro to micro: Tracing the expansion and consequences of community supervision. *Annual Review of Criminology, 3,* 261–279

Phelps, Michelle, and Ruhland, Ebony. (2022). Governing marginality: Coercion and care in probation. *Social Problems, 69,* 799–816.

Phoenix, Ann. (1994). Practicing feminist research: The intersection of gender and "race" in the research process. In Mary Maynard and June Purvis (Eds.), *Researching women's lives from a feminist perspective* (pp. 35–45). Taylor & Francis.

Pleck, Elizabeth. (2004). *Domestic tyranny: The making of American social policy against family violence from the colonial times to the present.* University of Illinois Press.

Potter, Hillary. (2008). *Battle cries: Black women and intimate partner abuse.* New York University Press.

Rajah, Valli. (2007). Resistance as edgework in violent intimate relationships of drug-involved women. *British Journal of Criminology, 47,* 196–213.

Rastegar, Darius A., and Fingerhood, Michael I. (Eds.). (2020). *American society of addiction medicine handbook of addiction medicine* (2nd ed.). Oxford University Press.

Reichert, Jessica. (2020). *Drug testing in community corrections: A review of the literature.* Illinois Criminal Justice Information Authority Center for Justice Research and Evaluation. https://icjia.illinois.gov/researchhub/articles/drug-testing-in-community-corrections-a-review-of-the-literature

Reichert, Jessica, Weisner, Lauren, and Otto, H. Douglas. (2020). *A study of drug testing practices in probation.* Illinois Criminal Justice Information Authority Center for Justice Research and Evaluation. https://icjia.illinois.gov/researchhub/articles/a-study-of-drug-testing-practices-in-probation

Reinharz, Shulamit. (1994). Toward an ethnography of "voice" and "silence." In Edison Trickett, Roderick Watts, and Dina Birman. (Eds.), *Human diversity: Perspectives on people in context* (pp. 178–200). Jossey-Bass.

Renzetti, Claire M. (1992). *Violent betrayal: Partner abuse in lesbian relationships.* Sage.

Renzetti, Claire M. (1998). Violence and abuse in lesbian relationships: Theoretical and Empirical issues. In Raquel K. Bergen (Ed.), *Issues in intimate violence* (pp. 117–128). Sage.

Renzetti, Claire M. (1999). The challenges to feminism posed by women's use of violence in intimate relationships. In Sharon Lamb (Ed.), *New versions of victims: Feminists struggle with the concept* (pp. 42–56). New York University Press.

Richie, Beth E. (1996). *Compelled to crime: The gender entrapment of battered black women.* Routledge.

Richie, Beth E. (2000). A Black feminist reflection on the antiviolence movement. *Signs, 24,* 1133–1137.

Richie, Beth E. (2012). *Arrested justice: Black women, violence, and America's prison nation.* New York University Press.

Richie, Beth E., Kanuha, Valli K., and Martensen, K. M. (2021). Colluding with and resisting the state: Organizing against gender violence in the U.S. *Feminist Criminology*, 1–19.

Ridgeway, Cecilia L., and Correll, Shelley J. (2004). Unpacking the gender system: A theoretical perspective on gender beliefs and social relations. *Gender & Society, 18*, 510–531.

*Rise.* (2020, October 20). 'Abolition is the only answer': A conversation with Dorothy Roberts. *Rise Magazine.* https://www.risemagazine.org/2020/10/conversation-with-dorothy-roberts/

Ristock, Janice L. (2001). Decentering heterosexuality: Reponses of feminist counselors to abuse in lesbian relationships. *Women & Therapy, 23*(3), 59–72.

Ristock, Janice L. (2002). *No more secrets: Violence in lesbian relationships.* Routledge.

Roberts, Dorothy. (2002). *Shattered bonds: The color of child welfare.* Basic Civitas Books.

Roberts, Dorothy E. (2014). Child protection as surveillance of African American families. *Journal of Social Welfare and Family Law, 36*(4), 426–437.

Roberts, Dorothy. (2018). Marginalized mothers and intersecting systems of surveillance: Prisons and foster care. In Yasmine Ergas, Jane Jenson, and Sonya Michel (Eds.), *Reassembling motherhood: Procreation and care in a globalized world* (pp. 185–201). Columbia University Press.

Roberts, Dorothy. (2020, June 16). Abolishing policing also means abolishing family regulation. *The Imprint: Youth and Family News.* https://chronicleofsocialchange.org/child-welfare-2/abolishing-policing-also-means-abolishing-family-regulation/44480

Robinson, Amanda L., Myhill, Andy, and Wire, Julia. (2018). Practitioner (mis) understandings of coercive control in England and Wales. *Criminology & Criminal Justice, 18*(1), 29–49.

Roddy, Ariel L. and Morash, Merry. (2020). The connections of parole and probation agency communication patterns with female offenders' job-seeking self-efficacy. *International Journal of Offender Therapy and Comparative Criminology, 64*(8), 774–790.

Roddy, Ariel L., Morash, Merry, and Bohmert, Miriam Northcut. (2022). Spatial mismatch, race and ethnicity, and unemployment: Implications for interventions with women on probation and parole. *Crime & Delinquency, 68*(12), 2175–2199.

Ross, Loretta. (2016). *University of Washington School of Social Work Commencement Address.* [Video]. YouTube. https://www.youtube.com/watch?v=NH52tMHwwQo

Roy, Debjani. (2012). South Asian battered women's use of force against intimate male partners: A practice note. *Violence Against Women, 18*(9), 1108–1118.

Safe and Together Institute. (n.d.). https://safeandtogetherinstitute.com/the-sti-model/model-overview/

SAMHSA. (2014). *SAMHSA's concept of trauma and guidance for a trauma-informed approach.* https://store.samhsa.gov/product/SAMHSA-s-Concept-of-Trauma-and-Guidance-for-a-Trauma-Informed-Approach/SMA14-4884

Sarachild, Kathie. (1975). Consciousness-raising: A radical weapon. In Kathie Sarachild (Ed.) *Redstockings of the Women's Movement* (pp. 144–150). Random House.

Saunders, Daniel G. (2002). Are physical assaults by wives and girlfriends a major social problem? A review of the literature. *Violence Against Women*, 8(12), 1424–1448.

Saunders, Daniel G. (2008). Group interventions for men who batter: A summary of program descriptions and research. *Violence and Victims*, 23(2), 156–172.

Saunders, Daniel G., Jiwatram-Negron, Tina, Nanasi, Natali and Cardenas, Iris. (2022). Patriarchy's link to intimate partner violence: Applications to survivors' asylum claims. *Violence Against Women.* https://doi.org/10.1177/10778012221132299

Scaia, Melissa P. (2017). *In their own words: Victims of battering talk about being arrested and convicted.* National Clearinghouse for the Defense of Battered Women. Google Drive. https://drive.google.com/file/d/1-jb8k1wdvnd3zR3-9fFu1pIdroWN4JTf/view

Schechter, Susan. (1982). *Women and male violence: The visions and struggles of the battered women's movement.* South End Press.

Sentencing Project. (2007). Women in the criminal justice system: Briefing sheets. https://static.prisonpolicy.org/scans/womenincj_total.pdf

Sered, Danielle. (2019). *Until we reckon: Violence, mass incarceration, and a road to repair.* The New Press.

Sewell, Alyasah A., and Ray, Rashawn. (2020, June 11). *The collateral consequences of state-sanctioned police violence for women.* Brookings. https://www.brookings.edu/blog/how-we-rise/2020/06/11/the-collateral-consequences-of-state-sanctioned-police-violence-for-women/

Shapiro, Janet R., and Applegate, Jeffrey S. (2018). *Neurobiology for clinical social work: Theory and practice, Second Edition.* W. W. Norton.

Shepard, Melanie F., and Pence, Ellen L. (1999). An introduction: Developing a coordinated community response. In Melanie F. Shepard and Ellen L. Pence (Eds.), *Coordinating community responses to domestic violence: Lessons from Duluth and beyond* (pp. 3–23). Sage.

Sherman, Lawrence W. and Berk, Richard A. (1984). The specific deterrent effects of arrest for domestic assault. *American Sociological Review*, 49, 261–272

Sherman, Lawrence W., Smith, Douglas A., Schmidt, Janell D., and Rogan, Dennis P. (1992). Crime, punishment, and stake in conformity: Legal and informal control of domestic violence. *American Sociological Review*, 57, 680–690.

Simmons, Aishah S. (Ed.). (2019). *Love with accountability: Digging up the roots of child sexual abuse.* AK Press.

Small, Mario. (2009). *Unanticipated gains.* Oxford University Press.

Smith, Carly Parnitzke and Freyd, Jennifer J. (2014). Institutional betrayal. *American Psychologist*, 69(6), 575–587.

Sokoloff, Natalie J., and Dupont, Ida. (2005). Domestic violence at the intersections of race, class, and gender: Challenges and contributions to understanding violence against marginalized women in diverse communities. *Violence Against Women*, 11(1), 38–64.

Sousa, Cindy A., Siddiqi, Manahil, and Bogue, Briana. (2022). What do we know after decades of research about parenting and IPV? A systematic scoping review integrating findings. *Trauma, Violence, & Abuse*, 23(5), 1629–1642.

Specht, Harry, and Courtney, Mark E. (1994). *How social work has abandoned its mission: Unfaithful angels*. The Free Press.

Stark, Evan. (2007). *Coercive control: The entrapment of women in personal life*. Oxford University Press.

Stark, Evan, and Hester, Marianne. (2019). Coercive control: Update and review. *Violence Against Women*, 25(1), 81–104.

Steinberg, Dominique M. (2014). *A mutual-aid model for social work with groups* (3rd ed.). Routledge.

Steinberg, Robin. (2023). *The courage of compassion: A journey from judgment to connection*. Penguin Random House.

Swan, Suzanne C., and Snow, David L. (2003). Behavioral and psychological differences among abused women who use violence in intimate relationships. *Violence Against Women*, 9(1), 75–109.

Sweet, Paige L. (2019). The sociology of gaslighting. *American Sociological Review*, 84(5), 851–875.

Sweet, Paige L. (2021). *The politics of surviving: Domestic violence in traumatic times*. University of California Press.

Tu, Joan, and Penti, Brian. (2020). How we talk about "perpetration of intimate partner violence" matters. *Journal of the American Board of Family Medicine*, 33(5), 809–814.

United Nations. (2015). *The World's Women 2015: Trends and Statistics*. Department of Economic and Social Affairs, Statistics Division. https://unstats.un.org/unsd/gender/downloads/worldswomen2015_report.pdf

United Nations. (2022). *Safe consultation with survivors of violence against women and girls*. Ending Violence Against Women Section. https://www.unwomen.org/en/digital-library/publications/2022/12/safe-consultations-with-survivors-of-violence-against-women-and-girls

van der Kolk, Bessel. (2014). *The body keeps the score: Brain, mind, and body in the healing of trauma*. Penguin Books.

Van Dieten, Marilyn, Jones, Natalie, J., and Rodon, Monica. (2014). *Working with women who perpetrate violence: A practice guide*. National Resource Center on Justice Involved Women. https://cjinvolvedwomen.org/resources/working-with-women-who-perpetrate-violence/

Venkatesh, Sudhir. (2002). "Doin' the hustle": Constructing the ethnographer in the American ghetto. *Ethnography*, 3(1), 91–111.

Victor, Bryan G., Henry, Colleen, Gilbert, Terri T., Ryan, Joseph P., and Perron, Brian E. (2019). Child protective service referrals involving exposure to domestic violence: Prevalence, associated maltreatment types, and likelihood of formal case openings. *Child Maltreatment*, 24(3) 299–309.

Victor, Bryan, Rousson, Ashley R., Henry, Colleen, Dalvi, Haresh B., and Mariscal, E. Susana. (2021). Child protective services guidelines for substantiating exposure to domestic violence as maltreatment and assigning caregiver responsibility: Policy analysis and recommendations. *Child Maltreatment*, 26(4), 452–463.

Violence Against Women Act of 1994 (1994, September 13). Title IV, P.L. 103–322, 108 Stat. 1902.

Virani, Alicia. (2021). *The financial impact of court-ordered batterers' intervention programs in Los Angeles County*. UCLA School of Law Criminal Justice Program. https://finesandfeesjusticecenter.org/articles/la-batterers-intervention-programs-costs/

Walfogel, Jane. (2009). Prevention and the child welfare system. *The Future of Children*, 19(2), 195–210.

Walker, Lenore E. A. (1979). *The battered woman*. Harper & Rowe.

Washington, Patricia A. (2001). Disclosure patterns of black female sexual assault survivors. *Violence Against Women*, 7(11), 1254–1283

Watkins-Hayes, Celeste. (2009). *The new welfare bureaucrats: Entanglements of race, class, and policy reform*. University of Chicago Press.

Watkins-Hayes, Celeste. (2019). *Remaking a life: How women living with HIV/AIDS confront inequality*. University of California Press.

West, Carolyn. (2009). "Sorry, we have to take you in:" Black battered women arrested for intimate partner violence. In Kathy A. McCloskey and Marilyn H. Sitaker (Eds.), *Backs against the wall: Battered women's resistance strategies* (pp. 49–68). Routledge.

Whitaker, Daniel J., Baker, Charlene K., Pratt, Carter, Reed, Elizabeth, Suri, Sonia, Pavlos, Carlene, Nagy, Beth J., and Silverman, Jay (2007). A network model for providing culturally competent services for intimate partner violence and sexual violence. *Violence Against Women*, 13(2), 190–209.

Worcester, Nancy. (2002). Women's use of force: Complexities and challenges of taking the issue seriously. *Violence Against Women*, 8(11), 1390–1415.

Yalom, Irvin. (2005). *The theory and practice of group psychotherapy* (5th ed.). Basic Books.

# Index

Founded in 1893,
UNIVERSITY OF CALIFORNIA PRESS
publishes bold, progressive books and journals
on topics in the arts, humanities, social sciences,
and natural sciences—with a focus on social
justice issues—that inspire thought and action
among readers worldwide.

The UC PRESS FOUNDATION
raises funds to uphold the press's vital role
as an independent, nonprofit publisher, and
receives philanthropic support from a wide
range of individuals and institutions—and from
committed readers like you. To learn more, visit
ucpress.edu/supportus.

www.ingramcontent.com/pod-product-compliance
Lightning Source LLC
Chambersburg PA
CBHW020856270326
41928CB00006B/737